A SLUMLESS AMERICA

A SLUMLESS AMERICA

MARY K. SIMKHOVITCH AND THE DREAM OF AFFORDABLE HOUSING

BETTY BOYD CAROLI

OXFORD
UNIVERSITY PRESS

Oxford University Press is a department of the University of Oxford.
It furthers the University's objective of excellence in research, scholarship,
and education by publishing worldwide. Oxford is a registered trade mark of
Oxford University Press in the UK and in certain other countries.

Published in the United States of America by Oxford University Press
198 Madison Avenue, New York, NY 10016, United States of America.

© Betty Boyd Caroli 2026

All rights reserved. No part of this publication may be reproduced, stored in a retrieval system, transmitted, used for text and data mining, or used for training artificial intelligence, in any form or by any means, without the prior permission in writing of Oxford University Press, or as expressly permitted by law, by license or under terms agreed with the appropriate reprographics rights organization. Inquiries concerning reproduction outside the scope of the above should be sent to the Rights Department, Oxford University Press, at the address above.

You must not circulate this work in any other form
and you must impose this same condition on any acquirer.

CIP data is on file at the Library of Congress.

ISBN 9780197793800

DOI: 10.1093/oso/9780197793800.001.0001

Printed by Sheridan Books, Inc., United States of America

The manufacturer's authorized representative in the EU for product safety is
Oxford University Press España S.A. of Parque Empresarial San Fernando de Henares,
Avenida de Castilla, 2 – 28830 Madrid (www.oup.es/en or product.safety@oup.com).
OUP España S.A. also acts as importer into Spain of products made by the manufacturer.

In February 1943, while President Franklin Roosevelt dealt with discouraging news from the war front, he took time to write a letter to a woman he had known since his teens, when their families vacationed near each other along the Maine coast. Fifteen years his senior, she no longer answered to the name his parents knew her by—Mary Kingsbury—and he addressed her by her married name: "My dear Mrs. Simkhovitch." After congratulating her and the organization she founded for leading the fight for decent housing for all, he assured her that he looked forward to the war's end and to working with her on their shared quest for "a slumless America." It was a goal she pursued her entire adult life, and the fact that safe, affordable housing still ranks high on the nation's list of urgent needs shows the enormity of that struggle.

Contents

1. When Nobody Talked About Housing — 1
2. Breaking Away — 16
3. Finding Answers — 29
4. Choosing New York — 44
5. "Friendly Aid" Falls Short — 57
6. Life of Jones Street — 76
7. Growing and Reaching Out — 96
8. Conflicts and Critics — 116
9. Keeping Reform Alive — 136
10. Gains and Losses — 159
11. National Breakthrough — 174
12. "Woman-Made America" — 191
13. "Pioneers Are Always Needed" — 206

Acknowledgements — 225
Notes — 227
Index — 263

I

When Nobody Talked About Housing

The two-story house in Newton, Massachusetts, where Mary Melinda Kingsbury was born in 1867 looked a lot like the houses around it, and indeed across the entire United States. With ample natural light in every room and outdoor space for recreation, it housed a family of four.[1] Before she became aware that others lived on stacked floors, with as many persons in a single room as in her entire Newton house, she didn't hear housing discussed. People talked about having a house or wanting a "nice" house, but "housing," especially with a capital H, never came up.[2]

Nor did the idea of leaving what the Kingsbury neighbors called their "Garden City" to live in a crowded metropolis like Manhattan, with nearly one million inhabitants by 1870.[3] Her parents, Frank and Laura Kingsbury, had both visited New York City and made brief forays of their own into the wider world, but they always came back to New England, convinced it was the best place on earth. They fully expected their only daughter to make the same choice, as their forebears had done since the 1600s.

Both parents had their own reasons for wanting to stay put. Frank Kingsbury had survived some of the Civil War's most perilous battles in Pennsylvania and Virginia, and he was constantly reminded of them by the missing index finger on his right hand. Many of his soldier buddies had not come back. For Frank, the good life after being mustered out of active military service was settling into a house just outside Boston, singing in the church choir, and working in local government.

The woman he married, Laura Holmes, had grown up thirty-five miles to the south, in Bridgewater, Massachusetts, where the town cemetery had tombstones of her ancestors on both the maternal and paternal side. Laura could trace her roots back to Roger Conant, the Englishman who helped wrest land from the Wampanoag native people in the 1620s.[4]

In Mary's autobiography, written long after she had left home, she related fond memories of her childhood, especially those trips to her mother's family in Bridgewater, which had "something softer about it than the Boston area. . . . [Bridgewater was] near the Cape with sandy soil and pine woods in which lady's slippers grew."[5] She extolled the "huge sycamore . . . [and] cinnamon roses at the doorway" of her grandparents' home, where she liked to sit and eat a supper of bread and milk "with little red checkerberries floating in it" and listen for the "whippoorwill."[6]

Her years in New England left an indelible imprint on Mary, and Frank and Laura Kingsbury provided strong models to follow. All her life, she retained their values and predilections. The energy with which she pursued goals, for example, was a family trait. The Holmeses, her mother's people—who supplied the Melinda in her name—had been held up as exemplars in helping others, especially the neediest. They openly opposed slavery when few of their Massachusetts neighbors would speak out on the subject. Laura Kingsbury liked to remind her daughter that when a fugitive slave knocked at the Holmes's door, they opened it, and every morning at breakfast prayer, they included an end to slavery in their supplications.[7]

Alongside firmly held principles, Laura Kingsbury maintained a deep curiosity about the world, and she was eager to explore the unknown. Brisk—almost brittle—in speech and presentation, she flirted with risk. At the age of twelve, she started a lively correspondence with her bachelor uncle, Jonathan Platt, who had gone to what seemed to Laura like another planet—California in the 1849 "gold rush." When his preteen niece offered to help find him a wife, Platt specified that it not be one who would "go off to the women's rights convention" (the Seneca Falls women's convention had taken place in July 1848) while he was left at home "to wash the dishes and feed the chickens and take care of the little bloomers."[8] He furnished young Laura with evidence of an entirely different life for girls her age in California, describing how they were put to work for long days, under a hot sun, "without any bonnets . . . carrying pans of dirt on their heads . . . steady as old men." He showed even less compassion for the "17 Chinamen" he employed, belittling their religious beliefs and ridiculing their eating habits. While he supplied the tools, they did all the work, and profits were split half and half.[9] "They call me Mister Platt," he wrote Laura, while he dubbed them "queer chaps . . . [who] have to pay $4 per month mining tax [although] some of them can't make much more than that."[10]

Reports such as these did not induce young Laura to go westward. She continued to keep track of her uncle's career, as he moved into public service, as a member of the Placer County school board and later the state legislature. But California was not for her. After earning a teacher's certificate while still in her teens, she went to live in Yarmouth, Massachusetts, where whalers' wives had a long history of asserting their independence. In that seaside community, she immediately became a favorite of students and parents alike, who warmed to her wit and fun-loving spirit.[11]

On her father's side, Mary had the example of his mother, Mary Homer Kingsbury, who had attended the Female Seminary in Ipswich, Massachusetts, in the 1820s, when it was known as one of the best girls' schools in the nation.[12] Under the direction of pioneer educators Mary Lyon and her friend Zilpah Grant (the two women who later founded Mt. Holyoke Seminary), Ipswich offered a rigorous curriculum, and students crossed paths—even if briefly—with these inspiring mentors.

That grandmother's intellectual curiosity enriched her own life as well as that of her offspring, but it was her musical training that had the strongest impact. Mary recalled how, as a child, she loved sitting beside her grandmother at the Chestnut Hill Church, listening to the clear singing voice ringing out above all the others. At home, Grandmother

Kingsbury kept a blackboard in the kitchen, to teach music notation and theory to any young folk passing through. She "took her music with her," her granddaughter remembered, and made it such a central part of her life that no day seemed complete without the sound of music.[13] Her grandmother helped shape Mary's belief that training in music should not just be for the wealthy or those headed to a professional career. Music belonged to everyone.

Instead of attending a four-year college that awarded a baccalaureate degree or even a female seminary, like Holyoke, Mary's mother opted for a less-expensive option.[14] Bridgewater had its own Normal School, and she could enroll there without leaving home. The "Normals," as they were called, offered education at low cost by allowing students to teach while continuing their coursework. After only a few weeks of training, students took over their own one-room school, and by alternating periods of work and study (nine weeks as teacher, then nine weeks as student), they earned enough to support themselves while meeting requirements for teaching certificates. Tuition was free for anyone who committed to teach.

Since teaching was considered "women's work," the Normal schools enrolled very few men. Only one in six of Laura's classmates at Bridgewater Normal School was male. She nonetheless found in that small number the man she wanted to marry. Frank Kingsbury, two years her junior, had come to Bridgewater from Chestnut Hill.[15] His older brother attended Williams College, and his younger sister enrolled at Wheaton Female Seminary in Norton, Massachusetts.[16] Why Frank ended up at Bridgewater is unclear. Perhaps, as the middle child, he was less favored by his parents. Or he could have been showing a frugal streak of his own. It wasn't his dedication to teaching. As soon as he earned his teacher's certificate in August 1859, he looked for a way to reimburse the Normal School (tuition was valued at $10 per term) without going near a classroom. He took a job on State Street in downtown Boston, working at the A. A. Frazar Company, merchants of metal fittings for ships. He hadn't forgotten Miss Holmes back in Bridgewater, however, and he began his letters to her: "My own darling Laura."[17]

When talk of an imminent war gained momentum in early 1861, Frank was twenty years old, too young to enlist without parental consent, which his mother refused to give. He was fully drawn into fighting spirit, however, and clearly identified the enemy as a batch of misguided Southern states that insisted on leaving the Union. While waiting to hear whether Virginia seceded, he deemed a negative decision important for both North and South: "Encouraging to us and sickening to the cherished hopes of the rebels."[18]

Correspondence between Frank Kingsbury and Laura Holmes indicates they agreed this was a fight to bring the Southern states back into the Union. Not a word about abolition or the abomination of slave owning. "Rebellion and secession must be crushed," Frank wrote Laura on April 15, 1861, two days before Virginia passed a resolution to secede. In preparation for battle, he and a friend took "two old guns" and went out in a field to drill in military tactics. By their second meeting, thirty-six other men had joined them. Frank continued to waver about enlisting, however, aware that his job at Frazar might not be waiting when he came back.

In the summer of 1862, Frank's thinking changed. His employers were urging him to sign up, especially after Newton received orders to furnish 106 soldiers, either men who joined of their own volition or those enticed with some monetary reward. He was inclined to enlist but wanted this to be a joint decision with Laura, whom he now meant to marry. He had already introduced her to his family, who signaled their approval, and she had managed to have him meet her parents "accidentally of course" when he came to pick her up when she was at the family home during a break from teaching.[19] Frank proposed marrying Laura before he left to fight, but a conversation with her on July 22, 1862, resulted in a mutual decision to wait.

New legislation gave Frank incentive to sign up without delay. To help states reach their assigned quotas, Congress provided both a carrot (a bounty paid to volunteers) and a stick (a draft if quota not filled.) The bounty, $100, was payable only after volunteers completed their service, but the 1862 law sweetened the reward, granting $25 immediately on enlistment.[20] That was the sum Frank Kingsbury collected when he signed up for three years. In his letters to Laura, he sounded almost exhilarated by his move. His morale had plummeted while working at Frazar, he admitted, and he had become "dissatisfied with myself, making very little progress in anything."[21] Now he saw a chance to change all that and do something that counted: "It will be said to my honor that I volunteered."[22] Indeed, he was right. More than a hundred years after he signed up, Mary's daughter spoke proudly of her grandfather's war record, adding, "He volunteered, you know."[23] He took enormous pride in his part in the war, using "Colonel"—though an honorary rank—for the rest of his life.

When twenty-one-year-old Frank joined Company K of the 32nd Massachusetts Regiment Infantry, he stood just under five feet ten inches in his military uniform, which he wore when he made a surprise visit to Laura's school in Yarmouth. One of Laura's students remembered how Miss Holmes had responded to a knock on the door. She exited briefly, and when she came back into the classroom, her cheeks were "flushed" and her eyes were "starry. [We girls] were thrilled . . . for teacher's beau had come."[24]

The young soldier that Laura Holmes introduced to her students that day was of a solid build, with blue eyes and light brown hair. These were all Kingsbury family traits, and Mary would resemble him, both in size and coloring. Showing the same propensity for leadership that would later distinguish her, he earned a quick promotion to the rank of sergeant major.[25]

Over the next three years, Frank witnessed some brutal battles. He emerged unscathed from Antietam Creek (where nearly six thousand men were killed and three times that number wounded) and from the horrendous fighting at Fredericksburg in December 1862, so deadly that *Harper's Weekly* called it a "massacre."[26] One soldier described a carpet of corpses, swollen and black, "one without a head, there one without legs, yonder a head and legs without a trunk . . . with fragments of shell sticking in oozing brain, with bullet holes all over the puffed limbs."[27] A somber President Lincoln turned even grimmer on hearing of the losses: "If there is a worse place than Hell," he lamented, "I am in it."[28]

With food and other supplies becoming ever scarcer, Frank persevered, even as scores of men around him deserted. Offered a clerkship that would take him out of battle but hinder promotion, he calculated his own personal balance sheet and concluded that fighting would bring more pay and "more honor."[29] Frank's understanding of honor needs qualification. When offered a captain's commission with a Negro regiment, he declined, writing succinctly to Laura: "Guess I won't take it."[30] That he felt no need to give his reasons suggests abolitionist sentiment in Massachusetts was limited. Boston may have been a center of antislavery protest, but not all Massachusetts residents supported the cause. The fact that a separate newspaper, *The Commonwealth*, was founded in August 1862 to advance the antislavery movement suggests that other newspapers had been judged lacking in fervency. Laura's family may have prayed for an end to slavery, but it took substantial bounties to entice soldiers to sign up to fight for that. Frank's letters mention "honor" and "pay" but not the plight of enslaved Southerners, and his daughter would later be criticized for showing a similarly limited commitment to racial equality when she fought for public housing in the United States.

Like many Americans, Frank Kingsbury had initially sounded optimistic about an early end to fighting. In November 1862 he predicted a quick victory "before another summer."[31] Only gradually would he learn how wrong he was.

In June 1863 Second Lieutenant Kingsbury headed for Gettysburg, Pennsylvania, which he reached just hours before the battle began that would take "half of all [the men] we took into this fight," including one dearly loved cousin.[32] Frank escaped with only minor injuries when a "ball" passed through the mane of his horse, grazing his body and wounding him in the chest. After a few weeks of convalescence, he was back in the field. Within months, however, he suffered more wounds, although he "was not obliged to leave the field."[33]

Then his luck turned. A shell exploded near him at Bethesda Church, Virginia, and a fragment struck his right hand so severely that his index finger had to be amputated. From his recovery station in Washington, DC, he wrote Laura on June 1, 1864, that he was "trying hard to get home" and if at first he did not succeed he would "use political influence. . . . I am bound not to stay here three weeks."[34] How he pled his case is unclear but by September 1864, he was at Boston's military base, Gallops Island, all field battles behind him.

Frank could now return to the question he posed to Laura Holmes a little over two years earlier: When could they wed? Since committing to each other in 1861, they had renewed their intentions at each meeting, and he had been writing her two or three times a week. Now she was ready. In applying for the marriage license, Frank fudged a bit on the difference in their ages, adding a year to his twenty-three to put him closer to Laura's twenty-five.[35] It was "near enough," he wrote her.[36] His daughter would later adopt similar strategy, altering dates to conceal the fact that she was seven years older than her husband.

After exchanging vows on January 4, 1865, Frank and Laura Kingsbury lived in military housing on Gallops Island in Boston Harbor. Although his employer provided an African American staff to do most of the domestic work, residents paid for their food, and that meant Laura had to budget. She had initially pitched in to help the cleaning staff, but then stopped, explaining to her sister: "I knew those 'colored women' snickered to think I was so green as to do their work for them, so I've given it up."[37] She could not so easily ignore the cost of food, however, especially after she learned that she would be charged $1.50 a day for the "table bill" of every friend or relative who came to visit.[38] Her parents lacked the means to contribute to their daughter's household. To get by, they had taken in boarders after she left home. Frank's parents, who were better off, sent the occasional food shipment (buttermilk, vegetables, lard pork, or a plum pudding), and Laura learned to discourage guests, especially those likely to linger at mealtime.[39]

Laura was not ready to relinquish all pleasure, however, and when a group of officers and their wives decided to go to New York in April 1865 to participate in the official mourning for the assassinated President Lincoln, she quickly added her and Frank's names to the list.[40] Excited about the prospect of seeing New York City for the first time, she got up at five in the morning to watch from the deck while her ship steamed into the harbor.

For someone from Newton, Massachusetts, it must have seemed that the entire world had converged on Manhattan that Tuesday to watch the huge, black hearse move the coffin of the slain president up Broadway from City Hall to Union Square, then turn left on 14th Street to reach Fifth Avenue and continue to 34th Street. The hearse, with sixteen horses pulling it, was only a small part of the procession, with 11,000 soldiers marching, one hundred bands playing, and countless thousands of singing groups, Masons, and ethnic organizations walking behind them. Laura Kingsbury did not record the specific locations where she and her group stopped to view the somber demonstration and hear church bells toll, and she struggled to find words to describe the scale of what she saw. She wrote to her sister back in Massachusetts: "Nellie, I don't exaggerate when I say Boston is no more to New York than Bridgewater [population 3,700] is to Boston [about 200,000]."[41]

The procession Laura Kingsbury viewed that day moved within yards of where she would later see her daughter marry and then become a national leader in improving urban housing. Laura would not have had the opportunity to enter one of the overcrowded tenements she passed that day, buildings where families doubled up to pay the rent on small, poorly ventilated apartments with scant access to toilets and little water for bathing and laundry. Nor did she know that a team of doctors was already investigating living conditions in the tenements of the Fourth Ward, through which Lincoln's hearse moved that day. The physicians' seventeen volumes of findings, *Sanitary Conditions of the City*, included a description of one plot of land only 240 feet by 150 feet with 20 buildings on it, housing 111 families within smelling distance of 5 horse stables and a soap and candle factory. The mixture of "filth and stench of this locality are beyond any power of description," one investigator wrote.[42] Disease was rampant, and one doctor noted that deaths went unmentioned: "The country is horrified when a thousand victims fall in an ill-fought battle, but in this city 10,000 die annually of diseases which city authorities have the power to remove, and no one is shocked."⁴³ That report made such an impression on the New York State Legislature that it passed the Metropolitan Health Act in 1866, establishing a Board of Health to deal with the horrendous conditions it described.

The newly married Laura Kingsbury apparently saw none of this, and she returned to familiar quarters in Boston Harbor at trip's end oblivious to the problems of the nation's largest city. Frank was mustered out of the army a few months later, and the couple went to live near his parents in Chestnut Hill, Massachusetts, where the "filth and stench" described in *Sanitary Conditions in the City* remained as foreign as the moon.

After Mary Kingsbury Simkhovitch became famous enough to be listed in standard reference works, such as *Notable American Women*, her family was described as wealthy, with "considerable" property consisting of "large real estate holdings in the Boston area."⁴⁴ There is little evidence for that conclusion in the family's extant records. Both Frank and Laura had pedigreed backgrounds, reaching back to the earliest English settlers, but no claim to fortunes. Both had low-cost education. After her marriage, Laura had minimal domestic help, and she recycled clothes, cutting up old garments to make doll outfits and dresses for her daughter, born two years after her marriage.⁴⁵ Laura occasionally earned a little extra money by sewing for others, including her younger sister, who received a bill for one dress Laura delivered: "material, $3.93; trimmings, $1.38; and labor, 50 cents."⁴⁶

Frank Kingsbury had steady employment in government jobs that conferred respect and supported a moderate lifestyle. He worked briefly for the US Customs Service, and then, while also serving as selectman of Newton, took a job in the state's Adjutant General's office in 1872. That gave him the right to don a military uniform, which he wore with pride in Newton.⁴⁷ His only son, Isaac William (Will) was born that same year, completing the family of four, and by the time Will turned eleven, Frank had the job that sufficed for the rest of his life: city clerk of Newton. The title accorded him recognition in the community, and his name appeared frequently (as Colonel I. F. Kingsbury) in the *Newton Graphic*, in connection with his work and as a tenor with church choirs.⁴⁸

When a local women's group met to discuss their voting rights in September 1887, they invited Colonel Kingsbury to speak. After one of their members, "Mrs. Claflin of Quincy," presented the argument that "women should vote in order to benefit their children and their country," Colonel Kingsbury went further. At a time when the state of Massachusetts had not amended its constitution on woman suffrage, he assured his well-heeled female audience they already had the right to vote. "Any woman who pays a personal or real estate tax may be registered to vote," he explained, and he gave them a list of places and times they could go to register.[49]

At his retirement in 1911, Frank was lauded as a model citizen, outstanding not only for his work and civic involvement but also the important part he played in the local Caecilian Society and the choir at the Church of the Redeemer.[50] An Episcopal church, it was located only a few steps from the Kingsbury home on Hammond Street.[51] Mary's parents had been stalwart members of the Congregational Church, but when the Reverend Henry Nash, a professor at the Cambridge Theological School, organized an Episcopal congregation in their neighborhood, they were quick to join. They liked Nash's progressive thinking, especially the part about the church's responsibility for social justice. The Kingsbury family's participation in Nash's church went beyond Frank's singing with the choir. He also became senior warden in the church, and Mary played the organ while still in her teens.[52]

Nash did much more than deliver the Sunday sermon in Newton. Each summer he led members of his congregation on a retreat to the north of Maine, in Washington County, not far from the Canadian border. Near the village of North Perry, Nash's group settled in cabins and spent their days hiking in the countryside, sharing campfire meals, and boating in the Passamaquoddy Bay. They soon encountered others escaping the summer heat of the Boston–New York area, and that is how Mary met Franklin Delano Roosevelt. His father, James Roosevelt, had acquired property at Campobello, on the Canadian side of Passamaquoddy Bay in 1883, the year after Franklin's birth, providing a cooler summer spot than Hyde Park for his family. Franklin learned how to sail his own boat in the Passamaquoddy, and after he married Eleanor in 1905, he began taking his own family to the expanding compound at Campobello. Neither Franklin nor his mother, Sara Delano Roosevelt, could identify the exact time of first meeting Mary, but their respect and sense of shared values never wavered.

Although Nash's church sponsored occasional projects to aid indigent Bostonians, the Kingsburys interacted mostly with people who looked like them. That makes it difficult to decipher what pricked young Mary's interest in the foreign and unfamiliar. Perhaps magazine illustrations of the time, showing Italian immigrants on city streets, each partnering with a monkey to entertain bystanders, whetted her curiosity. When her uncle asked the five-year-old Mary what she would like him to bring back from an upcoming trip to New York City, she replied, to the consternation of her mother, "a hand organ [accordion] and a monkey."[53]

Laura Kingsbury was occasionally amused by how serious and mature her young daughter sounded. After learning that preschool Mary was asking for coffee and tea with her meals when her mother was absent, Laura warned her that drinking tea could make her look old and wrinkled. In some alarm, Mary insisted that her mother feel her face "directly" to see if the aging process had already begun. That afternoon, she was overheard instructing the hired help: "I shall not have any more tea to make me grow old."[54]

From her mother, Mary learned to disdain household tasks. Circumstances continued to require that Laura manage her home carefully, but she did so without serious involvement or concentration. "Domestic duties worried rather than interested her," according to her daughter, whose living arrangements as an adult almost always included domestic help.[55] The adult Mary rarely ventured into the kitchen, and never learned to use a can opener or perform other household chores that most of her peers took for granted. She liked to eat, but showed little interest in how her favorite dishes were made. Only on a rare occasion did she surprise her guests with something she had prepared herself. During one of the family's summer vacations in Maine, she disappeared for a couple hours and then came out of the kitchen with an angel food cake. "We didn't know you could bake," one guest blurted out, and Mary replied evenly: "Well, I can read."[56]

Like her mother, Mary preferred directing her energy to tasks of the mind rather than preparing plates to please the palate. Laura always found time to compose a witty verse and study a foreign language. She maintained an active interest in theater until so advanced in age she required a wheelchair to get to performances.[57] Until her death at ninety-four, Laura continued to correspond, compose, and pronounce freely on various matters. In that long life, she could not help but exert a strong influence on her daughter.

But as is so often the case when the first child is a girl, father and daughter developed an exceptionally close relationship. As a youngster, Mary took long walks with Frank, and when she became an adult, he, more than Laura, approved of the choices she made. "My mother viewed with distrust" the settlement work, Mary later wrote, "but my father understood why I was drawn to the life of crowded neighborhoods."[58]

In bearing and speech, the adult Mary mirrored Boston Brahmins, and she was known to claim privileged origins in her public statements. In a 1946 interview, she contrasted her own upbringing with that of children in the crowded New York neighborhood her settlement house served: "I never had the social advantages which [they] have now. . . . I had to go to private schools."[59] Her autobiography included a more accurate account, mentioning her teachers at Newton public schools: Miss Roberts, who stressed deportment for eight-year-olds, and Mr. Kent, who laced teaching mathematics with sarcasm for his young charges' efforts.[60]

Since most biographical sketches stick to the "wealthy" and "privileged" depiction of her family background, with the implication that the Kingsburys bankrolled Mary's achievements, some clarification is appropriate.[61] An abundance of evidence, including letters written by and about the Kingsbury family, shows that they lived comfortably as property owners for generations but that Frank and Laura had neither means nor inclination for philanthropy. Their contribution to Mary's life's work was not money but mindfulness. Laura's intellectual bent constituted a legacy to her daughter, and Frank's dedication to public service helped shape her. Sociologist Stephen Kalberg, after examining the records of fourteen settlement movement leaders who became activists, concluded that they came from "devoutly religious homes" with education high on the family agenda.[62] Mary Kingsbury Simkhovitch certainly fit that pattern.

In the "parochial but solid" part of the nation where she grew up, Mary observed that "the substantial virtues of truthfulness and honesty were so deeply inculcated as to be taken for granted."[63] But a sense of superiority permeated it to the core, and the twelve million immigrants flocking to the United States between 1870 and 1900 occupied a distinctly inferior stratum. Seven out of ten docked in New York, and although some fanned out across the continent, many stayed, making Manhattan 42 percent foreign born by 1890. For most of Mary's Massachusetts friends, who firmly believed "New England came first and America second," a city with nearly half its population born on another continent was both suspect and tainted. Indeed, she noted, "To say that a person was 'New Yorkey' was to lift eyebrows while smiling."[64]

As Boston's population expanded westward after the Civil War, farmland was cut up into lots for single-family homes, and the tiny villages that made up Newton took on a different look. The term "suburb" had not come into common use in America, and one resident provided a label that seemed to fit Newton: a "cluster of beautiful villages" forming a "Garden City."[65] Villages on Newton's northern ring (Newton Corner, West Newton, Newtonville, and Auburndale) had the advantage of the Boston and Albany Railroad running through them, providing access to Boston and other commercial centers. Villages on the southern perimeter, including East Newton (later named Chestnut Hill), where the Kingsburys had once owned sizeable tracts, lagged in getting rail lines.

The growing population of the villages soon presented problems. Individual households could no longer be sure that the water from their individual wells was safe or that their neighbors' sewage received adequate treatment. Newton leaders began talking of "improvement" for their "Garden City" to provide a public water supply, sewage disposal, and spaces for parks. This was not the highly regulated Garden City of Ebenezer Howard and others, who advocated rental housing on carefully laid out grids, with designated service centers and recreation areas.

The improvement societies in Newton's villages wouldn't dream of touching home ownership or erecting multifamily dwellings. They just wanted to keep residents in their Garden City safe.

Mary's move from that narrow, homogeneous population into a wider world where government-subsidized housing was accepted public policy has gone unexplored, although her role in changing Americans' priorities cannot be denied. From her Garden City background, she came to realize that the values sustaining less-populated parts of America came up short in rapidly growing cities. Industrialization and urbanization imposed a new reality, she reasoned, and the laissez-faire capitalism so prized by most Americans could not handle the consequences when factories in large cities drew workers into overcrowded tenements. Mary Kingsbury Simkhovitch's story is unique to her, but it is central to the struggle to put housing with a capital H on the nation's agenda.

2

Breaking Away

To escape the tradition-bound lifestyle her parents had chosen and start carving her own path to activism and reform, Mary Kingsbury needed a burst of energy and a supportive network. She found both after graduating from Boston University (BU) in 1890. But not immediately. Compared with her two most famous colleagues in social reform—Jane Addams and Lillian Wald—she had a sluggish start.

Mary could have initiated a break with Newton when the time came for college, but she opted to commute daily from home to BU seven miles away and accessible on the new railway line. Neither she nor her high school friend, Ida Davis, "had any longing to leave home," she later wrote. "The life of girls shut off and congregating with one another didn't appeal to us."[1] Although BU later became one of the nation's largest private universities, its College of Liberal Arts in Mary's time numbered only 150 students and a faculty of 10. That fostered an egalitarian community, she decided, like the coeducational midwestern colleges.

BU had other advantages. An article titled "Can a Poor Girl Go to College?" appeared in the *North American Review* not long after Mary and Ida made their choice, and it singled out BU as especially congenial to women of limited means because of its admission policy and scholarship program.[2] Besides asserting a commitment to coeducation in its charter ("Ladies will be admitted to all the privileges of the college on the same conditions as gentlemen"), BU boasted a male faculty that took women seriously.[3] One of Mary's favorites, Thomas Lindsay, who taught there for decades, left the strongest impression and may have influenced her decision to major in Latin, his specialty.[4] She found it "thrilling" that he involved students in his research, invited them to his home, and listened to what they said.

Other favorites included philosophy professor Borden P. Bowne, whose description of his student years in Germany may have triggered Mary's later decision to go there to study. She remembered him as an "excellent destructive teacher" who led his students in questioning everything they thought they knew. "To have learned how to distrust any message is the beginning of wisdom," she later declared.[5]

Although Mary did not have the camaraderie of dormitory living, she spent long days on campus, attending classes, studying in the lounge, and socializing with other members of the sorority she joined. She knew Kappa Kappa Gamma discriminated against some students simply because of a "local taboo" or the "wrong" last name, and one of those excluded became a good friend. Anne O'Hagan, who was both popular and smart, "was never invited to join [a sorority]," Mary recalled, "because she had an Irish name and was a Catholic."[6] Already showing a willingness to overlook injustice in favor of what she saw as a greater good, Mary noted the sense of community fostered at the sorority house. A personal bonus came in her junior year when her sorority sisters selected her to represent them at a national convention in Minneapolis, her first big trip on her own.

Closer to home she made an even bigger discovery. In Boston's West End, she began volunteering her time at St. Augustine's, an African American Sunday School, founded as a mission in 1884 by her Episcopal church.[7] Much more than a place of worship, St. Augustine's functioned as a community center, offering classes in woodworking, printing, and other subjects. Mary played piano for Sunday services and accompanied the choir, but what she took away from leading St. Augustine's Primrose club counted for much more. The teenaged members of Primrose invited her to their homes, providing her first up-close look at how crowded, poorly maintained housing stunted opportunity. As a fourteen-year-old, she had gone to a Boston tenement with her Sunday school class and met an elderly woman surviving in cramped quarters without sufficient food or fuel.[8] The scene seemed so alien to anything Mary knew that she dismissed it as "staged," but what the Primrose girls showed her was shockingly authentic.

Mary saw how urban poverty affected lives in multiple ways, from infant nutrition to teenager delinquency, from neglected healthcare to crippled old age. Half a century later, she described the indelible effect of her first exposure to slum housing: "The steam and noise and smell and congestion were too much for one new to this side of life."[9]

After graduating from BU with a bachelor's degree in June 1890, Mary did what most women graduates did at the time—she remained unemployed and continued living with her parents. In accounts of her life, she omitted the eighteen months between graduation and taking her first job, but her brother, Will, who was still living at home at the time, filled in the blanks. Decades afterward, when she was near death, and he, an experienced physician, wanted to summarize her medical history for her doctors, he noted that after graduation from college, she suffered from lumbago (muscle and joint pain in the lower back), "severe and protracted," along with "severe asthma" that rendered her nearly an invalid.[10] Laura Kingsbury's references to Mary's "limping" and hair loss at that time add to the evidence that she was not well in her early twenties.[11]

While Mary was virtually incapacitated, her two closest friends from college, Anne O'Hagan and Ida Davis, proceeded to make lives for themselves. O'Hagan, who had always known she wanted to write, moved to New York and went to work as a journalist. Davis, who had already agreed to marry her high school sweetheart, William Ripley, as soon as he completed his Ph.D. in economics at Columbia, was keen on starting a family. Of the three, only Mary held back, unwilling or unable to move on. Often described by her contemporaries as the most beautiful woman they had ever seen, she had suitors, including a college classmate, Bernard Berenson, who likened her shoulders to those of the Venus de Milo statue. Although he later became a world-renowned art critic, he made a distinctly negative impression on Mary, and her brother labeled him "pure poison."[12]

The eighteen-month period of postgraduate lethargy ended in November 1891, when Mary began substitute teaching in the Somerville

High School and commuting from her parents' home only a few miles away.[13] Teaching Latin to recalcitrant teenagers proved disappointing. Unlike her mother, who thrived on conversations with young people and never lost patience, Mary felt frustrated. She disliked grading papers so much that she later admitted she sometimes just threw them away rather than wade through the many mistakes made by her "backward students."[14] Constant checking on their progress in memorizing Latin conjugations and declensions bored her, and discipline was a problem. It was not so bad when the boys behaved themselves, she admitted, leaving the impression that much of the time they did not. At the end of the 1893–1894 academic year, she resigned, having taught less than two years, and she rarely referred to the experience afterward.

The dissatisfaction with teaching may have served as prime impetus for trying something new, and instead of going back to her sickbed, Mary enrolled as a "special student" (meaning she was not working toward a degree) at the Harvard Annex (later named Radcliffe) in Cambridge. Up to that time, she had made traditional choices, and her decision to major in Latin at BU and write her thesis on the "dative" showed a classical bent.[15] But now a series of events and new acquaintances pushed her in an entirely different direction.

Mary later described herself as a "practical sociologist," drawn into her life's work "through curiosity as to the causes of poverty and human inadequacies of various kinds and a desire to help people to meet their difficulties as intelligently as possible."[16] In other words, it was an intellectual magnet, not an emotional one, that drew her, and the origins of that change are best traced to the academic year she spent at the Harvard Annex when she was twenty-seven years old.

The Kingsburys' Episcopal minister in Chestnut Hill, the Reverend Henry Sylvester Nash, played a big part in getting her to the Harvard Annex. Mary had gotten to know him in her early teens, on those summer retreats her family took with him in Maine, and he remained a magnetic figure for her as long as he lived. His achievements after an obscure beginning provided a model for what one individual could do.[17] Born in 1854 in the small central Ohio town of Newark, where his father had gone to preach after leaving Kentucky because of the slavery issue, Nash taught himself Latin. While on a trip east to visit relatives, he applied to Harvard and was admitted, graduating three years later at age twenty-four. Incredibly learned, he had the ability to concentrate amid any distraction, and a family member reported that he could compose sermons and books while "children careened around him and even made a daisy-crown and set it on his head."[18] Popular as a minister to his congregation in Chestnut Hill and as a teacher at the Episcopal Theological School in Cambridge, he gained a national reputation. When he died in 1912, the *New York Times* referred to him as the "foremost New Testament Scholar" of his time.[19]

Nash's remarkable scholarship only partly explains what drew Mary to him. Charismatic and funny, he put great emphasis on physical training and deemed "football the most spiritual of all games."[20] At the summer colony in North Perry, Maine, he was "always dean," Mary remembered, "witty and the life of every party." For the text of his Sunday evening talks, he would take "the clam, the high tide, the potato patch or the last colony baby." Mary remembered him as a dedicated activist without being an "iconoclast." He disdained self-importance and sometimes amused his friends by declaring that his only hope for the hereafter was that "the Lord would permit him to carry the garbage pails in purgatory."[21]

Very much a man of this world, Nash "despised the scholar who took no interest in our corporate life." He thrived on talk about American politics and history, and he publicly advocated for the vote for women when that was not a popular position to take.[22] This combination of intellectual and physical prowess, accompanied by a strong moral conscience and selfless assistance to others, impressed Mary deeply. No one can read her papers without recognizing the special relationship that existed between her and this minister and family man who was thirteen years her senior. As long as he lived, she spent summers near him, and the rest of the year, the two corresponded. To the end of her life, Mary, who was notoriously inaccurate about dates and frequently wrong about her own children's birthdays, could recall the exact date that Henry Nash died.[23]

It was Nash, who, in 1894, arranged for Mary to live with the family of an old friend of his, the Reverend Francis Tiffany in Cambridge. That intervention was both significant and revealing. Since Cambridge is within commuting distance of Chestnut Hill, Mary might have continued living with her parents, as she had done for her undergraduate degree, but she did not. Tiffany and his wife took in a few boarders every semester to supplement their income, and it was in their house at 11 Hilliard Street that Mary first encountered the home as salon, a lively center of debate and stimulating conversation. Everyone sat around the kitchen table in the evening, helping themselves to a cocoa brew that was always kept simmering (and called simply "stove"). Tiffany had traveled widely, and he was provocative with his "wise reflections," as he entertained his boarders with recollections of time spent in Palestine.[24]

Tiffany stood out as one of several Episcopal ministers in Boston who sought to enlarge the church's scope, and the deeply religious Mary admitted they changed her thinking. The Reverend William Dwight Porter Bliss, who started a subsidiary organization, the Brotherhood of the Carpenter, was particularly influential. His sermons emphasized that religion went beyond an individual's relationship with a deity; it affected that person's dealings with all mankind. Aiding those in need belonged on the list of what defined the human condition. Often called the "social gospel," this interpretation of religion figured in multiple reform movements in late nineteenth-century America, affecting factory conditions, housing availability, medical treatment, recreation facilities, and education.

Social gospel priorities in the United States fit nicely with an import from England—the "settlement house movement," which one historian identifies as a "striking production" of "transatlantic social Protestantism."[25] Originating as Toynbee Hall in London's heavily immigrant East End in 1884, this first settlement house "settled" young male college graduates next door to impoverished families. Word quickly spread of this experiment, and Americans started dropping by for a look. Stanton Coit, alumnus of Amherst and Columbia, apprenticed at Toynbee Hall for three months and returned to the United States to set up his own settlement house on New York's Lower East

Side in 1886. Originally male-run, his Neighborhood Guild changed its name to University Settlement in 1892 and partnered in operations with the female-run College Settlement a few blocks away on Rivington Street.

Unlike the English settlement house, the American version was much more likely to be founded and run by women. Jane Addams included Toynbee Hall on her first European tour in 1887 and then followed up with two more visits before opening Hull House in Chicago in 1889. Vida Scudder's trip to London for graduate work included a tour of Toynbee Hall, and she immediately saw the potential for adapting the idea in the United States. She accepted a job teaching English at Wellesley and observed that many young women just out of college had trouble finding a professional niche and had to settle for living with their parents. In a settlement house, single women would have the respectable option of residing in a female community because they were there to help others. To parents and neighbors who saw a woman's role as wife and mother, the benevolent mission of the settlement house helped justify it as an acceptable, temporary alternative to marriage. Much like a convent, it provided the liberty of living with other women, freed of the demands of family.

Before Addams's Hull House opened, Vida Scudder went to work creating a network of women to support and staff settlements in the United States. She started with invitations to alumnae of the Seven Sisters colleges, and, when positive response came back, moved ahead to form (with Helena Dudley of Bryn Mawr, Jean Fine and Helen Rand of Smith, and others) the College Settlements Association.

Boston's Denison House, founded in 1890, was one of the association's first achievements, and it quickly attracted a roster of unusually talented, motivated women. On a fall day in 1894, when Mary Kingsbury was just starting classes at the Harvard Annex, she made her way to Denison House in South Cove, one of the most congested parts of Boston. The neat, brick building at 93 Tyler Street appeared noticeably pristine compared with the derelict three-story structures around it. No laundry hung on lines strung from its windows, and its walls had none of the dark splotches left by peeling paint. An oasis, Denison House stood out, with neat draperies at its windows, a freshly painted white door, and cleanly swept steps.

The first room Mary would have entered (which she later learned to call the "green room") looked a lot like parlors she knew in her youth: polished mahogany furniture under framed pictures on the walls. But the people who sat in Denison's "green room" and stood at desks in the foyer looked nothing like her Newton neighbors. Elderly women in tattered skirts, young mothers clutching babies and asking for milk, excited teens vying for spots on athletic teams—all contributed to a picture of a bustling but orderly place where something important seemed to be happening. Mary experienced a settlement house for the first time, and it was life-changing.

In a short time, she came to see how Denison House's interior differed from neighboring tenements. With the significant increase in immigration after the Civil War, Boston's share of the newcomers nearly doubled its population between 1870 and 1890.[26] New York City still rated its moniker of "Golden Door," but Boston and other large American cities (including Philadelphia and Chicago) showed immigrants' definite preference for urban life over rural.

Industrialization provided a magnet, drawing workers to cities, and competition for housing near the workplace caused rents to rise. Without any laws to stop them, landlords turned what were once mansion-type single-family dwellings into lodgings for dozens as they chopped large rooms into cubicles. As rents soared, families doubled up, and some augmented their income by taking in boarders. Others made money by turning living space into multipurpose worksites—for home sewing or making candy and dried flowers. Kitchen tables served not only for eating but also for sleeping and manufacture.

Even the most conscientious homemaker could not offset the hardships that such intense crowding produced: lack of sufficient running water and adequate toilet facilities, no space to separate the sick from the healthy, and sleeping areas lacking a window or any ventilation. In such conditions, the newly arrived Irish, Italian, Jewish, and Syrian families found themselves living in slums. When college-educated women moved into 93 Tyler Street, their neighbors had to wonder why they would choose to live there. Some wrote off settlement workers as naïve and ineffective, doing nothing more than "teaching the poor to eat with a fork," and later they would be accused of "slumming."[27]

Historians have taken a more positive view, and one credited the early settlement leaders as part of a "female dominion" that helped women advance in the professions, especially in new fields like kindergarten teacher, athletic instructor, and researcher in social conditions.[28] Activists such as Scudder, Addams, Florence Kelley, and Molly Dewson amended the old "cult of true womanhood" prescription that limited women to their own households, where they served as moral center, physical caretaker, and education manager. By the end of the nineteenth century, the "female dominion" had widened the playing field, so that formerly domestic duties became community responsibilities, and women took leading roles in investigating factory conditions, instituting baby clinics, and legislating rules and regulations for urban housing. Preparing for these new jobs required advanced education, and the reformers pushed for more colleges to open their doors to women. Networks formed for mutual support, leading to a plethora of women's clubs, including one that proved very important to Mary—the Women's Educational and Industrial Union (WEIU).

Molly Dewson, born in 1876, went to work for the WEIU after graduating from Wellesley. She later joined the National Consumers' League and other activist groups that put her in Eleanor Roosevelt's orbit, and after the Roosevelts moved into the White House in 1933, Dewson headed the Women's Division of the Democratic National Campaign Committee. As she helped propel competent women into important government jobs and shape progressive legislation, she noted the critical part women of her generation had played in preparing for these changes. For her, the New Deal was a culmination of "what us girls and some of you boys have been working for so long it's just dazzling."[29] Dewson did not single out Mary Kingsbury as one of the players, but she certainly qualified, as others later noted.

Among the women supporting Mary in her move into another world, Emily Balch, a temporary resident at Denison House in its early days, stands out. Although only a few months older than Mary, Balch, daughter of a prominent Boston lawyer who once served as Senator Charles Sumner's secretary, had already studied at the Sorbonne and embarked on an academic career by the time Mary met her. Balch's friend Helena Dudley headed Denison House for a brief period, and she also joined Mary's list of remarkable female role models.

It is impossible to say which of the settlement house women Mary met in Boston left the largest mark on her, but the little-known Helena Dudley was unquestionably significant.[30] Nine years older than Mary, Dudley had come east from Colorado to study science, first at the Massachusetts Institute of Technology and then at Bryn Mawr. Her subsequent introduction to the settlement house idea changed everything, and she dropped plans for an academic career and went to Denison House in 1893, just when the nation was entering a severe economic downturn. She initially concentrated on relief work—helping people get enough to eat and a place to sleep—but soon turned to more permanent reforms, organizing sewing rooms to provide women with paying jobs and opening public baths to improve hygiene.

Dudley, Scudder, and their co-workers in the College Settlement Association made a point of combining charitable work with academic research. Scudder was one of the few who managed to keep a faculty appointment while proceeding with settlement work, but the need to combine charity with scholarship and reform concerned them all. Writing in the *Annals of the American Academy of Political and Social Science* in 1894, Dudley insisted that in the debate over charity and reform, no clear line could be drawn, but when "people are hungry and hands are idle, relief work must be carried on."[31] The question of whether to focus in time of great need on immediate relief or long-term changes would become a lifetime concern for Mary.

Settlement work was not for everyone. Mary's BU friend Anne O'Hagan accompanied her on one of her assignments from Denison House and later described that time in a Boston slum as "one of the memorably dreary afternoons of my life."[32] After taking a sick child to a doctor, getting a diagnosis, and then going back to the tenement to instruct his mother on his care, O'Hagan could not wait to return to her own world of plentiful baths and neatly combed hair. But Mary was undaunted, O'Hagan noted. She wanted more such missions, like a "shining St. Joan, fair and radiant and armed with a sword."[33]

Leaders in the College Settlement Association looked to Jane Addams for counsel and advice on especially difficult problems. But mostly they improvised, dealing with one request or exigency after another: helping a new mother care for a sick infant, assisting a grieving family obtain funds for a burial, teaching English to Italian newcomers, directing a dramatic production, lobbying for public baths, and putting amateurs together for a concert. Every settlement was a hybrid: part education, part economic aid.

During Mary's one year at the Harvard Annex, the school had not yet formed an official relationship with Denison House (that would come in 1899), but the college's student roster matched the settlement staff in diversity and promise. Among the 255 students enrolled at the Annex, fewer than half were working toward either a bachelor's or master's degree. The others, including Mary Kingsbury, were "specials" enrolled for noncredit. They stood out from the others as the most promising, and college officials judged them "apt to be the ones who soonest make their mark after leaving us."[34]

Among the more flamboyant of the specials was Gertrude Stein who, though younger than Mary, had already experienced much more of the world. Raised partly in America and partly in Europe, she had been orphaned and left with a substantial income for life when she showed up at the Annex in 1893. Her intellectual preferences ran more to the philosophy classes taught by George Santayana and the psychology lectures of William James than to the social sciences favored by Mary. Still, in a student body of 255, paths easily intersected.

Faculty at the Annex was 100 percent male, most of them moonlighting from teaching male classes a few blocks away. One of Mary's favorites, Professor William Ashley, augmented the $3,000 salary from

Harvard by offering a course at the Annex.[35] His decision was fortuitous for Mary, who later singled him out as "the most provocative and stimulating of all [my] teachers.... [He] was a driver and he expected solid work."[36] She received plenty of individual attention since only eight women enrolled in his Elements of Economic History, devoted to Western Europe and England from the Middle Ages to the end of the 1800s. She was one of only two students in his graduate seminar.[37]

None of Mary's other professors provided the excitement that Ashley did, but together they helped divert her from the classics of her undergraduate degree and ignite an interest in the social sciences. Her course selection that year indicates a definite shift to foreign affairs and women's issues: Constitutional History of England before 1500, Modern European History, and a new sociology course that promised to examine the "significance of the status of women and of the family."[38] None of these courses had even the slightest connection to her BU thesis on the Latin dative.

If Mary was seriously considering a career in university teaching, she might have opted to work on a doctorate. But the Harvard Annex did not offer one at the time. That degree was still a relatively new one in America in the 1890s, even for men. Yale had granted the first three in 1862, but a woman did not earn a Ph.D. in America until 1877, when Mary's alma mater (BU) broke the ban.[39] By the time she earned her bachelor's degree in 1890, women held only about 1 percent of the doctorates in the United States, and although that percentage would grow slightly in the decade that followed, it stood at only 6 percent by 1900.[40]

These pioneer female Ph.D.'s sent a mixed message to young women like Mary, because most of them chose either to remain single or marry too late to bear children. For Mary, who insisted large families were happiest and seemed at that point in her life intent on having a sizeable brood herself, it was not easy to visualize the combination of Ph.D. and homemaking mother.

By the summer of 1895, Mary was poised for transition. That one academic year had made an enormous difference. Her courses at the Annex, the women she met at Denison House, and lively discussions at Reverend

Tiffany's home all combined to give new direction to her life. In this community of scholars, activists, and world travelers, she found the courage to do what few of her contemporaries managed. Fortuitously, she received a $600 grant (equal to about $22,000 in current dollars) from the Women's Industrial and Educational Union, an organization which gave recipients wide latitude in how (and where) they used their grants. With money in hand, Mary had her chance to break away from Boston, and on July 16 she sailed for Europe.

3

Finding Answers

In biographical sketches of herself, Mary Simkhovitch liked to include "studied in Berlin." That simple phrase did not begin to capture what happened in the fourteen months she spent in Europe, how her goals took shape, as she found answers to her questions.

The start was unremarkable. She joined hundreds of other Americans going to Europe for graduate study in the late 1800s. Universities in Germany were particularly popular, and the trend to enroll there accelerated after 1870, reaching a peak in the mid-1890s. She applied for a passport on June 8, 1895, and a few weeks later joined Cambridge friends in New York for an onboard sailing party. As they left Fulton Pier on the *Noordland*, the ship's manifest listed her as "MMKingsbury," alongside "LHKingsbury." Unlike the other students, Mary had her mother with her. At age fifty-six, Laura Kingsbury had taken Mary's good fortune at winning the $600 scholarship as an invitation to herself. Entirely convinced that no young woman should travel without a chaperone and knowing the family budget did not permit hiring one, she determined to go herself. Dissuaded in her teens from going west to join her uncle, she welcomed this opportunity to see an even more enticing part of the world.

Mary described the ocean crossing as "eventful." On its first day out, the *Noordland* struck a small fishing boat that had gone off course, and later, passengers sighted an iceberg. They also witnessed the burial at sea of an elderly German immigrant on his way back home to die. A bad storm sent Mary to her cabin the second day out, and she remained there for most of the crossing, unable to lift her head from the pillow. Besides seasickness, she suffered from what was reported as "rheumatism." At journey's end, her mother, who stood the trip well and never missed a meal, felt obliged to tip staff heavily because "Mary required so much service."[1]

The entire Kingsbury family had engaged in long discussions about how to pay for this trip because the $600 scholarship would not suffice. Two small inheritances Frank had recently received, one from his father and another from an uncle, would help, and their Newton house could be rented out for $1,000 a year while Frank boarded with relatives and Will stayed in a college dorm.[2] But there were taxes and debts to be paid, including one to a Bridgewater bank, as well as tuition for Will, who was beginning his senior year at Harvard. When Frank estimated his wife and daughter needed $2,000 more than Mary's scholarship provided, the ever-frugal Laura insisted she would see that they managed on less.

Details of that year are far better preserved in the mother's letters than in the daughter's because Laura, feeling guilty about leaving her husband at home, insisted on sharing her impressions with him. Sometime in the future, she mused, she and Frank might be able to make a similar trip together, but only if "our children are prosperous."[3] They could never permit themselves the pleasure if they had to pay from their own pockets.

After nine days at sea, Mary and Laura got their first look at Europe when they disembarked in Antwerp. Losing no time, they promptly shipped most of their baggage on to Eisenach so they could travel less encumbered. Keen to economize, they stayed at Antwerp's Grand Miroir Hotel, which was, Laura explained to her husband, "not first class, [but] friends have found it good enough."[4] Busy touring the city's cathedrals, museums, and other attractions during the day, they bought cheap tickets for evening concerts, which Mary judged equal in quality to anything she had heard in America.

Both women understood the importance of graduate study to Mary's future, especially if she expected to qualify for a professorship. Laura failed to comprehend why her daughter disliked teaching high school, but she understood that universities paid better. A faculty member could earn $1,500 a year.[5] Even if acquiring the requisite graduate degree meant spending time as far away as Europe, a professorship sounded very good.

Wellesley was only a few miles from Newton, and Laura assured Frank that if Mary got a job there, she could commute and live with them.[6]

The prospect of study in Germany came with caveats. More than one of Mary's favorite instructors at Boston University and the Harvard Annex had touted the academic excellence of German universities, but stories abounded of how women found a cool welcome in some of the graduate classes. One American scientist, Ida Hyde, a decade older than Mary, had been shocked and angered by her reception in 1893, and she titled the bitter article she wrote later about her experience "Before Women Were Human Beings." Although invited to Europe by a Strasbourg professor who had heard of her impressive experiments in zoology and biology, Hyde received little help from him after she arrived, and her fellow students, unaccustomed to seeing a woman in a science lab, treated her like a "freak."[7] She managed to earn a doctorate degree in 1896, thus becoming one of the first women to do so in Germany, but it came "magna cum laude" rather than "summa cum laude" because one professor held out against the rest of her committee and refused to confer "highest praise" on a woman.

Whatever her worries about how she would be treated in Berlin, Mary apparently thrived on European air. Soon after arriving in Antwerp, Laura reported that her daughter was walking "with little noticeable limp."[8] Within two weeks, that ailment disappeared entirely. Mary felt better than she had in years.

Making their way 300 miles east by train, the Kingsburys arrived in picturesque Eisenach, where Mary planned to immerse herself in German before starting classes in Berlin. It is unclear why she chose Eisenach, but it was certainly cheaper to rent two rooms there than in Berlin, one of the most expensive spots in Europe. Eisenach was the birthplace (in 1685) of Johann Sebastian Bach, a fact that music-loving Mary would have noted. The landlady at the small boarding house the Kingsburys chose offered another advantage—she doubled as tutor in German—and thrifty Laura managed to get herself included in Mary's lessons "without additional cost." By the end of the winter, she predicted, she would be able to "speak it fairly."[9]

In their meals at the boarding house, Mary and her mother received a thorough introduction to German cuisine, which Mary liked a lot more than her mother did. "Yesterday we had cucumbers served in what looked like buttermilk," Laura complained in a letter to Frank, "and even Mary skipped it. I never touch such messes."[10] As for "German housekeeping," Laura found nothing good to say on the subject and promised that when she returned to Massachusetts, "I shall doubly appreciate our civilization."[11]

In October mother and daughter proceeded to Berlin (after a brief stop in Weimar) and Mary immediately conferred with Emily Balch, the only other American woman attending the Friedrich-Wilhelms-Universität that year.[12] In discussing the courses to take, both women agreed that they should seek out the very best professors, although that meant competing with hundreds of men for seats. In order not to call attention to themselves, they vowed to behave "modestly" and take "a back seat and make the best of the situation."[13] University officials had made clear that the right to attend classes did not mean matriculation—no credit would be granted. The courtesy had been extended because, unlike their German counterparts, the American women could be counted on to pack up and return to the United States without expecting their mentors to find them jobs.

Kingsbury and Balch prepared to accept limitations, though they chafed at the obstacles raised before them. Mary wrote her father that some professors were so "bitterly opposed to the whole movement [for women's education] that they won't allow a woman to cross the threshold of their lecture rooms."[14] She appreciated those who defended her right to be there, and one professor gained her special approbation for making his support for women's rights perfectly clear. After male students smirked through his description of the "debased condition of women," he chastised them: "If anyone here sees anything amusing in what I have just said, I can only say he has utterly failed to comprehend me."[15]

Mary squeezed in as many courses as she could, including a seminar that met four evenings a week, while her mother dealt with practical matters of lodging and food. After advertising in a local paper for rooms,

Laura realized her German wasn't yet up to dealing with the hundred-plus replies that came in, and she hired a local woman to help her choose a place that was centrally located and "not Jewy."[16] Laura's antisemitism is apparent in other letters. When Professor Hirschberg and his wife invited Mary to a "swell dance," Laura made sure that Frank knew that "*of course* she doesn't go."[17]

In assessing Berlin's cultural institutions, Laura lacked the words to express her enthusiasm. "I can never tell you," she wrote her husband, "how I enjoy being in the midst of all this and hearing so much of interest.... Everything here is massive and rich and you feel that the Germans never mean to be second in anything."[18] By December, she was spending three mornings a week at the Berlin Museum of Antiquities, and in the evening she often went with Mary and her friends to a musical event. To economize, they bought the cheapest seats, up in the fourth balcony, "where a German woman rarely sits. We prefer to go once a week at 50 cents," Laura explained, "rather than once a month at two dollars." Mary even offered to forego buying "the new blue serge suit" she wanted so she could afford tickets for more music.[19]

Lectures formed the centerpiece of Mary's days, and she planned carefully to take advantage of the most valuable offerings. Adolph Wagner, a renowned professor of economics, was deemed "so especially good in his course on socialism" that sometimes one thousand students showed up to hear him lecture.[20] In such a large gathering, it is remarkable that Mary managed to meet the man she wanted as her partner in life.[21]

Professor Wagner's class also provided the basis for what became her life's work. She arrived in Germany just as intense debate over laissez-faire capitalism was peaking, and although she did not identify as a socialist, Wagner's brand of socialism, calling for the extension of government into transportation, housing, and recreation facilities, made sense. She disliked what seemed like excessive state intervention (such as obvious police surveillance at political meetings), but she appreciated the range of services available in Germany to all, including the lowest-paid urban worker.[22] Wagner called it "state socialism," without the craziness and occasional criminality of revolutionary socialism.[23]

Branded later as "municipalization," this segment of Wagner's agenda grew out of his observation that what sufficed in rural and sparsely populated areas was neither feasible nor adequate in crowded urban areas. He was not unique in recognizing the change and advising remediation. In England, Birmingham's mayor, Joseph Chamberlain, had reaped his own share of attention in the 1870s, when he spearheaded new government services for his city. Deeming gas and water supplies, parks, and recreation spaces a responsibility of government, he came to stand for what some called "municipal socialism."

Mary, who grew up among people who put the highest value on individualism and self-reliance, began readjusting her priorities to fit Wagner's thesis. Times had changed. In farmhouses and small towns, waste removal could be left to individuals, but in crowded city housing, with residents stacked on multiple floors, it required supervision and regulation. Not surprisingly, Wagner's critics dubbed him father of "sewer socialism."[24]

Wagner's focus on cities is understandable, given that his adult years witnessed the same rapid urbanization in his native Germany that altered the United States between 1871 and 1900. The number of Germans living in cities of 100,000 or more quadrupled, and the resulting congestion caused misery and health hazards not previously known. Germany stood at the forefront of European efforts to assign cities responsibility for providing and regulating essential services, and when Mary toured publicly financed housing projects and rode city-operated transport, she found the "municipal socialism of Berlin . . . visionary, exhilarating, imaginative and well worth copying."[25]

The Paris Universal Exposition of 1900 was still in its early planning stage when Mary, in Berlin, began a long examination of how Americans differed from Europeans. The exposition highlighted those differences in stunning detail. Fifty-six countries participated, and besides their individual pavilions, thematic displays (on industrial, commercial, scientific, and cultural developments) demonstrated how the new upstart North America had its own ideas about what to show off. One historian notes that the British exhibited maps illustrating extensive poverty in their midst, the Belgians touted low-cost housing they had provided, the

Germans (although sounding imperialistic) touted a social vision emphasizing learning and art and proudly pointing to the social insurance available to German workers for the previous sixteen years.[26] While the French pavilion showed the benefits of mutual insurance and savings societies, the US counterpart, "behind its classical false front, was about business" and the rosy future of capitalism. That was exactly the mindset Mary Kingsbury took to Europe in 1895. It is not the one she came home with in the fall of 1896.

Exposure to new thinking may explain the change that Emily Balch saw in her American friend. Comparing the Miss Kingsbury she had met at Denison House in Boston with the woman enrolled in Berlin, Balch much preferred the latter. "[She is] nicer, or at any rate more interesting than I remembered her and it is great fun to have someone to discuss one's ideas with," Balch wrote home at the end of September 1895. "She is one of those persons who look so well and capable that it seems as if you must catch something of both. She has, moreover, the advantage of being a lady which a great many very nice people are not."[27]

Time spent together in Germany cemented a lifelong friendship between Mary Kingsbury and Emily Balch. They did not agree on everything, and Kingsbury never fully embraced Balch's socialism or her convictions on pacifism. Their mutual respect and loyalty, however, remained unshakeable. In 1946, when Balch became the second American woman (after Jane Addams) to win the Nobel Peace Prize, Mary wrote that she recognized in Berlin that Balch was "a leader in human fellowship, whose modesty, selflessness and daily practice are a shining example to younger women everywhere."[28]

Balch's impressive list of contacts boosted her value as a friend. A former classmate of hers at Bryn Mawr, Alys Smith, had just married Bertrand Russell, and the newlyweds had come to Berlin the winter of 1895–1896 to do research. When Balch introduced them to the Kingsburys at a concert, Laura could hardly conceal her excitement. She found "the Honorable Mr. Russell of England soon to be Lord Russell," still very young, but "we told Miss Balch that we were proud to know a lady with such distinguished acquaintances."[29]

Several male students had their eye on Mary Kingsbury, and Balch evaluated them in letters to her father. She dismissed one of the American suitors as "a very nice fellow if not especially cultivated." Another was worse. Although "very attentive to Miss K and introduces her to Statistical Bureaus and lots of German influential people [he is] very disagreeable." For the most part, the men "simply take no notice of us [women]. . . . No one ever opens a door for you or says 'excuse me' if he bumps into you."[30]

Laura Kingsbury gave a fuller picture of the competition for Mary's favor. Although five men called in one day, she reported in October, "not one of them succeeded [in seeing her], because she was out."[31] In another letter, Laura mentioned an "Austrian count" and a professor but said nothing of the young Russian who had already caught Mary's attention.[32] Either Laura failed to notice her daughter's interest in Vladimir Simkhovitch or she chose to ignore it in hopes it would evaporate.

Emily Balch noticed. In a letter to her "Dearest Papa," she described a tea she had given for twenty people, including "a little Russian whom we see a good deal of in a way, named Vladimir Simchowitsch" [sic].[33] Balch probably did not know that Vladimir, while briefly out of town, had begun writing letters to Miss K that began *"meine Geliebte"* ("my beloved").[34]

Mary apparently kept thoughts of Vladimir to herself and continued exploring Berlin in the company of her mother, who chaperoned the adult daughter as if she were an adolescent. In one instance, when Mary went out with a "Harvard postgraduate," Laura assured Frank that she had been observing the young man for a while and felt confident of his honorable intentions. Otherwise, "I would not have let her go with him alone of course."[35]

Mother and daughter agreed they should avoid "Americans by the hundreds" because they had come to "see Germany."[36] Laura fretted about the high cost of living in Berlin, and she admitted it "fairly frightened" her to realize that the amount Frank had estimated was "not much out of the way." She found it "appalling—so far in excess" of anything she had imagined, but no matter how hard she tried, she could not economize further. Unexpected charges kept popping up. Mary needed to see a doctor about the hair loss that started during her illness after college graduation, and she had other unforeseen expenses, such as the payment of 10 pfennigs every time she hung up her coat at the university.[37]

Determined to see as much of Germany as possible, Mary arranged to go with Laura to Dresden during the Christmas break. She justified the expense by noting that if they traveled third class and stayed in a cheap pension, the excursion would not cost much more than remaining in Berlin. That level of travel, with bare-wood seating in trains and third-class waiting rooms, meant "conquering your pride," but mother and daughter did it "bravely."[38] To have missed seeing the outstanding art galleries of Dresden would have been "idiotic."[39] Mary used the time to have a "long tramp" in the countryside and gear up for what she expected to be more difficult classes in the spring.[40] According to her mother, her health was better than ever, and she ate "like a pig."[41]

Laura's letters show very little of the curiosity about other cultures that piqued her daughter's interest, and she erroneously concluded that Mary's opinions mirrored her own. Writing to Frank about Christmas Eve services in a Greek church, Laura noted that they could not get seats and that "Mary was too much disgusted to stand it out." Assuming her daughter's feelings lined up with hers, Laura wrote that the ceremony and "of course the strange language intensified the repulsion we felt."[42]

In what seems like an odd choice for the most important Christian holiday of the year, the Kingsburys attended a Russian service—perhaps Mary hoped Vladimir would be there. Laura judged this experience even worse than that of the night before with the Greeks. She wrote Frank that a room full "of Russians affected both Mary and myself as being as far apart from us in race as though they were Chinese or Japanese."[43]

In fact, Mary was drawn to those who brought something "foreign." She found them deserving of attention, and she praised the "great pluck" of an aunt who had moved to multiethnic New York.[44] Within days of arriving in Berlin, Mary boasted to her father that seven different nationalities lived in her pension—German, French, Russian, English, Dutch, Cape Colonial, and American. "We try to be a credit to our country," she continued, adding that she felt a special magnetism to one group.

Without mentioning anyone by name, she wrote, "The Russians show up very well. They are always very interesting."⁴⁵

At the university, Emily Balch and Mary Kingsbury managed to gain acceptance from some of their classmates. Both women were elected "unanimously" to the Staatswissenschaftlicter Verein (Political Science Club), and Laura bragged to her husband that they were "the first two women in Germany so far as we know who have ever been admitted to such a club."⁴⁶ She evidently did not know that Vladimir Simkhovitch and two of his friends had founded the Verein, and he would have had a big voice in who joined it.

Before her mother's scheduled return to Newton, Mary wanted to use time on spring break to travel south with her, through Bavarian Germany and Italy. Several classmates agreed to join her for parts of the trip, and one of them—a Mr. Slade—set out with Laura ahead of the others on March 2. Mary was still finishing a speech scheduled for March 6 on the status of women in America. Much more than a simple seminar paper, it was to be given before a distinguished audience of more than a hundred jurists and professors, and she had to deliver it in German.

Satisfied that she had made a good impression with the speech, Mary joined her traveling companions in Munich and proceeded to Verona and then to Venice. The city struck Mary as magical; her mother dismissed it as dirty and undeserving of their time. Concentrating on its hygiene rather than its thousand-plus-year history, Laura wrote home, "It stands to reason it can't be healthy. All the basement stones are dripping with moisture and the rats peep out from among the piles and scurry away to their holes again."⁴⁷

For the month that the Kingsbury women traveled through Italy, mother and daughter continued to express very different opinions. Laura found the Italians exasperating, especially in matters of money, and she struggled to stay one step ahead of them so as not to be cheated. Although she waged a never-ending battle to cut costs, she found that she and Mary were spending $5 a day in Venice, and placed part of the blame on locals for overcharging. "We are well up in all the tricks of the crafty Italians," she assured Frank, "and between us manage to circumvent them pretty often."⁴⁸

Exposed for the first time to a distinctly Latin culture, Mary was "enchanted with the beauty" and began to think of wine as part of a meal rather than a vice.[49] That enchantment grew as she made her way southward, to Naples, Sorrento, and Capri's Blue Grotto. A trip along the Amalfi coast on Palm Sunday was "the grandest drive of our lives," she wrote. For nearly four hours, she and her mother skirted the Mediterranean coast "in glorious sunlight," so close to the road's edge that they could "drop gloves into the sea below." Laura, finally excited about something other than money and what she judged as inferior cultures, wrote her husband, "I have seen gardens and I have seen gardens but never this side of paradise will my eyes again behold a garden like that behind the cloisters which I saw last evening in the full moonlight." She urged him to read "Longfellow's poem of Amalfi—he calls it paradise."[50]

In Rome for Easter Sunday, Mary and Laura joined the thousands filling Vatican Square for the holiest day of their year. It was easy to feel the key role this place played in the history of Christianity—in a way "no history [book] can ever make you feel"—but the ritual was decidedly foreign to those steeped in American Protestantism. Laura objected to the "pomp" and decided her "little Chestnut Hill Church" meant "much more."[51] Mary had a very different reaction. The "holy" sites of Italy intrigued her and she singled out Assisi as the spot she could return to many times, "with the feeling that it is truly a significant, a holy place."[52]

As the Kingsburys made their way back north and stopped for a few days at Lake Como, their plans for the coming year remained unclear. Laura had set a date for sailing back to United States; Mary kept mulling over her options. She needed money to stay in Europe and had applied for fellowships and corresponded with the "powers that be" to keep her name in the minds of people who awarded scholarships.[53] When word reached her on April 15 that her current scholarship would be renewed, it meant another year in Germany was possible, though she was leaning toward returning to America. When Laura left Mary to go to Paris and then to Antwerp to board the ship for New York, her daughter still had not made up her mind. At least she had not shared any decision with Laura, who sailed without knowing when she would see her daughter again. Fortunately, Mary's health was no longer a worry. The Old World evidently agreed with her, and while she might decide to remain in Europe, her mother much preferred the "civilization" of New England.

Uncertainty prevailed as Mary made her way back to her classes in Berlin. If she remained in Germany, she needed to live in a cheaper city and had discussed with Emily Balch the advantages of the university in Göttingen, where the cost of living was a fraction of that in Berlin.[54] As Mary struggled with choices, she kept returning to the one person central to any decision she made: Vladimir Simkhovitch. Despite Laura's careful chaperoning during the year, Mary had had plenty of chances to see him without her mother's knowing. After first encountering him in Wagner's class, their paths crossed often, and his inducting her into his Political Science Club in January increased opportunities for them to spend time together.

Vladimir showed his interest in Mary in many ways. Around Christmas, he inscribed photos of himself to her two best friends in America—Ida Ripley and Anne O'Hagan.[55] The inscription on one, "As a remembrance of the silks I gave you," implies this was not his first communication with Ripley, and the message indicates he was seeking her approval.

The inscription on the photo Vladimir gave Mary after her return from Italy offers even firmer evidence of his intentions. On the back of the large, studio-produced picture of six-year-old Vladimir in a bespoke suit, he wrote in German:[56]

> "Mary:
> To you belongs my present [time]
> To you belong my hopes for the future
> Accept, also, my memories of my past.
> Vladimir"[57]

Emily Balch claimed Vladimir was "captivated" by Mary from the day they met, and she thought she knew why. Both women had been "curiosities" at Berlin, but Mary was "the most beautiful woman" Balch had ever seen. In addition, Mary possessed a "delicious warm voice . . . intellectual vigor, originality and character."[58]

Vladimir remained a puzzle to Balch, and she judged him a curious enigma. Only twenty at the time she met him, he appeared "clever, high strung, fearfully enthusiastic, really a boy and yet in some ways a man. There is something so attractive about him and at the same time very pathetic."[59]

Dichotomies abound in various descriptions of Vladimir Simkhovitch. Some of his fellow students found him self-centered and arrogant, while others noted that he could be genuinely caring of others. Even his most determined critics recognized his wit. When Mary had much earlier requested from New York an accordion and a monkey, she was putting in child's language her wish for a life out of the ordinary, and she had evidently found that in Vladimir.

Physically, she appeared the larger and sturdier of the two—full figured, blonde, blue-eyed, with skin so clear and light it appeared nearly translucent. Although only a fraction of an inch shorter than she, Vladimir's frame emphasized his slightness, and his unruly hair and darting dark eyes conveyed a cagey quality that contrasted with her solid centeredness. While Mary projected a sense of knowing what she was about, with no surprises, Vladimir embodied the mystery of a multilayered identity. His resistance to supplying much information about his origins added to the enigma.

As Mary continued pondering what to do about further study, she made a decision that could not have pleased her mother. But Laura, now back in Newton, didn't know. For nearly two weeks in July 1896, Mary strolled the streets of Paris with Vladimir, enjoying its museums and talking about the future. Together they agreed on a plan. She would return to New York and enroll at Columbia University while Vladimir went back to Germany and completed his doctorate at Halle University. Then he would join her in America.

That important decision behind her, Mary proceeded with her plan to meet Emily Balch in London at the end of July to attend the International Socialist Workers and Trade Union Congress. The well-connected Balch had procured press passes for them both through "a London friend of Karl Marx," giving them the "wonderful chance to hear all the debates and see at close range famous labor and socialist leaders of that time."[60]

Marx's daughter and son-in-law attended the conference, along with Fabian Socialists George Bernard Shaw and Sidney and Beatrice Webb. These were the same people Emily and Mary heard Professor Wagner discuss in his lectures in Berlin, and now they appeared within arm's reach. Eight hundred delegates came from countries around the world. The meeting left an indelible impression on Mary.

Her other stop in London was Toynbee Hall, the pioneer in settlement houses. Unlike Denison House in Boston, Toynbee was a male operation, started by clergyman Samuel Barnett and his wife, Henrietta. Eager to put what they considered the social responsibilities of their religion to work, the Barnetts had come to East London as newlyweds to live in one of the city's worst slums. Despite their religious training and affiliation, the Barnetts did not consider themselves missionaries; proselytizing was not on their agenda. At Toynbee Hall, Mary recognized how an organization identified with one religion could look unwelcoming to those with different beliefs, and she formed the deep and lifelong conviction that religious observance had no place in a settlement house.

Toynbee Hall provided another lesson. Mary learned that the Barnetts had made little progress toward their goal of making a difference in the world until they enlisted recent graduates of Oxford University. By settling a cadre of young, ambitious men in Toynbee Hall, with the agenda of studying the neighborhood and interacting with the men and women who lived nearby, they could make a change. The Barnetts named the men's residence Toynbee Hall, a salute to a young Oxford tutor, Arnold Toynbee, whose untimely death in 1883, at the age of thirty-one, was attributed to overwork helping the poor. Whitechapel, where Toynbee Hall opened on Christmas Eve 1884, was undergoing a population change as Eastern European Jewish immigrants replaced English and Irish residents. The newcomers needed language instruction and other adaptive strategies. The Barnetts did not delude themselves that they could provide everything, but they could foster respect on both sides of the class divide, resulting in gains for all. The Oxford men, headed for careers in politics and business, would learn about a population they didn't know, and the slum dwellers would gain language and work skills to give them a way out.

By the summer of 1896, when Balch and Kingsbury visited Toynbee Hall, they were hardly pioneers—they added to what was looking like a female brigade. Jane Addams, Ellen Starr, Vida Scudder, and others had already made multiple visits and had set up their own settlement houses in the United States. A contingent of American males also looked to Toynbee Hall as an example. It was the women's names, however, that made bold print.

Because sleeping quarters were a defining feature of the settlement house and propriety dictated not mixing the two sexes, most were designated primarily for one or the other. That didn't mean all the work at the settlement was done entirely by one sex—it meant that dormitory space was reserved for one sex while the other took sleeping quarters close by and came in for work assignments, meetings, and meals.

By August 1896, with the Toynbee Hall visit behind her, Mary was ready to return to New York. It had been a pivotal year. Lessons in Wagner's socialism, firsthand exposure to Germany's experiments in public housing and other services, meeting world-famous socialist figures at the London Conference, and seeing Toynbee Hall in operation combined to alter her thinking and change her career goals. Equally important, the romance with Vladimir Simkhovitch had pushed ideas about a cloistered or female-centered life out of the picture. She was in love. She wanted a career, but she wanted a family, too. She had set a goal that subsequent generations of American women would call "having it all."

4

Choosing New York

In mid-September 1896, when Mary steamed back into New York Harbor, she got a different picture from the one her mother saw at Lincoln's death procession in 1865.[1] Each of those three decades had added large numbers of immigrants to the population, many coming from Europe. The scene that the young Laura Kingsbury struggled to portray had become even more complex. Still limited to the island of Manhattan (the other boroughs would not officially become part of New York City until 1898), the number of people claiming a place to sleep there had nearly doubled. Intent on living close to the jobs they found at the city's port, factories, and construction sites, they settled for cramped quarters in derelict buildings. Profit-minded landlords took advantage of the fact that four out of ten New Yorkers had been born in another country. They lacked the language, contacts, and experience to protest their exploitation.

Wiser and more traveled than when she had sailed fourteen months earlier, Mary Kingsbury was much better prepared to deal with a metropolis of this size. Formerly unsure of herself and a bit sickly, she now had stamina, direction, and focus. No more mention in family letters of rheumatism, limping, and hair loss. As she prepared to make decisions about where to live, study, and work, she had someone else to consider besides herself, and that complicated things. Vladimir Simkhovitch, who routinely described his family as "rich," made very clear that he was on his own now. If he came to join her, as promised, she would have to support them both, at least for a while.

Combining that responsibility with Kingsbury's other priorities was more appealing in multiethnic New York than in any other American city. She later wrote, "I was drawn to the idea of plunging into life where it was densest and most provocative."[2] No metropolis in the nation matched its excitement and bustle, its opportunities, and its cultural offerings. Long noted for its heterogeneous population and its rough (some would say, crude) edges, Gotham seethed with change. The colorful fragments of its neighborhoods shifted and rearranged themselves too fast for anyone to chronicle.

Anne O'Hagan, Kingsbury's classmate at Boston University, had already settled in the city, renting an apartment on Irving Place, just above 14th Street, and writing articles on multiple subjects for some of the nation's most popular periodicals. One piece in *Munsey's* dealt with current events (Cuba); the next with a literary figure (Cyrano de Bergerac). O'Hagan's daily routine incorporated a wide range of persons and ideas, and when Kingsbury moved in with her, she began exploring the city with O'Hagan's "delightful companions."[3] The renewed association of the two women proved fortunate. Kingsbury's introduction to "the life of the city and its writers was wide," she later wrote, and "New York worked its charm upon me."[4]

O'Hagan's neighborhood showed the results of a change in immigrants. New arrivals from southern and eastern Europe, especially Italians, Greeks, and Russians, were replacing the Irish and German accents of those who came earlier. In a short walk from O'Hagan's apartment, Kingsbury could hear a dozen different languages. She could hear several just by sticking her head out the window, and it was under the tutelage of her journalist friend that she got her next lesson in immigrant life.

It seems more than likely O'Hagan knew about Vladimir. He certainly knew about her because he had inscribed a photo of himself for her the previous winter. If she and Mary talked at all about him and what American city would suit him, New York would surely emerge the clear favorite. Variety was important to him. He needed a place where he could find exotic foods, art markets, and a good chess game. Kingsbury realized that his heavy Russian accent would have branded him an outlier in much of the United States, but in New York, where so many others were foreign-born, he would fit right in.

Another plus for New York was its distance from Laura Kingsbury. Mary could hardly forget her mother's disdain for Vladimir in Berlin, how she had brushed him off like some disagreeable insect on an afternoon teacake. His penchant for kissing everyone, both male and female, struck Laura as decadent, and his wit, appreciated by others, left her cold. She could hardly ignore him since he was usually the center of attention, but she made no pretense of liking him. As far as she was concerned, he did not begin to measure up to the young men who had been courting Mary since she was old enough to be courted. To Laura Kingsbury, Vladimir Simkhovitch was just a sorry representative of an inferior people whose Eastern Orthodox Christianity included too much incense and too much gold.[5] That disdain would have multiplied exponentially had she known that he was, in fact, Jewish.

Mary had her own reasons for choosing New York. She felt drawn—as had young Americans for generations—to its energy and variety. Later in her life, when questioned about why Italian immigrants stuck to large cities rather than spreading out into rural, open spaces farther west, she defended their choice as perfectly understandable. Italians liked cities for the same reason she did, she explained; they found them more interesting.

One of the most powerful of Gotham's many attractions was Columbia University, located in the East 40s at that time, within walking distance of O'Hagan's apartment. It wasn't convenience, however, that made Columbia the obvious choice for Kingsbury. Its faculty, reputedly the best in the nation in the "new" social sciences, offered her the chance to continue the intellectual journey she had begun at the Harvard Annex. Echoing the Christian Socialist clerics whom she had earlier encountered in Boston, Columbia's professors, many of whom had studied in Europe, encouraged moving beyond textbook treatment of the past to include consideration of the contemporary world.

The virtual wall between Columbia and gritty downtown began to fade as professors introduced students to "fieldwork" and encouraged them to exit the library and investigate how people lived—their homes and working conditions, hygiene, and political alignments. Richmond Mayo-Smith, at the forefront of this change, had studied at the University of Berlin before coming to Columbia in 1877. He advocated treating the entire city as "the natural laboratory of social science, just as hospitals are of medical science," and he dispatched students to work at charitable institutions around the city.[6]

One prodigious, inventive mind attracted another, and Columbia's faculty in Kingsbury's field boasted a roster of intellectual pioneers. Some among the all-male faculty welcomed females into their classes and encouraged everyone's participation in discussion and research.

The most exciting of her mentors were not much older than Kingsbury, and she later singled out several as influential. Edwin R. Seligman, six years her senior, had started teaching at Columbia when he was only twenty-seven, but had already studied in Berlin, Heidelberg, Geneva, and Paris. A man of broad interests, he had not yet authored the books on fiscal policy and taxation that would earn him a national reputation, but she could see that his sensibilities fit hers. The son of a banker, Seligman was pioneering progressive reforms in housing and education for low-earning New Yorkers.

Other significant figures at Columbia included John Bates Clark, who had studied in Germany and Switzerland before returning to the United States. He added his voice to those urging fellow academics to expose their students to new thinking. For the very first sociology professorship in the United States, Columbia hired Franklin Giddings in 1894, about the same time that James Harvey Robinson started teaching what became an enormously popular course in European intellectual history. Rather than stick to military and diplomatic subjects, Robinson urged his colleagues to incorporate anthropology, sociology, and psychology into their syllabi for what he was calling the "new history."[7]

Decades later, when Mary Kingsbury Simkhovitch wrote her autobiography, she named all these men as her teachers. It is an impressive list. But it is important to remember that she did not actually earn another degree. Columbia's records for 1896 to 1898 list her as "in attendance" at classes in economics and social science, sociology and statistics, economics and finance, French, and history.[8] Other women at Columbia at the same time pursued doctorates, and one of them, Elsie Clews (soon to become Elsie Clews Parsons) became a good friend of Mary's. But adding a Ph.D. after her name did not appear to be Mary Kingsbury's goal, suggesting that she had already discarded the idea of college teaching for something more activist.

The greatest value of those years at Columbia may well be the contacts she made; many of the names on her list of professors turn up later as advisers and supporters in her professional life. At this early stage in her career, they offered a third layer in the process of changed thinking that began at Harvard Annex and grew in Berlin. The fact that these same professors stood as towering figures in Vladimir's chosen field provided an additional bonus.

At the beginning of her second year at Columbia, when the campus moved farther north to Morningside Heights, Miss Kingsbury left Anne O'Hagan's apartment and relocated to a more densely populated section of Manhattan. Situated east of the Bowery and north of Delancey, 95 Rivington Street sat in the area Jacob Riis had already exposed to uptown New Yorkers (and the rest of the nation) in his 1890 book, *How the Other Half Lives*. Riis's photos of dim and dingy rooms crowded with hungry-looking children and their poorly clad elders sent shock waves beyond Manhattan and stamped for a century the Lower East Side as destitute.

The façade of College Settlement at 95 Rivington Street, where Kingsbury moved in September 1897, stood out from the rundown tenements around it, much like Boston's Denison House did on Tyler Street. Originally an "old-fashioned mansion" with large, high-ceilinged rooms and intricately modeled woodwork, Number 95 had once housed a wealthy New York family. After they relocated to put some distance between themselves and the immigrants moving into the area, the building was divided into multiple units. The combination of too high occupancy and too little maintenance produced rapid deterioration, and by the time the College Settlement Association rented it, volunteers had their work cut out for them. With a major cleanup and refurbishing, they transformed it into a "Palace of Delight," according to an article in *Lippincott's Monthly Magazine*. The once-dismal structure became an inviting place of "delicately tinted walls, . . . well-bound books on the cabinet shelves, and the objects of *virtu* scattered about with the careless grace that suggest the presence of cultivated women."[9]

Although founders of the Rivington Street settlement came predominantly from the Seven Sisters colleges, they lacked the financial resources of their Ivy League brothers, and they could not provide free lodging to all who volunteered to teach and work there. College Settlement, unlike Toynbee Hall, began charging a few cents to those who used their services and could afford to pay. Volunteer workers like Mary Kingsbury paid for their lodging out of what they earned at the settlement.

The number of "college girls" on Rivington Street varied from week to week, with some moving out to follow other opportunities while others moved in. Sleeping space was limited, but six to ten women typically resided at the settlement, intent on making contacts with their neighbors. To overcome reluctance of immigrants who wanted nothing to do with them, the "college girls" reached out to the neighborhood children, offering them picture books, and engaging them in games, hoping to arouse the curiosity of their parents and draw them to the settlement house for classes in hygiene and crafts. Even if the parents refused to enter the premises of 95 Rivington Street, they might become more receptive to home visits, thus giving settlement workers a chance to monitor their sanitary facilities and eating arrangements.

As word spread about 95 Rivington Street, boys in the neighborhood began requesting their own separate clubs and recreation facilities, and men were hired to lead them. The basement became one of the favorite spots in the house, combining a lending library with a lounge for reading and listening to music. The backyard, covered with trucked-in sand, offered rope swings and space for gymnastics. The College Settlement offered one amenity that most settlements did not—public baths for women. These proved extremely popular, and on hot summer days, dozens of women walked miles and paid the ten-cent entry fee to take a shower.

Soon after she arrived, Kingsbury met the head worker, Jane Robbins, a superb model to follow. Daughter of a prosperous Connecticut couple, Robbins attended Smith College and taught school in Kentucky before deciding to enter the Woman's Medical College of the New York Infirmary in 1887. By the time she completed her medical degree, she had joined the settlement movement, where she encountered situations that had not been part of her school's curriculum. She had to improvise as she went along, learning about unfamiliar immigrant customs, local politicians on the take, and corrupt law enforcement.

Robbins's initiation into life on the Lower East Side was an eye-opener. The policeman who stopped by 95 Rivington had mistaken its all-female lineup for a brothel, and he blithely informed the director what his regular shakedown was going to cost her.[10] Robbins, who had previously considered herself aloof from what she considered sordid dealings in finance, now realized she would have to play along to get along. Boys in the Italian neighborhood gave her another lesson. As Robbins later explained to an anti-Tammany gathering of the Women's Municipal League, the boys introduced her to a game called "election," which involved thrusting a piece of paper in another person's hand and saying, "Dere, now, is some money, an' you kin vote."[11]

When Robbins left College Settlement in January 1898 to confront other challenges, Kingsbury replaced her as head worker in charge of operations. Although this was her first attempt at managing a staff, she excelled and gained glowing reviews from the settlement's board. She streamlined assignments, turning many of the head worker's tasks over to assistants so that she had time for promoting the settlement movement to outsiders. The board sent her to Elmira, New York, to speak to the "sociological section of the Elmira Academy of Science," and laudatory reports came back. The board applauded how quickly Kingsbury "showed a grasp of the situation and a power of organization which enabled her to make a decided advance" in how the organization ran. Previous directors had closed the house during summers to give staff time off. She kept it open, with fourteen workers on hand.[12]

A common thread ran through all the American settlement houses, but Kingsbury recognized that each had a slightly different emphasis. One put greater importance on physical education or job training, while others (including that of Lillian Wald, originally named the Nurses' Settlement) stressed hygiene and health. Vida Scudder's College Settlement Association allied closely with academics, and its definition of a settlement became Kingsbury's: a "graduate school whose university is the outer world."[13]

Settlements like hers, with entirely female staffs, encountered misogyny, and Edward Cummings, the Harvard Annex professor whom Kingsbury had admired as both tough and brilliant, was among the guilty. He compared American settlement houses to England's and concluded the Americans were unprofessional and lacked the cool observation and shrewd administration essential to successful community organizations. Because so many of them were directed by women, he implied they lacked organizational skills.[14]

Vida Scudder defended her sisters, arguing that women needed time and that the "amateur quality" would diminish, although she hoped it would never entirely disappear. It was exactly that zestful enthusiasm that stood as the settlement's greatest value. "It has been said," Scudder continued, "that if half a dozen young men got together, they would instinctively form a club, but the same number of women would evolve a home."[15] The "hominess" was desirable, she concluded: "A settlement stands primarily, not for the application of a method, nor for the accumulation of fact, nor for the evolution of theory. It stands for a purely spiritual ideal; for life, which is an end in itself."[16]

Scudder skipped over one important function of the settlement: providing a place where ambitious, well-educated women like herself could connect and support each other both professionally and in their personal lives. It was a need that the brilliant, well-traveled Scudder understood well, as did her good friend Helena Dudley. Much like medieval convents that offered women an escape from authoritarian males and a chance to live in a small community under female management, social settlements attracted women like Dudley and Scudder.[17]

Neither married, and Scudder defended single-sex households as rich and full. "I want to register my conviction," she wrote in her autobiography, "that a woman's life which sex interests have never visited, is a life neither dull nor empty nor void of romance."[18]

It was in that heady period, when Kingsbury was on her own in New York, studying at Columbia and residing at the College Settlement, that she published her first scholarly article. In a special issue of *Municipal Affairs* devoted to "women's work in city problems," she outlined how the eighteen settlements then operating in the New York area differed. In what sounds like a class paper for one of her Columbia professors, she noted that only a few were run by women: the Neighborship Settlement in Brooklyn, Whittier House in Jersey City, and three in Manhattan: Lillian Wald's Nurses' Settlement, Hartley House in the West 40s, and the author's temporary home on Rivington Street.[19] She made very clear that no matter how wholeheartedly settlement workers attacked problems, they could never manage to provide safe, affordable housing for all without "state intervention."[20]

While a resident on Rivington Street, Kingsbury studied Yiddish and immersed herself in the daily lives of Russian Jews, who shared a religion with the Germans her mother had disparaged. Residing among Italian immigrants who came from the same places she had visited with her mother, Kingsbury got to know families torn apart by piecemeal migration, a tortuous process in which a father immigrated first and then sent for his wife and children later. She worried about young mothers trying to feed their families on the meager earnings their husbands brought home, not always on a regular schedule. She bathed new babies and talked with young girls about how to make better lives for themselves without rejecting their families' traditions and love. She organized boys' clubs to keep them off the streets. Unlike Lillian Wald, who focused more narrowly on health services and practical assistance, Kingsbury and her College Association co-workers liked to theorize and talk about how to investigate living/working conditions, and then promote legislative reforms to improve them. It was during the 1897–1898 year, she later wrote, that she caught the excitement of this "kind of university with the lessons hot from the griddle."[21]

Mary Kingsbury, who had come to Manhattan not entirely sure how to merge academic life with the social services, found her answer on Rivington Street. In the settlement house, she had both. Sharing dormitory space and dinners with other educated, highly motivated young women provided an ongoing seminar in ideas. Working every day alongside her immigrant neighbors gave her the incentive to look for solutions to their problems. "There began my long life in the settlements," she later wrote. "I have never regretted that decision [to live on] the old East Side [with] its ferment of poverty and learning, of tenements and sweatshops, of drama, of striking personalities, of political change....Its impact upon a young New England woman was terrific." She singled out that "long period of my education [as] the most exciting chapter, for here everything was tested."[22]

Initiation in political campaigning figured in that education, and it would later serve her well as she proceeded with her most significant achievement—a national housing law. While Toynbee Hall men considered settlement house residency as a political apprenticeship, the same advantage did not prevail in the United States, where political machines, like Tammany Hall in New York, controlled access to political careers and played a big role in victory on Election Day. Since a settlement house could hardly align with an organization over which it had no control, leaders like Jane Addams and Vida Scudder had set a pattern of avoiding party labels and favoring individual candidates who promised to promote needed reforms. That operating mode served Kingsbury in the 1897 election, when she took the equivalent of City Politics 101. She ferreted out the candidate whose ideas most mirrored hers and stood up for that candidate, without regard to party labels.

The Eighth Ward, where College Settlement was located, had a challenger for the job of ward leader, currently held by a flashy, diamond-fingered, ineffective boss, and Kingsbury wanted him out. In this, the first mayoral election uniting all five boroughs, she deemed the progressive Seth Low, then serving as president of Columbia University, far more amenable to her agenda than any of the other candidates. From the steps of College Settlement, she spoke out for him and for other favorites.[23]

Seth Low lost, but many of the contacts Kingsbury made in that campaign lasted a lifetime. Among the most notable were Henry Moskowitz, who later married Belle Israels, a top adviser to Alfred Smith, governor of New York and Democratic presidential candidate in 1928; Felix Adler, a leading educator and founder of the New York Society for Ethical Culture; and Josephine Shaw Lowell, a Staten Islander who shed her widow's weeds to become a primary force in New York's community service and leader of the Charity Organization Society. With access to powerful people like this, Kingsbury might have settled in at 95 Rivington Street and stayed a lifetime.

Ties to her small-town background still pulled, however. One day she took a walk westward, crossing streets teeming with immigrants, then an African American quarter, before arriving at the relatively less-populated blocks west of Washington Square. After the dense crowds on Rivington Street, this seemed like "open space." Its "quaint provincialism" appealed, "like another country," and she would later return to the Ninth Ward [later known as Greenwich Village] to make her life there. But she could never forget Rivington Street's "hold on [her] heart.... Once life on the East Side has been experienced, one can never say good-by. The East Side is always rising, like a genie in Arabian tales, to inquire, to confront."[24]

Soon after that walk, Kingsbury had to leave College Settlement. Staying on was not even an option. Vladimir had been writing loving letters to "Dear Molly" during the time they were separated, and in the summer of 1898, he followed up with the clincher: He was on his way to New York to marry her. Despite the accolades Mary picked up for the months served as head worker at 95 Rivington, she knew the female enclave had no place for a husband.

Circumstantial evidence suggests that the two enjoyed some time together in the interval, between Mary's departure from Europe in 1896 and Vladimir's arrival in New York two years later. Mary acknowledged spending the summer of 1897 at the British Museum "for study," and proof for that comes from the passenger list of the ship *Manitoba*, which sailed from New York on May 30, 1897, with "MMKingsbury" aboard.[25] She made the return crossing ten weeks later. Vladimir's whereabouts during those ten weeks are less clear, but an anecdote he told later places him in London with her. On a solo trip to England in 1913, he returned to a coffee shop he had formerly frequented, and the waiter lamented the absence of his "lovely lady."[26] The wiry, garrulous extrovert had evidently made a memorable impression alongside the solidly built, blonde Mary, and the summer of 1897 looks like the only time the two could have been in London together.

Even after receiving word of Vladimir's imminent arrival in New York, Mary hesitated to tender her resignation. Not until he had sailed from Bremen on the *Friedrich der Grosse* in mid-August 1898 did she give notice she would be leaving Rivington Street by October 1. He had been talking so enthusiastically of his plan to emigrate that his German friends started calling him "our future American."[27] Mary, more reluctant to reveal a romance, had kept her co-workers in the dark, and only after she was sure of his arrival did she confess her engagement. She sprang it on her housemates late one evening as they were getting into their nightgowns and preparing for bed. In one fell swoop, she showed them Vladimir's picture and left them flabbergasted with the announcement that she meant to marry him.

Working with foreigners was familiar to settlement workers. They all did that. Marrying one was something else. Wealthy male settlement house workers sometimes took a romantic interest in the young immigrant women they met, and occasionally a marriage resulted. The reverse situation, in which a native-born American woman linked her future with that of a poor immigrant man, was almost unthinkable. Mary McClure, who was in the room the night Kingsbury revealed her plans, remembered vividly fifty years later the excitement that she and the others felt: "We were thrilled, and I doubly so, by his being a Russian."[28]

Vida Scudder, who lived her adult life in partnership with a woman and once wrote that there were not enough good men to go around, was also present that evening, and she had some misgivings about Mary's announcement. Many decades later, she could laugh at her own apprehensions, though she admitted she had been worried when Mary "turned out the light one evening and pacing up and down, informed my rueful ears" of her engagement to a Russian named Vladimir.[29]

Kingsbury's friends weren't being dismissive when they referred to him simply as "a Russian." That was about all she told them. The fact that the photos he inscribed for Ida Ripley and Anne O'Hagan were still in Mary's possession when she died suggests she kept a lot to herself.[30]

It's not clear how much Vladimir told Mary about himself and his family. The photo he gave her before she left Berlin, showing him as a boy of six, carried an ambiguous inscription that was more about her than him. She could infer a bit from the photographer's Warsaw label, the elegant outfit of the young subject, and the setting. They all supported Vladimir's claim that he came from a family of means and had received a classical education, including study of Latin, Greek, and Old Slavonic.[31] The Latin came in handy during their courtship in Berlin. They normally conversed in German, but when either struggled for a word, a Latin cognate sufficed, and Mary had reason to be thankful for all that time spent on the Latin dative.

Whatever family wealth Vladimir may have enjoyed in his youth, he had warned Mary that he would arrive penniless in America, and she passed that on to her dormitory sisters. They took note, and Annie Ware, one of those present when Mary revealed her plan to marry, expressed concern. The two women had a lot in common (growing up in Massachusetts, attending Harvard Annex, traveling in Europe, working together at New York's Social Reform Club) but this announcement indicated a radical diverging. Ware wrote a mutual friend: "Mary Kingsbury is going to marry a Russian . . . who speaks no English whatever and is coming to America to live. He is son of a very wealthy Russian family who disapprove of the engagement so they will be poor."[32]

Ware added, "Mary insists she will not mind," and there is no evidence that she ever did. The Massachusetts girl who had wished herself out of New England's staid confines had matured into a woman who coveted a bit of the foreign, unfamiliar, and unpredictable. In Vladimir, she had found a man more exciting than any she had ever known, and he was coming to New York to marry her. It would be up to her to find a way to support them both—and to do this in the second-largest city in the world.

5

"Friendly Aid" Falls Short

As Mary Kingsbury prepared for her thirty-first birthday in September 1898, she had a lot on her mind besides welcoming Vladimir. The past four years had been life changing. That eye-opener time at the Harvard Annex, then a widening of her view of government in Berlin, followed by study with innovative professors at Columbia, topped off by accolades collected as head worker at the Rivington Street settlement combined to launch a bigger life—one that left its mark. Not merely on those whose paths crossed hers, but on a nation. Jane Addams and Lillian Wald had already made headlines with their settlement houses; Mary K had a wider agenda.

Details of how to proceed remained unclear. In the field she knew best—settlement work—she appreciated what others had done but saw the limitations of private initiatives. The article she published that year underlined her conviction that "state intervention" was necessary to satisfy human needs. Settlement houses provided only bandages on the wounds resulting from unsafe housing and working conditions. Government would have to intervene.

As she examined her job options, trying to balance personal need and professional opportunity, financial considerations came out on top. After Vladimir's warnings that he had nothing, she might have turned to her parents, but she knew they would balk at supporting her and a husband, especially one from Russia. The job she took would have to accommodate them both, providing a substantial salary and living quarters appropriate for a family. If those were the only considerations, the opening for a head worker at the Friendly Aid Society on East 34th Street looked like a perfect fit. It paid an annual salary of $1,000 (about three times what a schoolteacher earned) and offered a separate suite for its head worker.[1] On Rivington Street, she had bunked with other female staff even after taking charge; the layout at Friendly Aid meant more privacy.[2]

In other ways, the job at Friendly Aid fit her about as well as ice skates on a polar bear, as she would soon learn.[3] Friendly Aid's board president and chief funder, Warren Goddard, had a deserved reputation as an outstanding citizen, who used his personal wealth for the good of his community. His benevolence, however, came with a lot of controls. He retained virtual veto power over all programming at Friendly Aid and had little regard for those whose opinions differed. Kingsbury's firm belief, formed at Toynbee Hall, that religion had no place in a settlement house, would have to bow to Goddard's dictate that a Unitarian service be held at the settlement house every Sunday evening. The name Friendly Aid carried the taint of top-down benevolence going from knowing haves to unschooled have-nots. She had already committed to the goal of an amalgamated community, a "matrix of understanding" for persons of disparate means working together.[4]

On the plus side of Friendly Aid, the neighborhood hosted an unusually long list of nationalities. Immigrants from Germany, Ireland, Italy, Sweden, and Russia formed the bulk of those who walked through its doors, joined by a smattering of other immigrants and native-born. Even if Kingsbury had tallied the pros and cons of the job and fully recognized the negatives, she had to face facts. With marriage only weeks away, she could not wait for something better.

Married couples and families rarely lived at settlement houses, and Warren Goddard's board had every reason to expect a single woman to occupy the head worker's suite at Friendly Aid. With dozens of new settlement houses opening across the continent and residents moving in and out, it's difficult to determine precisely how many had spouses or young children living with them. Perhaps the most visible example was that of Graham Taylor, a Congregational minister, who, while teaching at the Chicago Theological Seminary, teamed up with three of his male students in an experiment modeled on Toynbee Hall. The men rented rooms in an immigrant neighborhood and set about helping recent arrivals from Ireland, Germany, and the Scandinavian countries. After other young people joined Taylor's group, they took the name "Chicago Commons" and moved to larger quarters at 140 North Union Street in October 1894. That provided space for Taylor's wife and four children to join him, and when a new five-story building became home for Chicago Commons in 1901, the Taylor family had their own floor, while a kindergarten and a variety of community activities occupied the floors below.[5]

Florence Kelley had already set an example for using a settlement house as childcare, but it was a temporary arrangement and occurred under duress. Kelley was seeking refuge from an abusive husband when she fled New York for Chicago in December 1891. She had preceded Mary Kingsbury by about a decade in going to Europe for graduate study and meeting a Russian student with political views much like hers. Against the strong objections of her parents, she married Lazare Wischnewetzky in a civil ceremony in Geneva, Switzerland, in October 1884 and took his name. But after his medical career faltered and he failed to achieve the success he craved, Wischnewetzky became "arrogant" and "menacing," according to Kelley's biographer, while Kelley's usual "confidence" deteriorated into "timorous" reluctance.[6] The couple's decision to relocate to the United States did not improve Wischnewetzky's treatment of his wife, and the man once described by his mother-in-law as an "upright man, a gentleman" became physically abusive, striking Florence repeatedly so forcefully that her face turned black from bruises. Fearful for herself, as well as her three children, all under the age of six, she made her way to Chicago, and after a brief time at a local Women's Christian Temperance Union residence, she installed them at Hull House for periods when she could not board them with other families.[7] Even after Kelley returned to New York in the late 1890s and lived briefly at Wald's Henry Street, she had one or more of her children with her. That didn't prevent her from proceeding with her reform work.

Although Mary Kingsbury would very likely have been aware of such flexible residency requirements at other settlement houses, her new employer at Friendly Aid apparently had a more restricted view, and she kept secret her plan to marry a few weeks after taking the job. Had she dared to mention Vladimir Simkhovitch in the interview process, she could have provided the board with a list of his impressive achievements. He was coming to New York from Halle-Wittenberg, touted at the time as the "center of intellectual life," and his doctoral dissertation was already scheduled for publication in Germany.[8] He was even getting his name in the *German Yearbook of National Economy and Statistics* with a book review he wrote.

The list of negatives was a bit longer. Native-born Americans funded Friendly Aid, and they did not see newly arrived Russians as equipped to help other immigrants. Vladimir's personal style, much as it enchanted Mary, struck many others as narcissistic and loud. One of his classmates in Germany, American Wesley Clair Mitchell, later became a good friend, but his description of their first meeting suggests how strong an impression Vladimir Simkhovitch made. On a visit to one of the university's most distinguished faculty members, Mitchell heard a "piercing musical shriek from the alcove off the [professor's] study." It was Simkhovitch, paying a call on the professor's daughter "whom he was entrancing with a critical account of the way in which the local opera [with its barrel-like prima donna] rendered Wagner.... What I had heard was Vladimir Simkhovitch's rendition of the Valkyries' call as they swooped down upon the stricken field to carry dead heroes to Valhalla."[9] The second encounter between the two men was just as memorable. Simkhovitch enlightened Mitchell on the "home life of the Romanoffs and certain very shaky branches on what passed for their family tree."[10]

Mary had witnessed Vladimir's exuberance, and she had equally registered his arrogance and tendency to demean others. He had dismissed one of the university's most illustrious professors as never "influenc[ing] anybody."[11] Vladimir didn't hesitate to show his attraction to the opposite sex, and a friend noted later that he "always put his arm around the girl seated next to him."[12] This was the man that competent, ambitious Kingsbury was about to marry—amusing and exciting to her, but not one that staid board members of Friendly Aid would likely appreciate, let alone want to employ. Nor would his princely affectations make him a candidate for a job in the service sector.

For his very first months in America, Mary didn't have to worry about feeding and housing Vladimir. He spent that time at Cornell University in Ithaca, studying English as a "foreign Fellow."[13] By December, however, when she was still settling into her job at Friendly Aid, he was back in New York City, and they set their wedding date for January 7, 1899.[14]

Their marriage certificate listed the vicar at the Chapel of the Incarnation, at 240 East 31st Street, as performing the ceremony, but Kingsbury credited her mentor, friend, and family minister, Henry Nash, as leading her and Simkhovitch in their vows.[15] The bride wore a white dress and carried a bouquet, but it was the groom, "just conquering our English" who most impressed one guest.[16]

No family attended, except the bride's brother and parents, who made the trip from Massachusetts despite qualms about her choice of husband. Frank and Laura Kingsbury knew little about Simkhovitch, but they had clear notions about what made a successful marriage. Coming from similar backgrounds, they had lived happily together for thirty-four years and could not imagine how their daughter with a husband from some faraway place in Russia could hope to achieve the same milestone. Simkhovitch seemed so odd—such a contrast to the clean-cut young men who had courted Mary in Newton. At least the best man was American. Ernest Bogart, a New Yorker whom Simkhovitch had met in Germany, came from Princeton, where he was teaching, to stand beside his friend and sign the registry, along with Mary's brother.[17]

After a short honeymoon at the Windsor Hotel in Atlantic City, the newlyweds took up residence in the head worker's suite at Friendly Aid, and the bride began signing herself "Mrs. Vladimir Simkhovitch." Unlike her mother, who struggled with housekeeping tasks, she had a full staff seven days a week. In fact, the settlement house ran much like a college dormitory, with Mary in the role of housemother. A hired cook prepared three meals a day for the entire staff to eat in the communal dining room, which was cleaned by Irish maids.

The new Mrs. Simkhovitch focused on managing the many activities Friendly Aid provided. Besides a kindergarten and a bank, she oversaw classes in cooking, history, civics, dramatics, and drawing. She juggled club meetings to attract different age groups and people of varying interests. The bathing facilities became so popular that she had to ration use and impose a small charge of 3 to 5 cents, depending on the bather's ability to pay.

The unexpected called for improvisation. When New York had its hottest June on record in 1901, causing horses to drop dead in the street and Bellevue Hospital to run out of space for sunstroke victims, Simkhovitch instructed her neighbors to fill their bathtubs with cold water and climb in as often as possible.[18] People without bathtubs could go to the hospital yard and request to be hosed down along with horses.

Friendly Aid's head worker did not presume to know all the answers, and she learned from her failures. After finding the meeting hall empty for a community discussion of city government, she mulled over possible reasons and concluded, "People as a rule are not interested in any abstraction. They come to meetings to oppose something rather than to favor anything. They come when they realize the importance of the issue."[19] This reinforced her belief that settlements should not be in the business of "foisting our own opinions or knowledge upon others but in discovering human interest, passions, and tastes, and in working from these as a base."[20]

This conclusion was amply verified when she scheduled a subsequent meeting on a subject closer home—the high rents being charged for substandard apartments. The neighborhood turned out in force for a discussion of how they could lower the share of their earnings that went to housing. She had already argued in her writings that government had to step in, footing at least part of the bill for providing enough safe, affordable housing, but recognized her view got little traction among those who continued to believe that private investors were the answer.

In one of her earliest attempts to change public opinion on this subject, she reached outside the walls of her settlement house on 34th

Street. Learning that Lawrence Veiller, head of the Tenement House Commission, was mounting an exhibit at 404 Fifth Avenue to show horrific slum conditions, she volunteered to help put together the maps, photos, and charts that would document his case for change. An estimated 10,000 people viewed the exhibit in 1900, and when pressure built for the New York State Legislature to enact regulations for existing tenements and those yet to be built, she went to Albany with others to lobby.

Given how overcrowded tenements became, outdoor space—for running and walking, conversing with friends, and enjoying fresh air—presented temporary relief and a refuge. Simkhovitch knew that play space for children was not an option in apartments too small to provide separate sleeping spaces for all. She saw the empty lot on First Avenue and 35th Street as an opportunity, and in a joint project with St. Gabriel's, the Roman Catholic parish, helped turn the vacant space into a public park.[21]

Recognizing that settlement houses had to network to be effective, she teamed up with John Elliott of Hudson Guild to unite settlement workers from all over the city. The dozen or so who met at Friendly Aid in 1901 called themselves the Association of Neighborhood Workers, and as the group grew in clout and number, its name changed in 1920 to United Neighborhood Houses of New York. It remained active into the twenty-first century.[22]

A head worker's primary responsibility, however, was to her own settlement, and Simkhovitch spent much of her energy supervising personnel, both residents who boarded at the settlement and volunteers who put in a few hours each week but lived elsewhere. Census takers in 1900 reported a total of six living at Friendly Aid. Along with Vladimir, the only male, she had the company of a longtime confidante. Anne O'Hagan, her friend since freshman year in college, had come to help at Friendly Aid while keeping her job at *Puritan*, a magazine for "gentle women." In addition, the census listed residents Carole S. Nye, a twenty-nine-year-old kindergarten teacher from Ohio, and two other single women (no occupation given) aged thirty and forty-six, also from the Midwest.[23] While O'Hagan earned money as a journalist, the others had independent sources of income or managed on what the settlement paid them.

By the time that census was taken, Simkhovitch was looking for a way out of Friendly Aid. She had always insisted that residents live simply, to diminish the divide between themselves and the less-prosperous population around them. Her staff agreed, but the Friendly Aid founders furnished their clubroom in plush red velvet sofas, presenting a jarring opulence to the impoverished men and women who had to walk by that room every time they entered the building. She also chafed at the fact that the founders insisted on Unitarian services in a neighborhood that was "practically 100 percent Catholic," and she objected to the board's censoring topics for discussion. When she scheduled an out-of-town speaker to come to her own suite of rooms to present the argument against annexing the Philippines—the result of the recent Spanish–American War—she had to cancel the event because board members regarded as "treasonable" any questioning of President McKinley's stand on the matter. She arranged for the speaker to appear at another settlement house, but questioned why her own employer would not permit a "free platform for discussion" of an important issue at the time.[24]

Friendly Aid's board members did not warm to Vladimir. They found him an unwelcome anomaly in what was largely a woman's world. An animated dinner companion, he appeared eccentric, even to seasoned settlement workers who had met their share of odd characters. He projected an aura of the disinherited aristocrat and was already cooking up schemes to make a fortune, or, as one relative later put it, "something to keep him in the style to which he would like to become accustomed."[25]

Vladimir insisted on waiting for a job to fit his talents, and for the first year of his marriage, he didn't earn a cent. To Mary's parents, it was unthinkable that their daughter labored long hours while her healthy mate sat idly by. She apparently shrugged off all criticism and remained convinced that a man with her husband's degrees and multilingual education could find a fit somewhere. She may even have turned to one of her former professors for help. In the fall of 1900, Columbia University hired Vladimir as "bibliographer and library supplemental," a job that paid less than half of what his wife earned but gave him access to Columbia's faculty and other resources. He soon made friends, and his review, in excellent English, of a book in German on the development of industry in Russia was published in Columbia's highly respected *Political Science Quarterly* in March 1901.[26] Signing himself Vladimir Gr. [Gregorievitch] Simkhovitch, he listed his academic affiliation as "Columbia," without specifying that he lacked faculty rank.

Just weeks after Vladimir's article appeared, Mary had a professional triumph of her own. She returned as "Mrs. Vladimir Simkhovitch" to her hometown to speak at Newton's Social Science Club. The women's study group had been meeting regularly for fifteen years, and most of the members remembered her as Frank and Laura Kingsbury's daughter, Mary Melinda.[27] Now she made her home in New York City and came to them as a published author with a Russian name and ties to universities in both the United States and Germany.[28]

Mrs. Simkhovitch chose to bring her world to them and talk about how immigration had altered large American cities, especially New York, so that it had become "a city of foreigners." She told her audience that when a friend with whom she was on a tram in New York had challenged her to "show [her] an American," she could only point to herself. The ethnic stereotypes, both negative and positive, that she used would have sounded familiar to her audience. She described Italians as "very ignorant, not very ambitious, . . . [but] good artisans." Jews struck her as a "varied bunch . . . either extraordinarily brilliant and attractive . . . or repulsive and degraded. . . . [But always] ambitious."[29]

The nucleus of her talk, however, emphasized her appreciation of the new immigrants and how they defied stereotypes. She found it a pleasure to live among them "day in and day out," observing "not only the evils, but also all the humorous and sunny sides" of tenement living. Witnessing their aspirations and fierce confrontation of obstacles had altered her entire outlook. As she explained to her Newton audience, only after "the insidious evils of life . . . rise up before one like a black shadow coloring one's whole mental vision" could one hope to gain a clear picture of the world, and it would "never look the same again as it did before [the exposure to life's evils] came."[30]

Simkhovitch wanted to clarify how city dwellers faced problems different from those of her small-town listeners. Schools mattered, she argued, since education remained crucial to other improvements, but simply building schools would not suffice. Young immigrants of both sexes were leaving the classroom at the earliest legal working age (usually fourteen) to take jobs available to them in manufacturing and the service sector. She was appalled at their ignorance on many subjects, including world geography and current events. Her audience would have concurred in her thoughts on schooling, but they had little context for judging her other proposals: addressing the need for stronger labor unions and new laws on housing. She was talking about a kind of housing foreign to them. Packing four families on each of multiple floors in a twenty-five-foot-wide building was simply incomprehensible to her Newton audience, accustomed to single-family houses on tree-lined streets. They had no idea what housing with a capital H meant.[31]

The Friendly Aid board members back in New York City didn't need to check on what their head worker was telling audiences in Massachusetts. They already knew her priorities, and their letter of reappointment in June 1901 included a mild reprimand. They offered to renew her contract "at the same salary now paid," and they expressed "the greatest satisfaction" with the sense of "hearty cooperation" among her staff who showed "devotion to the work and an enjoyment in its prosecution."[32] Along with its praise, however, the board hinted at the dangers of a director becoming too ambitious, reaching out in multiple directions, and spending too much money. They wanted the house to run at a profit, not at a "loss as at present," and they directed her to raise rates on the food that residents ate.

Simkhovitch's pregnancy, not yet showing when she received that letter, became very evident in the following months, giving the board additional reason to want her out. At age thirty-four, this was her first pregnancy, and she sounded practically giddy in a letter to a friend. When her delivery date passed, she wrote that she had considered ways to induce labor on "the Recalcitrant" and had decided to ask Julia, who swept floors at Friendly Aid, to let "me take a turn at her job."[33]

Stephen's birth on December 29, 1901, doubled the male population at Friendly Aid, and for a board already concerned with space allocation, this was troubling. One board member wrote Simkhovitch that the director's suite could be better used for the work of the settlement rather than "to provide accommodations for husband, nurse and child."[34]

The nurse had been a problem from the beginning, and it may well have been the hostile attitude at Friendly Aid that contributed to the difficulty. When the first nurse hired turned out to be "unreliable," Simkhovitch "launched" baby Stephen "upon the cold world of bottles," and then asked her good friend Elsie Clews Parsons to find her another nurse. When the replacement turned up her nose at the Simkhovitches' living conditions, Mary sent the nurse and baby off to Parsons at her country house "for a few days."[35] Stephen was only five months old, and this was the first of what would be many separations from his mother. Much as Simkhovitch praised motherhood, she had no compunctions about entrusting her children to others' care. After thanking Parsons for being a "foster mother," she admitted the sight of Stephen's empty bed made her uneasy, but she still postponed arranging for his return.[36]

Simkhovitch mixed mothering news with business in subsequent letters, and after she revealed plans to start a settlement house of her own, Parsons threw her wholehearted support behind it. Daughter of a New York banker, she was both ambitious and extremely well connected, having married the equally pedigreed and wealthy Herbert Parsons in 1900, after earning a Ph.D. at Columbia. Eight years younger than Simkhovitch, she soon outran her in both maternal and academic achievement, and her familiarity with the Social Register meant she had an edge in lining up deep-pocketed supporters for any project she chose. After Parsons agreed to chair the finance committee, Simkhovitch requested her help in getting distinguished people on the governing board: "I am relying on you to catch Mr. Sloane, Mr. Hare and Miss Cutting."[37]

While hatching plans for exiting Friendly Aid, Simkhovitch still had to deal with its board members, whom she described as "high minded" but naïve.[38] They weren't bad people, just misguided, and they acted like Lady Bountiful, observing from a distance how the other half lives. That wasn't the way she wanted to run the organization. The value of a settlement house, she later wrote, "is not so much in the rendering of specific services . . . as in the fruitful knowledge obtained through firsthand contact with the people in the neighborhoods."[39]

The Friendly Aid board's letter on May 10, 1902, made clear that she would have to leave. Rather than renewing her contract, the board noted its intention to follow a less ambitious route than she had wanted and to "concentrate our efforts on the present House rather than, for the time being, greatly extend our work." This meant hiring "a head worker of more simple methods and less far-reaching efforts."[40] Regardless of the diplomatic phrasing, the board wanted the Simkhovitches out, and Mary's contribution would soon be diminished in Friendly Aid's records. After their annual reports were deposited at the Social Welfare History Archives in Minnesota, curator David Klaassen noted that there was "absolutely no reference to Mary Simkhovitch, so it may be that she didn't leave on the best of terms."[41]

Several of Simkhovitch's co-workers joined her in the exodus. Friends wrote supportive letters, noting their disappointment with the board that fired her. Josephine Shaw Lowell, the highly respected elderly widow associated with New York City's Charity Organization Society, called the decision a "great calamity all round."[42] Other letters mentioned Simkhovitch's baby, and one of the more conciliatory board members pointed out: "Even if you would be willing [to let the child live in the settlement], the Board is not willing to take that responsibility and if the baby got scarlet fever or anything happened, they would never forgive themselves that they had allowed him to be there. I don't think there is one person on the Board who has children who would bring up her children there and I suppose they feel that [you should not either]."[43]

Simkhovitch insisted her son had nothing to do with her leaving Friendly Aid. "Let us have no rubbish about my resigning on account of the baby. . . . I resigned only because I was asked to. For mercy's sake, let us not lie about it. If the Board wants a change, they have a perfect right to have it and that's the whole of it."[44]

As the rare settlement worker with a family, she received a few envious notes from childless colleagues. One concluded a letter with a reference to the baby, "Bless his heart. How much will you take for him? I'd buy him high today. I'm lonely."[45] If that was meant as a compliment to Simkhovitch combining mothering with a career, she didn't acknowledge it. Her reply didn't even mention Stephen. In her eyes, she led a seamless life in which babies and speeches, articles and meetings, a husband and a settlement house all fit neatly together. That inclusive view would eventually undergo revision, but she began a firm believer.

Her next career move could not have happened so quickly had she not already been preparing, and in her book *Neighborhood*, she admitted the formulating of plans to start a settlement of her own had started months earlier. Two weeks after receiving the letter terminating her tenure at Friendly Aid, she filed incorporating papers and named five of the most prominent men in New York as her backers.[46] She later characterized them as representing a variety of approaches to social problems, but their function was less intellectual than practical—to give her undertaking legitimacy and provide financial credentials. Friendly Aid had Goddard's money and the Unitarian Church behind it; College Settlement had Ida Scudder's Association of College Women contributing money. Simkhovitch had to round up her own guarantors. She would later need another board of managers to make decisions about the working of her settlement—its programs, staff, and outreach. The incorporating board did not participate in day-to-day operations, but it was essential to validating the settlement's founding, and the fact that a relative newcomer to New York City could line up such a prestigious group indicates the respect she had already garnered. Always mum on any congratulation for herself, she showed no surprise that these five busy, very accomplished men agreed to back her.

Three of her incorporators came as representatives of the city's religious melting pot of Protestants, Jews, and Catholics, and they had all shown a genuine commitment to community service. Henry C. Potter, one of the most respected Episcopalian bishops in the nation, ministered to the cream of New York society at the Grace Church on Broadway at 10th Street, but his belief that "religion should minister to the whole man" spurred him to set up schools and infirmaries to serve the entire community.[47] In a nod to prospective Jewish contributors, Simkhovitch turned to Felix Adler, a German immigrant who had rejected the theistic teachings of his family's Reform Judaism in order to unite a mixture of social reformers, including theists, atheists, agnostics and deists, in the Society of Ethical Culture.[48] Attorney Eugene Philbin, a Catholic known for his network of government officials, had already invested considerable time and energy in helping charitable institutions.

The two men who completed the board had outsized reputations reaching well beyond New York. When Jacob Riis, the Danish journalist, published his exposé *How the Other Half Lives* in 1890, he had changed thinking about immigrants. Carl Schurz, the first German-born member of the US Senate and a member of President Rutherford B. Hayes's cabinet in the 1870s, remained a nationally respected figure.

With her board in place, Simkhovitch needed a name for her new settlement house. Addams and Wald had used place names, Hull House (for the family that once owned the mansion) and Henry Street, but Simkhovitch hadn't zeroed in on a definite location. Without the backing of the College Women's Association (or any other organization), she was on her own, and she chose an academic-sounding tongue twister: Cooperative Social Settlement Society of the City of New York. Later, after she and her colleagues put down stakes in Greenwich Village, the settlement would acquire the name that stuck—Greenwich House—but its legal name remained as set forth in its 1902 constitution.

The founding documents of the Cooperative Social Settlement Society, and particularly its constitution, specified that it would serve "a part of the city where no 'neighborhood house' existed," and that it would operate differently from others. Its organizers pointed to the very earliest settlements as models to emulate because, they, unlike those who came later, were "simply groups of persons living in a neighborhood for the mutual advantage of neighbors and residents." In what sounds like a slap at Goddard's Friendly Aid Society, the founders faulted churches and other associations that began funding settlements but insisted on control, wresting decision-making from both resident workers and those they helped. If holders of the purse determined the agenda, settlement living became "a method rather than a distinct form of life."[49]

The Cooperative Social Settlement Society, as its name suggests, sought wide participation of persons with differing perspectives. Simkhovitch and the other founders understood that sponsors deserved a voice, but so, too, did those who taught the classes and led the clubs. The Settlement Society's treasurer used phrases in his first report that made this clear: "It was in order to preserve the stability and resourcefulness of organization, while recognizing the fact that the residents in the Settlement must necessarily share in its management, that this Society was formed."[50]

With all that Simkhovitch had on her mind in early 1902—new baby, getting out of Friendly Aid, trying to start a settlement of her own—it is difficult to see how she found time to write an article for the *Political Science Quarterly*. Titled "Friendship and Politics," it reiterated her commitment to working outside the political system to initiate social reform.[51] Rather than piggyback on either a Democratic or Republican agenda, she advocated immersing oneself in a community's problems, figuring out a solution that fit each one, and then backing the political player most likely to advance it. Her pragmatic approach was a strategy for making progress on community projects without risking charges of "socialist" or "un-American."

In June 1902 Mary set off with husband and five-month-old son for the trip to North Perry, Maine, where her parents still vacationed. She had already introduced her husband to the community of Episcopalians, headed by her mentor and friend, Henry Nash, and he had become as fond of the area as she. Except in extreme circumstances, such as the war in 1917–1918, the couple left New York every summer, made their way north, and for two or three months relished a respite from urban sounds and stresses. In 1918, they purchased their own aptly named Mansion House near the town of Robbinston, Maine. But in the early years of their marriage, more moderate accommodations served, and they had multiple opportunities to observe young Franklin Roosevelt sail his boat *New Moon* on the water separating their home from his. After his marriage to Eleanor, Campobello became the couple's favorite retreat.

As the 1902 summer sojourn began, Mary was again pregnant and concerned about dealing concurrently with another baby and a new settlement house. After briefly considering putting professional goals on hold, she changed her mind and wrote Elsie Parsons on June 27 that she was now "inclined to go right ahead with my plan [for the new settlement house] just the same for I should arm myself with a secretary, etc."[52] She expected the second baby's delivery, just fourteen months after the first, to be easier, and she liked the idea of providing Stephen with a "comrade . . . his own age to love and fight with."[53] With a delivery date set for February 1903, she felt confident she could be back at work by April. Responsibilities at the newly opened settlement should be light those first few months, she predicted, consisting mostly of learning about the neighborhood and getting acquainted with those who already lived there.

Before she left for Maine, Simkhovitch and her co-workers had agreed on locating their new settlement somewhere west of Washington Square. The difficulty was finding adequate space at a reasonable price. Soon that part of New York would become internationally famous as the bohemian enclave Greenwich Village, but in 1902, it was just a neighborhood struggling to accommodate an increasing influx of immigrant families and single laborers looking for cheap housing near their jobs.

Two of her associates at Friendly Aid, Paul Kennaday and Mary Sherman, had signed on to her new project, and they took the lead in finding a site. In late July Kennaday wrote they had located something that might work—a three-story brick house at 26 Jones Street. Buildings on both sides of it—another three-story house on one side and a paper-box factory on the other—were both due on the market soon, and that would provide, he wrote, "plenty of room to grow if we are able." On the negative side, Kennaday listed a damp cellar, some partitions to be removed to let more light into the dark middle rooms, and the need for a thorough cleaning and paint job. With $2,000 already collected, he suggested renting the house for three years and using the remaining $1,500 for repairs. Residents who signed on to the project and paid rent would supply "the running expenses of the house," and, he noted with considerable optimism, "before long, the public would pay for the rest."[54]

Although Kennaday and other members of the finance committee sounded enthusiastic about 26 Jones Street, they insisted on pleasing Simkhovitch. "That," he wrote her, "after all, is the point to get what you want!" The committee's chief reservation concerned her infant son, or as one letter put it, "in regard to the street on Stephen's account."[55] That anxiety was understandable. Jones Street stood out as a particularly unsavory place to live, with a high infant mortality rate and two gangs, the Hudson Dusters and the Gophers, battling for dominance. About half the buildings on the block were crowded tenements of six stories, and five of them hosted saloons on the ground floor.[56] Even though it was a twenty-four-hour trip down from Maine, Kennaday thought it imperative that Simkhovitch see Jones Street, and he offered to schedule a finance committee meeting while she was in the city so that others could share their thinking on the property.

After a quick investigation, she enthusiastically approved Kennaday's choice. In a letter she wrote after returning to Maine, she made no mention of baby Stephen or the second child due a few months later but applauded the ethnic mix in that part of the city. "The situation is good. The population is varied; the colored [sic] population is said to be moving out, but Bleecker Street is Italian and Jewish and there are also . . . some French people in the neighborhood." Memories of her trip through Italy six years earlier may have influenced her view on one subject. She considered the growing Italian colony "a good thing," and added, "There is relatively very little work done in New York among Italians and at present there are more Italians coming to New York than any other nationality."[57]

Firming up a location was a major achievement, and Simkhovitch thought it essential. On August 18 she wrote from Maine, "I feel sure that we shall have no difficulty in getting the relatively speaking small sum necessary for the first year if we have a House; whereas I don't believe we shall be able to raise money at all for an object totally in the air."[58] Since she and her family would all live rent-free at the settlement and take their meals there, she announced she would accept no salary for the first year. Her practical-minded friend Parsons might have swayed her on that matter because Simkhovitch wrote her to announce a change of mind. She could manage everything, she assured Parsons, "as long as I shall be drawing a salary."[59] Jane Addams, Simkhovitch's model in so many ways, had a sizeable inheritance to help finance Hull House, while she had no cushion of family funds for Greenwich House.[60]

Although she faced uncertainties and major decisions in the summer of 1902, Simkhovitch pronounced those months "lovely." Vladimir gained sixteen pounds, and baby Stephen thrived on "Jersey milk."[61] Before returning to New York, she deposited Stephen with her parents for a few weeks so that she and Vladimir could house hunt. They had vacated their quarters at Friendly Aid in early June, and at summer's end, they checked into a boarding house just around the corner from it, at 229 Lexington Avenue. She disliked boarding, which meant not having her own kitchen while dealing with "a baby & a pasteurizer," and she wanted to be closer to 26 Jones Street.[62] It would be weeks before she could move in, but she intended to keep an eye on the renovations. Vladimir thought it folly to set up a place of their own for such a short period, but his wife prevailed, and for one of the very few times in her adult life, she managed domestic matters for her own household.

From the apartment she and Vladimir rented on King Street, Mary could take a short walk over to Jones Street and assess the condition of number 26. Kennaday had not exaggerated when he described it as needing work. Once a comfortable home for a single family, its three floors had been transformed into multiple small compartments, each housing a family or a group of boarders. The increased occupancy had not coincided with a refitting of essentials, however, and the water supply, toilet facilities, and waste removal remained shockingly inadequate. She saw a building in "an unimaginably filthy condition . . . dirt . . . vermin . . . the entire plumbing system and more than half of the gas piping had to be entirely renewed . . . no central heating."⁶³ With money raised by her associates and the labor of volunteer staff, she knew 26 Jones Street could be converted (like Denison House and 95 Rivington Street) into something far more attractive and useful. Her neighbors, in cramped quarters on the same street, did not have that option.

Anne O'Hagan continued to combine her day job in journalism with helping Mary, and she joined in the cleanup. Always the reporter, she took time to record one of the few descriptions that survive of the building at that time: a "fine mahogany-doored, brick-fireplaced old house" that had been "debased into a particularly crowded and dirty tenement." The prospective residents and volunteers tore down the partitions between rooms to make lighter, larger spaces on the first and second floors. In the basement "after dinner lounge," they painted what O'Hagan claimed were the first pumpkin-colored walls ever seen in Greenwich Village. After planting ivy to camouflage the bleak factory wall on one side of the backyard and buying minimum furniture, they proclaimed the "first Cooperative Social Settlement underway."⁶⁴

In the four years following Mary Kingsbury's shocking revelation to her friends at College Settlement, she managed not only to marry the Russian but also open a settlement house of her own. Located in one of the most vibrant sections of New York City, it would thrive well into the following century, a model for community centers across the nation. That a young newcomer to the city, without financial resources of her own, could accomplish this is remarkable. That it was a woman who achieved this while also starting a family (for whom she was sole financial support) underscores why the comic book series on Diana Prince later singled out Simkhovitch as a "Wonder Woman of History."

6

Life of Jones Street

On Thanksgiving Day 1902, the Cooperative Social Settlement Society of the City of New York officially opened, and spirits were high that evening as Mary and Vladimir Simkhovitch sat down to dinner with the nine men and women who had volunteered to work with her. The room still smelled of fresh paint, and some of the furniture looked shoddy, she later wrote, but "we felt somehow born again. We were all young together. Everything was ahead of us. Full of enthusiasm and zest, we plunged into the life of Jones Street."[1]

Nebulous as that sounds about plans and goals, it captures the spirit of the group that day, and it signaled a milestone for its founder. By opening the settlement house, she had made her career choice. No lofty professorships for her, with a limited teaching load and liberal time off. As director, she would be available twenty-four hours a day, living on the premises, sandwiched in between a factory on one side and an overcrowded tenement on the other.

Finding an affordable space in an appropriate neighborhood for her "matrix of understanding" had not been easy, but Simkhovitch pegged it essential. When Paul Kennaday notified her the previous summer that he had found a boarding house on Jones Street, a block or so from Washington Square, he omitted a lot. Even a quick look underscored its lacking the stately elegance that Henry James memorialized in his 1882 book, *Washington Square*. Vladimir described Jones as a "dirty, sunless street and, as if ashamed of its appearance, no sign betrayed its name." He laughingly related how he had once offered a quarter to a child to direct him to Jones Street, only to be told (after surrendering the quarter) that he was already on it.[2] Only one block long, connecting Bleecker with West 4th, Jones Street lacked the space to develop some "good" parts along with the "bad," and with its multiple saloons, it gained (and retained for years) the reputation of an "under-serviced slum."[3] With its unpaved surface and no public bathhouse or playground nearby, it offered little to families with small children. A few blocks away, the "Negro Plantations" comprised housing for about one-fourth of the city's Blacks. Instead of a "melting pot," this section of New York had the dynamism, as Simkhovitch later wrote, of a "boiling kettle."[4]

The neighborhood's low buildings and irregular, narrow streets appealed to her, and she likened it to a small town. In fact, Greenwich, as the area was once known, had in earlier times been a town, separate and distinct from New York at the southern tip of Manhattan. Because Greenwich escaped inclusion in the grid pattern imposed on much of the island in the early 1800s, it remained a testament to a previous era. Its crisscrossing roadways and odd-shaped houses survived while the rest of the city underwent carving into wide avenues and perpendicular, numbered streets, lined by uniform buildings. Since Sixth and Seventh Avenues did not yet extend below 14th Street when the Simkhovitches moved to Jones Street, she could see the whole stretch, from Washington Square to the Hudson River, as a village within a bustling city.[5]

The area's unofficial moniker, "American Ward" (a result of its high percentage of native-born residents) no longer fit by the time Greenwich House opened. The census of 1900 listed 5,000 immigrant families, who had come from many countries but tended to live alongside those who spoke their language. On Jones Street, Irish and Irish Americans predominated, making up about 40 percent of the total, while another 25 percent came from various parts of northern and western Europe, especially Germany, France, and England.[6] Those percentages changed after 1900, however, when Italians began arriving in larger numbers, reaching a peak in 1907. As Simkhovitch predicted, families fleeing the southern part of the Mediterranean peninsula would become the dominant ethnic group in the neighborhood. Their church, Our Lady of Pompeii, and their mutual aid societies would compete with Greenwich House for loyalty and support.[7]

The heavily immigrant neighborhood welcomed the Simkhovitches warmly, according to Mary, who thought it was the "baby [Stephen] in his carriage" that "set us right" with them. "After all it was a family that was coming, a family with other friends, too, friends who were going to live with us."[8] She failed to mention what curious bystanders would have noticed—that this family was about to increase. The mother pushing the carriage was noticeably pregnant. On February 23, 1903, Mary gave birth to a baby girl, Helena. To the disapproval of her next-door neighbors, she started parking the newborn "in her warm basket" out on the fire escape.[9] In her memoir, Mary tossed off Helena's birth as "another baby" without further identification, either as to name or sex.[10]

A look at Simkhovitch's professional calendar proves she had seriously underestimated what running a settlement would involve that first winter. Within the first two months of operation, Greenwich House started a kindergarten, several boys' clubs, a station of the Penny Provident Bank, a small circulating library for children, a lunch club for the factory girls next door who came over twice a week for hot food (which they paid for), and classes in English, sewing and upholstery, basket-making, cooking, and dancing.[11] Far from being the removed overseer, Simkhovitch kept busy into the ninth month of her pregnancy, teaching teenage girls in the afternoon and workingwomen in the evenings. She processed applications for new clubs, including one for teenage boys, called the American Scientific Association. Its "high-sounding" name came from one of the members, she explained, and then won the "instant approval" of the others.[12]

Young boys coming to Greenwich House triggered Simkhovitch's special concern. They "flock to the House in large numbers," she explained, "and we have little to offer them. . . . [T]hey don't want to be talked to. They want to *do* something, and the best thing they can do, the thing that interests them most is manual work, and the best kind of manual work is carpentry."[13] After calculating that Greenwich House needed $175 to equip one of its rooms with a "proper carpentry outfit" and another $300 to pay an instructor [total equivalent to more than $17,000 today], she set about raising the money.

Her board of managers and co-workers contributed to the effort, but she considered herself primarily responsible. Without a rich banker or family money behind her, she had to come up with a variety of ways to encourage donors, and she wanted to reach those with moderate incomes, not just a few deep-pocketed philanthropists. The membership program designed in the very first year of operation did just that. Life memberships went for $500 and sustainer tags for $100, but there were also lesser memberships at $25 or even $5. Greenwich House innovated what would become a staple of charitable giving: using the incentive of matching funds. Settlement workers went out with the message that one enthusiastic backer had promised to give $250 for every $1,000 raised in small donations, and with that inducement, donors handed over $5,000.[14] Wealthy New Yorkers, including Felix and Frieda Warburg and Gertrude Whitney, reliably contributed every year, writing checks for hundreds or even thousands, but Simkhovitch saw success as reeling in many donors of small amounts. Contributions often came in kind rather than cash: a subscription to a labor magazine, a Ping Pong set, or bed linens to be lent to households with bedridden patients. She made sure to thank every single donor, whether for a check of five digits or a set of pillowcases.

Even with careful management, expenses rose much higher than anticipated those first years, and when coffers ran low, Simkhovitch had to work extra hard. In 1903 she estimated she would need an additional $5,000 (equivalent to about $165,000 in today's money) to continue the kindergarten, clubs, and classes already started.[15] Settlement workers with jobs or family inheritances added to the communal fund and reached out to others for help. When Vladimir claimed that some of them went begging on the streets, tin cups in hand, he exaggerated, but not by much.

A board of managers met monthly to deal with money matters, evaluate current offerings, and brainstorm on changes and additions. Fortunately, the officers of the initial board of managers boasted considerable experience in social services. Edward T. Devine, who had come from the Midwest to work at the Charity Organization Society of New York and teach at Columbia, served as president. W. Franklin Brush, a founder of the East Side Settlement, took on the vice presidency. Secretary Mary Sherman, the lone female among the officers, had worked with Simkhovitch at Friendly Aid.

The charter of Greenwich House, as it was generally known, stipulated that decision-making be shared, and that after a brief probationary period, every worker would sit on the board of managers so that "the original conception of a Settlement as a leading household in a given community is retained."[16] Unlike Friendly Aid, where financial backers comprised the board that made all the important decisions, Greenwich House envisioned a broader base. In January 1904 a neighborhood person was added to the board of managers, and Simkhovitch valued the additional viewpoint.[17] Although not every decision would be unanimous, she wrote, the "general policies and plans are all worked out in common. The Board of Managers of the Society is composed of members of all three groups—subscribers [donors], workers [staff] and neighbors—and no great change can take place without the consent of them all."[18]

Space allotments at 26 Jones Street kept shifting, but in the beginning the top floor served as dormitory for half a dozen female residents who paid rent according to their means. The first two floors had one central room for gatherings, several classrooms, and a suite for the Simkhovitch family. Bathing facilities took up much of the basement; the backyard became a "beer garden without beer," as the minutes of one board meeting had it.[19] Around the big dinner table in the middle of the largest room on the first floor, residents gathered in the evening to discuss the events of the day, local politics, or whatever came to their minds. Monday night was sacrosanct time for staff to meet, summarize the week's events, and plan for the days ahead.

The building at 26 Jones Street could not begin to provide space for all that Greenwich House offered, and like other settlement houses, it rented additional rooms nearby. Male residents slept at 88 Grove Street, and the various clubs and departments (pottery, music, dance) used temporary makeshift locations wherever they found them.[20] The drama department sometimes resorted to spreading a tarp across the street and staging their productions in the open. By the time the three-year rental on 26 Jones Street was up, the treasurer reported enough money on hand to purchase additional space.

Activities, whether pleasurable, like dancing, or instructive, like civics class, popped up and then gained momentum or faded away, depending on the vigor of those who led them and the enthusiasm of the participants. By 1905, forty-six different classes and clubs met at Greenwich House, including cooking classes for girls; carpentry for boys; and pasting, sewing, and housekeeping classes for their mothers. A remarkably wide range of skills enriched the program, including clay modeling, chair caning, music lessons, and the making of brushes and lace.[21] On the fun side, the settlement added outdoor concerts and Thursday night socials, featuring storytelling and refreshments. After its asphalt paving in May 1904, Jones Street got its first streetlights, and Greenwich House sponsored outdoor dancing.[22] With something for every age group, it became one of the most popular spots in that part of New York. Crystal Eastman, later famous as feminist, activist, and founder (with her brother Max) of the socialist journal *Liberator*, wrote him that Greenwich House was "the place of all places" she wanted to go. "If I can get in there and make them like me, I shall consider my future made as far as real living goes."[23]

Engaging with families remained the keystone of the operation, and Simkhovitch brought in a doctor to focus on the most vulnerable. Hans Zinsser, who later acquired an international reputation as an expert bacteriologist, came to Greenwich House in 1906, as a recent graduate of Columbia Medical School, and saw a problem he could solve. In those days of poor refrigeration, babies became dangerously ill after consuming spoiled dairy products, and in summer heat, fatalities soared. Zinsser teamed up with Simkhovitch to install more cold-storage space at Greenwich House and then schedule regular milk deliveries. That meant mothers had access to safe milk for their babies, and the death rate fell almost immediately.

To give tired mothers a break from the drudgery of cooking and cleaning, Greenwich House arranged for dozens of them to take their children on day trips outside the city. In the green hills of New Jersey or Westchester County, they could picnic in sunshine and fresh air, forgetting for a little while the cramped, dark quarters where they lived the other days of the year. To lighten the load of mothers with several young children at home—an experience with which she could of course identify—the settlement house designated space for a nursery school, to be funded by subscribers and nominal fees from the parents whose children attended.[24] None of these activities was unique to 26 Jones Street, but the numbers they reached put their part of Greenwich Village on the map.

While Greenwich House addressed needs as progressively as it could, not everything could be solved at a class or club meeting. Conflicts among ethnic groups posed an immediate problem, and racism was particularly virulent. In the early summer of 1903, an Irish saloonkeeper on Jones Street assaulted a respected Black man without any apparent provocation. It was, Simkhovitch reported to her board, "The most dramatic event of the month."[25] To worsen an already bad situation, no verdict resulted when the case went to trial. It had to be tried again because two Irish men on the jury refused to find their countryman guilty. More violence followed, and fights broke out on Jones Street almost nightly.[26]

Simkhovitch appealed to her neighbors to "stiffen up [their] moral backbone" and take a stand against such injustice, but her own backbone was soon tested. Showing the same pragmatic accommodation as in her college years, when she justified her sorority's exclusion of Catholics, she announced at a monthly meeting of the Greenwich House board that she wanted to move Blacks out of the settlement's main building and into rented space nearby. "[T]he feeling is so keen against them," she explained, "that it would not do [to have them come to 26 Jones Street] even if there were room."[27]

The concentration of Blacks around Minetta Lane, a couple minutes' walk from Jones Street, could hardly be ignored, and she had originally arranged for both their participation in events and an evaluation of their economic condition. At an early board meeting, she described the "colored people of the quarter" as "for the most part highly respected and law abiding," and when they requested a separate meeting place, she proposed a social center for them "on a very small scale."[28] Almost every board meeting the first couple years took up the question of how to serve the Black community, leading to the establishment of a separate library, bank station, and a scholarship to investigate the standard of living in Minetta Lane and explain why the mortality rate among African Americans exceeded that in the rest of the city.[29]

But activities at Greenwich House were not integrated, and in March 1905 its director went further in promoting a color line. She took full responsibility for the change, calling it her "own personal feeling... that our interest as a Society [in the African American community] should now cease."[30] In fact, she continued visits to African American households but on a small scale.[31] Blacks were discouraged from enrolling in classes or clubs, and they virtually disappeared from activities on Jones Street. They lacked a voice in decision-making at the settlement because no African American sat on its incorporating board or any of its other boards at the time.[32]

This exclusion was not unique to Greenwich House—it characterized most settlements before 1945. Historians have concluded that although early settlement house leaders held as a central tenet that mixing ethnic groups promoted tolerance, this did not apply to Blacks. Committed to helping white immigrants, they "largely ignored the parallel situation of African Americans when they began to replace whites in settlement neighborhoods," as one historian put it.[33] The common justification for not integrating was that whites would refuse to participate.[34] The customary solution was for the settlement house to leave the area or stay and either operate a separate, small venue for Blacks only (Hull House established a small center for African Americans) or serve Blacks in their own homes (Greenwich House made home visits).[35]

That did not mean Black communities lacked social service centers. Many were sponsored by (or had close association with) churches, a version of assistance that the National Federation of Settlements, which was founded in 1911, disdained as "mission" work motivated by the desire to proselytize and convert.[36] Simkhovitch, who helped found the National Federation of Settlements and served for a time as its president, remained strongly committed to her Episcopal faith and made a church stop almost daily, but she remained adamant that religion had no place in a settlement house. Dedicated Roman Catholics and Protestants of various denominations would find too much to divide them, and a settlement's mission was to unite people.

With their focus on new immigrants and a residency option for staff, settlement leaders like Simkhovitch had little reason to incorporate community service centers that lacked these features into their federation. No predominantly Black organization joined the Federation of Settlements until 1926, although a variety of neighborhood organizations operated in African American sections of several cities.[37] One of the most notable was the Neighborhood Union in Atlanta, started by Lugenia Hope Burns about the same time Simkhovitch opened Greenwich House.

A Midwesterner, born in 1871 in St. Louis and educated in Chicago, Burns arrived in Atlanta in the fall of 1898, when her husband took a job at Atlanta Baptist College [later named Morehouse]. As resident on a college campus in a slum neighborhood, she was soon introduced to the appalling conditions in her neighbors' homes. After the birth of her son in 1901, she became acutely aware of the absence of playgrounds and parks that Blacks could use, and she resolved to change that. In 1908 she formed the Neighborhood Union, a nonreligious organization of Blacks that lacked the residential quarters of a Greenwich House but replicated many of its offerings, including a library and job training. During the twenty-seven years she served as president of Neighborhood Union, Burns directed a long list of programs. She and her allies met with local officials—the mayor, city council, and Sanitation and Health Departments—to petition for a more equitable distribution of services in health, housing, and recreation to all six of Atlanta's Black neighborhoods. Her biographer, Jacqueline Anne Rouse, admits Burns's Neighborhood Union did not succeed in all it undertook but was still "the strongest and most visible community-controlled agency for Blacks in Atlanta.[38] Much of that achievement came from its "aggressive, conscientious, and totally committed founder." Burns's Neighborhood Union became a model for other community organizations, both in the United States and abroad.

Like Burns, Mary Simkhovitch, pragmatic as she was, had a broad agenda. Besides running Greenwich House, she reached out to the wider community, as she had done at Friendly Aid, and word of her leadership spread. Within months of opening her settlement, she formed one of the earliest neighborhood associations in Manhattan: the Greenwich Village Improvement Society, with the establishment of public baths and a lending library at Hudson Park topping its list of goals.[39] The Association of Neighborhood Workers, which she had started in 1901, reported 192 members by October 1904.[40]

Her focus remained on her neighborhood, which had plenty of problems, and she zeroed in on housing conditions. Tiny, cramped apartments, barely large enough for families to eat and sleep, deteriorated when pressed to serve also as workplace. She saw how beds were rolled up and kitchens turned into manufacturing centers, as children joined adults on the job. Within earshot of Greenwich House, boys and girls not much older than her Stephen pasted petals on artificial flowers and cracked nuts for the candy their mothers produced at home to be sold elsewhere. That had to stop, she argued, and in March 1903, when her second child was less than a month old, she journeyed to Albany with Lillian Wald and others to urge the state legislature to enact restrictions on child labor.[41] The resulting laws, although less than she would have liked, were among the strongest in the nation. This was Simkhovitch's first foray into labor law, and it would not be her last.

While banning young children from the workplace was comparatively easy, controlling their mothers' working conditions took more effort. In Simkhovitch's neighborhood, mothers of small children rarely worked outside the home, but they added to household income by taking in boarders or engaging in home manufacture of one kind or another. Sewing was popular, especially for women who owned sewing machines or were willing to take out a loan to buy one. A pile of trousers for seaming or jackets for buttonholes could be brought home, "finished," and then returned when ready. These "home finishers" typically earned less than half of what shop workers earned for the same task, but it was difficult to improve their lot without also chopping off a major source of income.[42]

Female factory workers proved easier to reach, and in 1900 about one in five factory workers in New York City was female.[43] Labor unions had typically taken little interest in them, partly because most were single women who viewed their employment as temporary, lasting only until they married. The prospect of attending union meetings, paying dues, and joining protest demonstrations did not appeal. Without a union backing them, they lacked the clout to put much threat into their call for better conditions, and factory owners had little incentive to pay a living wage and maintain a safe workplace. Even the length of the workday was the boss's prerogative, and women who balked at long hours risked losing the job they had.

In 1904 Simkhovitch joined in a cross-class initiative to help female factory workers. Using the same formula as in settlement houses, she and her college-educated colleagues lined up as "allies" with factory workers to form the Women's Trade Union League (WTUL). That meant anyone trying to organize a strike, find a meeting place to discuss strategy, or fund bailouts for those arrested would all have the cooperation and backing of women who had never set foot in a factory. In the WTUL, Margaret and Mary Dreier, independently wealthy daughters of a successful businessman, joined forces and became friendly with Leonora O'Reilly, who had started working in a shirt factory when she was eleven years old.[44] With backup from their "allies," working women like O'Reilly gained confidence to speak up and demand changes. Simkhovitch's active role in the WTUL diminished after 1914, when a split occurred between middle-class allies and workers over which of the two workers running for president should be elected. But until then, and throughout the union's formative years, she played a key role, and she maintained her membership in WTUL for decades.[45]

With so many projects in play, Simkhovitch needed the rest and relief she found during summers in Maine. While in North Perry in 1903, awaiting word from her friend Elsie Parsons about a new baby, she wrote her a letter that revealed something of her feelings on career and family. After calling the pregnant Elsie a "Lucky woman," she continued, "The baby habit fastens on one—once one is started on that road one can't afford to be without a comparatively new one!"[46] Indeed, Simkhovitch exuded in private letters a satisfaction with family life that she rarely admitted in public. In another report of that Maine summer, she emphasized how she valued her family role apart from the exhausting professional mission she had set for herself: "[A]s usual all is peace. . . . The babies flourish, V[ladimir] takes to fishing and I enjoy the domesticity of the entire situation. Down here [in Maine] I'm just plain wife, mother, and no tinge of anything else."[47]

Those summer months in Maine did not suffice to keep her children healthy, however, and Mary's resolve to raise them in a settlement got tested when Stephen was five. She had stoutly defended keeping her infant son with her at Friendly House, but after he was diagnosed with a particularly virulent form of pneumonia a few years later, she questioned that decision. Searching for the very best care until he recovered, she installed him in a private sanatorium in Portland, Maine, where he had "a nurse just for himself." Confident he didn't require his mother's presence to mend, she assured a friend that he would be expertly cared for while she proceeded with her work in New York. Four-year-old Helena went to a "general caretaker," and then Simkhovitch asked Parsons to take her daughter "for a little while."[48] The immediate priority (once Stephen recovered) was finding a place near enough Manhattan that Vladimir and Mary could live with their children in an open, rural setting but commute to jobs in the city.

Removing Stephen and Helena from Greenwich House meant they lost access to the adventuresome, energetic young adults who worked there, available to babysit and lead them in games. The original nine who helped open 26 Jones Street grew as word of the settlement house's success spread. Some of the newcomers were recent college graduates, unsure about what they wanted to do with their degrees. Others were older and came from small towns to try life in a big city. They moved in and out, shifting and rearranging their lives according to financial necessity, career goals, and romantic interests. Only those with some means of support could stay very long because although room rent could be paid in either cash or work hours, everyone had to pay for food.

Of the ninety-eight staffers who remained more than a month in the first decade of the house's operation, women outnumbered men by almost three to one (seventy-three to twenty-five). Most of the women remained less than a year and then left to take jobs in other settlements, to teach, inspect tenements, work for charity organizations, or go into nursing. A few, including the Italian Countess Lisi Cipriani, returned home. Thirteen of the women married, two of them finding their husbands at Greenwich House. Male residents, faced with more job options, went into a wider variety of jobs, including university teaching, law, architecture, and nonprofit organizations.

Among those who put in a few hours each week at 26 Jones Street but lived elsewhere was Crystal Eastman, who saw her dream about getting to Greenwich House come true in 1906. At age twenty-four, she already had a master's degree from Columbia University and two years of teaching experience when she relocated to 12 Charles Street and enrolled in law school at New York University. The move put her in Vladimir's orbit. He had been a mentor at Columbia, but now the relationship turned romantic.

Crystal wrote her mother, Annis Eastman, that her friendship "with Dr. Sim" was one of the "RICHEST THINGS I have found in New York so far."[49] The mother, with whom Crystal corresponded often, recognized the shift in feelings and issued a warning. She had met Vladimir and admitted, "[M]y impression was not of the pleasantest."[50] She knew he was married and questioned Crystal about the propriety of his evening visits. "I wish I knew what Mrs. Simkhovitch thinks of all these things," Annis wrote her daughter. "I would pin any faith to her sanity and morality rather than to his, although his nature and manner may be sweeter."[51]

In the spring of 1907, while pursuing her law studies, Crystal Eastman earned $16 a week at Greenwich House, supervising children in the evening and leading a girls' club. That gave her time to see Vladimir, and after she summoned him out on Jones Street to hear serenading one evening, their relationship apparently altered. He wrote her that everything had "changed" and it was "the most wonderful of all God's miracles."[52] Although Vladimir destroyed many of his personal papers, Eastman retained the letters he sent her, and those filed at the Schlesinger Library suggest that they were intimate for at least a year. The married father of two waxed eloquent in one his letters to Eastman (written "Tuesday after dinner"): "My dearest, you are talking of love in your letter, what does it mean? O, Crystal, your agony is double agony to me. Is it really love that you still have for me?"[53] On another occasion, he revealed his thoughts on their relationship: "Thank God, a great deal of you has become a part of myself.... I am grateful, grateful for the little that is still mine." Then he noted his one regret: "I am so sorry that I have nothing to give you."[54]

His wife appeared not to notice Vladimir's relationship with Crystal. Or perhaps, she thought it a passing phase, not deserving her attention. She incorporated Crystal into the household, as she did many of the other young volunteers, to babysit Stephen and Helena and take them on outings. Fourteen years younger than Mary, Eastman liked being mistaken for the children's mother, and they apparently liked it, too.[55] They could see that their own mother seemed "so much older" than the mothers of their friends.[56]

On one overnight trip to the house in Mt. Kisco, north of Manhattan, where the Simkhovitches went occasionally to escape the city, they took Crystal along, and something may have happened to sharpen Mary's perception and push her to act. Or Vladimir may have acted on his own. He abruptly (and reluctantly, according to his letters) ended the affair, and Crystal left New York, to resume work on a survey of factory conditions in Pittsburgh.

Notwithstanding his infidelity, Vladimir contributed significantly to his wife's settlement in the early years. Using the connections he made at

Columbia University, he provided contacts that helped make Greenwich House a "graduate school in the community." Even after adding adjunct teaching to his "supplemental worker" assignment in the library, he did not merit full faculty status, but the multilingual, ambitious Vladimir quickly earned notice and recognition. When Russian Prince Georgy Lvoff in St. Petersburg needed to arrange the forwarding of Americans' contributions to his campaign for democratic reform in 1907, he sent a telegram to Vladimir.[57] Columbia's professors counted on him for leads to wealthy donors, and when the renowned anthropologist Franz Boas need to raise money to purchase a "linguistic library," he turned to Vladimir. It was a "valuable collection and it would be of enormous use to the Anthropology program at Columbia," Boas wrote, if only "My dear Dr. Simkhovitch" can find a donor.[58]

Professor Boas appeared on Vladimir's list when he put together Greenwich House's Committee on Social Investigations a few months later.[59] Charged with overseeing research projects at the settlement house, the group included Mary Simkhovitch's former professor Edwin Seligman, along with other Columbia faculty: Edward Devine, Franklin Giddings, and Henry Seager. Exceptionally well qualified to oversee research on the social and economic aspects of city living, the committee guided fellowship holders in collecting information and publicizing their findings. In its first few years of operation, the Committee on Social Investigations funded and oversaw the completion of three important research projects, all of them headed by women.

Greenwich House's first publication, *Tenants' Manual*, was aimed at newcomers to New York, whether from rural America or other nations. It listed laws protecting renters from greedy landlords, instructions on banks and legal aid associations, current interest rates on borrowed money, and other useful information.[60] Although the manual sold too few copies to return a profit, it underlined Simkhovitch's early commitment to improving living conditions.

The manual's title emphasized how the vocabulary for housing had changed with industrialization and urbanization. Rural Americans might talk of "tenant farmer" as one who worked the land and lived in a building owned by someone else. More likely, in local parlance, that person was "a renter" or, in the case of southern Blacks, "a sharecropper." The word "tenant," coming from the Latin "tenere" [to hold], implies both a temporary and inferior status, since the occupant is only a "holder." In 1867 the New York State Legislature codified the tenant's status by passing a Tenement House Law. It defined "tenement" as a structure housing more than three families.[61]

That Tenement House Law, passed the year Mary Simkhovitch was born, broke new ground as the first in the nation to set minimum standards in housing. It outlined acceptable size for rooms, prescribed adequate ventilation, and mandated a toilet (usually a privy in the backyard) for every twenty residents. New York State thus put itself in the vanguard on the regulation of housing, registering the fact that its biggest metropolis, Manhattan, received an increasing number of immigrants every year. With the steamship shortening the trip (and cost) from Europe and factory jobs mushrooming, New York's "golden door" gleamed ever brighter, and population was increasing by about 24 percent each decade, with the greater concentration below 14th Street. In a city with plots typically twenty-five-feet wide and buildings three or four stories high, landlords chopped up spaces to turn them into multiple dwellings. The owner of 26 Jones Street made sleeping cubicles for boarders, while neighboring 31–33 Cornelia Street bunched multiple families on each floor.[62]

In 1879, when Simkhovitch was still attending a Newton school, New York State attempted to upgrade its city housing with a law that required all rooms in new tenements to have a window. The law didn't dictate location of the window, and builders introduced the dumbbell-shaped building to meet legal requirements without guaranteeing much light or ventilation. The dumbbell's indentations on both sides, with one building placed up against another of dumbbell shape, produced a small shaft, providing residents (except those fortunate enough to live on the top floor) with little more than a dumping ground for refuse and garbage.

Greenwich House's *Tenants' Manual*, published in 1903, gave details of a new law, passed in 1901, to correct the shaft loophole, increase access to toilets, and mandate other improvements. But that attempt to upgrade improved housing conditions, like those preceding it, did not begin to clear the most notorious slums, and Greenwich House had one of them, dubbed "The Rookery," right around the corner, on Washington Place. Simkhovitch made a point of showing it to Frances Perkins (later labor secretary in FDR's administration, the first woman to hold a cabinet position) when she came to visit. Perkins was appalled at the "firetrap" she saw, infested "with rats and vermin of all kinds" and under the control of two gangs, the Hudson Dusters and the Gophers.[63]

In line with her firm belief that the first step in change was exposure of the problem, Simkhovitch turned to Elsa Herzfeld, who had already investigated similar living conditions in the West 40s for the Hartley House settlement. At her invitation, Herzfeld began gathering details on the Rookery's nine small wooden structures. She reported that these shanties housed two hundred people of nine nationalities, in conditions both shocking and dangerous. Among the "crooks, loafers and bums" who lived there were many who engaged in prostitution, domestic abuse, unregulated manufacture, and violent crime. The scathing indictment of the Rookery, published first in 1906 as *The Alley* and then as *West Side Rookery*, listed Mary Simkhovitch as coauthor with Herzfeld.

In Simkhovitch's opinion, those crumbling little houses were beyond saving, and she favored razing them entirely—although she did not provide a plan for sheltering those uprooted. That strategy of concentrating on physical structures while letting the human factor work out its own solution continued to define her approach, and she used it later when favoring the extension of Sixth Avenue to demolish substandard housing in the Minetta Lane area.[64]

Greenwich House's second publication under the direction of Committee on Social Investigations looked at a related subject: how immigrants spent their money. That topic was the brainchild of one of the settlement's workers, Louise Bolard More.[65] A graduate of Wellesley, More was teaching cooking classes at Greenwich House when she noticed how her students differed in culinary preferences and spending habits. With help from the Greenwich House Committee, she obtained funding to interview one hundred families and analyze their explanations for buying what they did. The results so impressed her Columbia mentors that she received additional funding for a second year, with the provision that she engage an assistant to live at Greenwich House and help collect data on an additional hundred families.

The results, published in 1907 as *Wage-Earners' Budgets*, showed housing a huge factor in family spending, second to food, regardless of total income or size of the two hundred families studied. Among some of the lowest income groups, rent claimed more than 30 percent of their earnings, and that did not include additional charges for light and fuel. After factoring in food that cost nearly half their income, little was left for anything else.[66] Ethnic differences did show up, with some of the least represented (Austrians, French, Scots, and Cubans) faring worst. For the largest groups (Irish English, Germans, and Italians, who made up 82 percent of the families surveyed) 66 to 75 percent of total family earnings went to food and housing.[67] Since it was common knowledge that families doubled up or took in boarders to come up with money at the end of the month, it is not surprising that Simkhovitch helped form the Committee on Congestion the same year that More's book came out.

Greenwich House's third publication may have originated with a member of the Committee on Social Investigation. Although Professor Boas later declined to have his name listed as a member of the committee, saying he had not been of help on the project, he had proposed the topic to be investigated. In a letter to "My dear Dr. Simkhovitch," on March 15, 1906, he suggested assessing the "physical and mental ability of the Negro child compared to the white child," and if there is a difference to find whether this is due to "social causes or to anatomical and physiological conditions?"[68]

The question perfectly suited Mary White Ovington, who had recently redefined her research interests. Two years older than Mary Simkhovitch, Ovington had also studied at the Harvard Annex, and she came to social work via a route even more circuitous than hers. Following graduate school, she returned to live with her wealthy New York family and take a job as registrar at the Pratt Institute in Brooklyn. It took only one year to convince her she wanted something more challenging, and in 1896 Ovington and a few of her friends opened a settlement house of their own in Brooklyn.[69] For the next half dozen years, she happily worked there, doing what she could to improve living conditions of her neighbors, and then, like Simkhovitch, she moved to a bigger arena.

The abrupt change for Ovington came in 1903, after she heard a speech by Booker T. Washington. Having just published *Up from Slavery*, he attracted national attention for redirecting attention to the "Negro Problem." Ovington admitted that she had always attributed racial prejudice to states south of the Mason-Dixon line, not to people who lived where she lived. Washington's speech opened her eyes, convincing her that racial injustice stained the entire nation, and she resolved to change that. Her first stop was Greenwich House to talk with its director because, Ovington explained, "Mrs. Sim" possessed that rare combination of "a deep sympathy and a clear head." Simkhovitch pointed out that Ovington knew "nothing about the people" she wanted to work with, and her research should begin with them.[70] With funding from Columbia, Ovington started gathering data under the guidance of Professor Henry Seager, who admitted he knew little more than she about the subject. Ovington's findings became a book and a classic: *Half a Man: The Status of the Negro in New York*. By the time it was published in 1911 (and praised in the *New York Times* for its combination of "genuine scholarship and charming literary style"), its author had already established herself as a leader in civil rights, having helped found the National Association for the Advancement of Colored People. Although Ovington never resided at Greenwich House, it played a key role in her professional life.

The work of Herzfeld, More, and Ovington, undertaken soon after Greenwich House opened, shows how quickly it claimed a special niche among New York settlement houses. Wald's Henry Street settlement might be getting more publicity because of its outstanding visiting nurse program, but Mrs. Sim was sprouting a research institute. In 1907 the newly formed Committee on Social Education boasted having one of the nation's foremost educators, John Dewey, as its chair. With a

Ph.D. from Johns Hopkins and distinguished professorships, he published *School and Society* in 1899, the book that established him as one of the nation's most innovative and respected thinkers on education. His transfer to Columbia University in 1904 conveniently put him inside the Simkhovitches' orbit, and they could not have dreamed up a more prestigious or influential chair for their Committee on Social Education. Its initial research focused on how speech and hearing limitations affected learning. Although Mary saw a lot of Dewey, his friendship with Vladimir was deeper, and the two professors corresponded warmly well into their old age.

Within a few years of opening its doors on Jones Street, Greenwich House achieved premier status among settlements. It offered the same range of services the others did, but it did more, functioning as a laboratory for investigating social problems and then activating the reforms to solve them. It attracted a talented and ambitious collection of workers and residents, including Frances Perkins, who claimed to have had her eyes opened at Greenwich House on her road to the White House. Central to the work at 26 Jones Street, Mary Simkhovitch combined the intellectual rigor of a college professor with the zeal of a union organizer as she made her way to a seat at the table of national reform. Other settlement house founders set lesser goals, and she sometimes had to temper her demands as she waited for public opinion and local leaders to catch up with her. Her mission in life did not change, however: to put safe, affordable housing on the national agenda and make public funds pay the bill.

7

Growing and Reaching Out

In May 1909 Mary Simkhovitch went to Washington, DC, to participate in the first national conference focused on housing. Its title, the National Conference on City Planning and the Problems of Congestion, reflected views of both its sponsors: Henry Morgenthau, a wealthy real estate developer, and Benjamin Marsh, of the Committee on Congestion of the Population, formed by Simkhovitch and her allies. As the only woman scheduled to address the mostly male gathering, she attracted special attention, and Joseph Cannon, the legendary congressman and Speaker of the House, admitted he misjudged her. He had joked about women speakers before hearing her but afterward paid her "a great compliment," according to a local newspaper.[1]

Simkhovitch gave one of her classic speeches at the Saturday evening banquet, starting with a colorful description of the Robin Hood pageant Greenwich House had recently staged on Jones Street and then detailing the horrible conditions of those who lived nearby. Her city block was home to 1,700 people from eighteen different countries, she reported, and the density was overwhelming. In a dark basement across the street from where she lived, "eleven people sleep in three rooms," and hers wasn't even Manhattan's most congested block: "There are forty-six others with a higher density." According to a recent investigation by the Neighborhood Workers' Association, more than three-quarters of the Manhattan families interviewed lived in "conditions recognized as overcrowded," defined as more than two persons to a room. Twelve percent of those surveyed lived five or more to a room. To get shelter, even in these congested, underserviced buildings, families cut back on food so that they could come up with rent, which was often more than one-third of what they earned.[2]

Before offering her plea for reform, Simkhovitch provided some background. The "five principal causes operating to produce congestion" were both economic and social, she explained. High rentals, which resulted in a small space-per-person ratio, and industrial conditions, which make it desirable for people to live near their work, were only part of the picture. She wanted her audience to understand that "social causes" were just as important. These included (1) "consciousness of kind," or wanting to live with people from the same place, with the same customs, of the same religion or race; (2) the powerful effect of custom and preferring the familiar to the unfamiliar; and (3) the advantages of city life—nearness of schools, religious houses, shops, theaters, modern plumbing in the home, and music in the park. She noted she shared something with the thousands who flocked to New York rather than heed advice to spread out into less-populated, rural areas: "The reason the poor like to live in New York is because it is interesting, convenient, and meets their social needs. They live there for the reason that I do; I like it."[3]

In proposing remedies to the housing problem, Simkhovitch emphasized that she spoke for herself rather than the Congestion Committee and that her recommendations were still in flux. Indeed, some of the solutions she proposed in 1909 disappeared from her later lists. She called for "two programmes—the long distance and the short distance." The long distance involved building in the peripheral areas of cities, providing cheap, rapid transit, prohibiting high buildings, and requiring careful inspection of occupancy and maintenance. That would take time, she admitted, but a short "good five years' job" could have immediate effects. It called for every city to make its own plan, so that each could coordinate efforts already underway to relocate people "from city to country." In what sounds like a slap at those who wanted to rely on private benevolence rather than government intervention, she called for "an organized opposition" to "charitable persons and societies" who thought their donations would solve the housing problem. She didn't have to explain that their contributions went mostly into landlords' pockets without doing anything to improve housing.

It's no wonder Simkhovitch's presentation impressed Cannon and other distinguished figures in the audience. She spoke from experience, about the street where she lived and the people she saw every day. A wife and mother of two, she had been director of Greenwich House for nearly seven years, and in overseeing its ever-growing agenda, the subject of housing kept coming up. The exorbitant costs reported in Louise Bolard More's 1907 book, *Wage-Earners' Budgets*, had not diminished.

Back in New York, Simkhovitch turned to activities run out of 26 Jones Street. At monthly meetings of the settlement's board, she did not preside but had a major voice in the group's decisions. Her reports emphasized the positive, with lists of recent additions such as classes and clubs formed and the engagement of celebrity intellectuals (like John Dewey.) But with every addition, the operating budget grew, and she had to figure out how to meet it.

As Mary's agenda pushed wider, so did Vladimir's, and in their separate spheres, they began to drift apart. With very different styles, they did not appeal to the same audiences. Her combination of Boston Brahmin poise and Tammany boss dedication attracted a devoted following, while his rapier wit put off as many people as it charmed. Neither spouse had a clear model for fitting individual ambitions alongside support for the other's goals, and as they moved across unfamiliar territory, they had to figure things out for themselves.

The couple's personal finances got a boost in 1907 when Barnard College offered Mary a three-year appointment as Adjunct Professor of Social Economy.[4] With more disposable income, she could consider buying property outside the city, preferably a small farm to accommodate Vladimir's agricultural interests as well as her own goal of placing the children in a rural setting. Stephen's bout with pneumonia had raised doubts about how safe it was to raise children in a congested area, and reports of high rates of tuberculosis and diphtheria on Jones Street reinforced thinking that country living was healthier.[5]

For V. G., as nearly everyone called Vladimir, the motivation to go rural was all about himself. He had written his doctoral dissertation on changes he witnessed in agriculture during his youth, and he spoke nostalgically of "Orla," his family's estate in Russia. He relished the idea of managing a farm of his own where he could implement some of the agricultural experiments that piqued his curiosity; he fancied competing in county fairs, showing off animals and products he raised himself. In his later years, when he owned property in Maine, he cultivated new varieties of delphinium and exotic peacocks. But in his early farming in America, he stuck to pigs, potatoes, and peaches.

The 108-acre farm that Mary and Vladimir decided to buy was located about forty miles west of Manhattan in a part of New Jersey that was still largely rural but within an easy train ride of Manhattan.[6] For help on the down payment, she appealed to her parents, who balked, fearing she was undertaking more debt than she could possibly repay. Laura Kingsbury wanted to make her misgivings perfectly clear, and in late 1908, while negotiations were underway, she wrote Mary a "business letter" explaining how she and Frank felt. They had looked forward, she explained, to the day when both their daughter and son, Will, would have homes of their own and "if our capital were such as to justify it" she and Frank would happily foot the bill in order "to give you each a home."[7] Laura admitted they simply lacked the means to make such a gift. They would, however, lend her a few thousand dollars toward a down payment, but they expected repayment of the loan at 5 percent interest. This offer stood only if she agreed to put the property in her own name, thus cutting out any claim from Vladimir.

Admitting that this "seems a very cold-blooded parental proposition," Laura apologized for setting these terms, and she tried to justify her reasoning: "Both your father and I want to be able to meet our own bills as long as we live and to do so must exercise reasonable prudence." These letters reinforce the conclusion that the Kingsburys had neither the funds nor the mindset to bankroll Greenwich House or maintain the Simkhovitch family.

If Laura had perceived the farm as a smart investment, she might have been inclined to help more with its acquisition, but she dismissed both Mary and Vladimir as ignorant about farming and easy targets for those who knew more. "You do not know how money will melt away in amateurish farming," she warned her daughter, "and [you will be] at the mercy of a farmer who may leave...in the busy season."[8]

Laura understood that Mary earned a good salary that "more than supports yourself and children as the most casual observer could not fail to perceive."[9] But what about the unexpected? What would Mary do if illness struck or if she found herself no longer able to work? Laura had little faith in Vladimir as a provider. In some of the harshest words she wrote about her son-in-law, she cautioned, without mentioning his name, "We fondly hoped to make for you and your children [a home] since you would never have one if we did not. We have in silence seen you bearing children and at the same time earning the greater part of the family's livelihood and no money laid by for a rainy day. You cannot keep this pace up many years, and it is the part of wisdom for you to prepare for the day when you cannot earn the money you are now doing."[10]

Despite all the warnings, Mary refused to back off from the farm purchase. She borrowed from her parents, took out a mortgage for the rest, and on April 14, 1909, became the sole owner of the farm in Readington Township, New Jersey, for $3,750.[11] In *Neighborhood*, she surely exaggerated when she gave the acreage as three hundred, with a herd of cattle that produced five hundred quarts of milk a day.[12] The deed, housed at the Schlesinger Library, makes it 108 acres, much too small to accommodate a herd capable of yielding a dozen ten-gallon milk cans a day. The closest rail stop was Whitehouse, and that was the name she and her family used for the farm, although (in a move that must have miffed her mother) she had stationery printed with "Orlanova," reminiscent of "Orla," the Simkhovitch estate in Russia.

Simkhovitch later described the years she owned that farm as "the happiest" of her life.[13] For her, Orlanova was idyllic, a "beloved" place with "an old stone farmhouse," a brook "wide and deep enough to swim in," and air perfumed by "sweetbriar rosebushes" and "swamp azaleas."

Although she typically chronicled her ancestors accurately, she took large liberties in describing aspects of her own life, as shown in her glowing words about life on the New Jersey farm. "Our hounds were playmates for the children, who with their governess lived happily during the week," she wrote, "but were happier still on the long weekends we could all spend together by the fireside in winter.... and [wander] up and down the hedges white with dogwood in the spring."[14] Once a year, Greenwich House staff came to Orlanova for a lobster party that lasted all night.[15]

That picture of warm fireside togetherness and group fun is not what her children remembered about Orlanova, and interviews, along with extant family letters and photos, reveal that they felt neglected and unhappy. Helena later talked about how she and her brother "ran wild" at the farm, with very little adult supervision. Only six when the farm was purchased, she recalled having little guidance on matters of hygiene, and her hair was rarely washed or combed.[16] Photos bear her out, showing waist-length hair that appears tangled. Her grandfather lent credence to her claim by noting in one letter that he was using Helena's bed because she found a place to sleep outside.

After Mary bought the farm, Laura regretted she had offered to lend any money at all because she feared Vladimir would now spend extravagantly, leaving Mary to "have to deprive [herself] of things in order to meet the interest payments." Ever the worrier, Laura wrote her daughter, "Suppose Stephen is taken sick again or Helena or you."[17] Vladimir's health had never much concerned her.

Much as the Kingsburys disagreed with what their daughter was doing, they had to admit she seemed satisfied with her lot. "It isn't that you ever complain by word or look," Laura wrote her, "but that you are doing the work of two people at least every day of your life is evident and where will it end?"[18]

Both Mary and V. G. raved about the farm for the first couple of years. They listed it as their official residence in the 1910 federal census, which recorded the family of four living in Readington Township, New Jersey, with the children's governess, Mary E. Allen, age fifty-three. Vladimir picked up a batch of blue ribbons for his poultry entries in East Coast fairs and competitions that year, and Mary boasted to her parents about the bountiful harvest of "375 bushels of corn and 65 big peach baskets of potatoes."[19] Another letter reported positive news on the animals: "Turkeys are laying, 11 pigs doing well.... We are far ahead of the other farms in the neighborhood."[20]

Enthusiasm for the rural life soon lagged, however, and Vladimir's collection of blue ribbons in 1911 numbered a measly five. Then none. He complained of overwork and stomach pains. Columbia University appointed him to a full faculty line as associate professor in 1911, increasing his salary to $4,000 (with half of that sum coming from his library job) and increasing his workload. As adjunct faculty, he had taught only one course each semester, but now he had two.[21] Mary lost no time deciding that he should turn over management of the farm to someone else "because it is [at Columbia] his future lies."[22]

Giving a very rosy (and possibly exaggerated) picture of her family's finances, Mary explained to her parents why income from the farm no longer mattered. In addition to her husband's salary, she earned $3,500, giving them a combined annual income equivalent to about $215,00 in current dollars. The couple had agreed that each would take $200 a month for personal expenses and designate the rest for the children's expenses and the farm's upkeep. Holding high hopes for Vladimir's academic future, Mary boasted that he had "new courses and lectures this year and his reputation at Columbia will depend a good deal on how things go now." Freedom from money worries is "absolutely essential for him at this stage in our life."[23] Eager to defend her husband against charges of extravagance, she wrote her father, "Vladimir wanted to know if I thought 2500 was too much for him and I certainly didn't because it is essential for his position at Columbia and in New York that he is not too cramped." Then, in a touch of humor that sounds more like him than her, she added that he could use any excess cash to "make a present to the farm of a load of manure."[24]

Vladimir's reputation as attentive husband did not merit the same wifely endorsement. His Don Juan proclivities were no secret at Greenwich House, and at a settlement birthday party residents sang a song they had composed about their director and her spouse. While Mary was "neat…sweet…handsome and fair…a fine, big-hearted, inspiring power," Vladimir was a "gay, witty lover of art…a foreigner…from God knows where." Then, while Mary listened, the residents zeroed in on what really made her husband tick: "At economic history/He is a perfect bear/Of mediaeval miniatures/He loves the very feature/But he'd part with every one of them/For any charming creature."[25]

Vladimir's wandering eye was not the only family problem Mary faced. From an early age, Stephen was an overly active, moody child who could be genuinely affectionate one minute and outright hostile the next. By the time he and his sister moved to the New Jersey farm, his grandmother Kingsbury, who visited there frequently and supervised the children's summers in Maine, was documenting Stephen's misconduct. He threw temper tantrums and uttered rude retorts. In a letter to her husband, Laura placed the blame squarely on Vladimir: "I believe if [Stephen's] father someday gave him a good spanking—no halfway work but to be remembered, it might do good."[26] Nothing she tried seemed to have any effect. When Stephen acted particularly hateful one day, trying to bite her hand, she warned him that he would not get a pony if he continued to misbehave, and he replied defiantly that he didn't care.

Frequent staff changes at the Whitehouse farm added to the children's perception of neglect. They liked their governess, Amy, who earned their special admiration for the way she put an injured dog out of its misery. She "took her pistol," Helena wrote her grandfather, "and went out in the pouring rain" and killed the dog. "She is a true sport."[27] But Amy left, and while Mary enjoyed a two-week cruise to the Caribbean with her friend Ida Ripley, another caretaker moved into Orlanova. Helena found the "new boss" much less to her liking. She is "boring," Helena reported to her grandmother, despite being "quite accomplished."[28]

After the move to Whitehouse, letters became the children's chief means of communication with their parents, who visited the farm only on weekends. They usually arrived separately, often bringing houseguests who claimed much of their attention and left them little time for Stephen and Helena. Bess Child, the governess who persevered at

Whitehouse more than a year, longer than any of the other caretakers, included in her written reports to Mary how much the children missed her. Hearing that she was due on Sunday, they were "just crazy for Sunday."[29]

Even the patient Bess Child grew discouraged with Stephen and threatened more than once to quit on his account. She remained, according to Laura, only because she "adored" Mary. Child eventually left the job to marry, and other caregivers came and went, with the Kingsbury grandparents filling in the gaps. Helena, who later spoke glowingly of her mother's professional accomplishments, admitted that in childhood she found her very distant, busy with her many projects, and detached from her children.[30]

New Jersey's 1915 census reported fourteen-year-old Stephen and his thirteen-year-old sister Helena living at the farm, without their parents but supervised by "creamery worker" Joseph Sprague and his wife, Ethel. Helena attended a local private school, Hartridge, in Plainfield, New Jersey, and made infrequent trips to Manhattan. Her recollections of time spent with her mother, when she put on her "best dress" for an opera or a concert, sound like a visit to an elderly aunt or grandmother. Stephen, also a student at the time of the 1915 census, had more trouble with school, and his academic record was peppered with infractions and failures. Even Frank and Laura Kingsbury, who doted on their grandchildren and stayed for weeks at a time at Orlanova when hired help was not available, continued to find Stephen difficult.

In the years that Stephen and Helena lived on the farm, their mother's professional reputation spiraled upward. Within her circle of reformers, she earned high regard as competent and reliable, ready to step in for any of the others without worrying about who got the credit. When Florence Kelley, head of the National Consumers' League, was called out of town in October, 1912, just when she had been scheduled to participate in a hot debate over the future of New York City schools, she asked Simkhovitch to represent her because she felt "sure," that she would "turn on all [her] powers of persuasion, and rout Satan and all his angels."[31]

Mrs. Sim did not merit the same praise on the home front. Regardless of her long record of promoting programs to keep teenage boys out of trouble, she had not found a way to help her own son. The woman who spoke so highly of family values was part of a family whose members did not all speak to each other. It was the most biting criticism of all that zeroed in on that failing: "She could mother the whole Village," her neighbors said, "but she could not mother her own children."[32]

Important people and media acknowledged her expertise and accomplishments. Eugene Meyer, later the publisher of the *Washington Post* and adviser to presidents, was an upcoming young securities buyer at Lazard-Freres when he first met her, and he gratefully acknowledged her influence on his thinking.[33] When Jane Addams received an honorary degree from Yale University in 1910, the *New York Times* turned the occasion into a salute not only to Addams but also to New York settlement workers. Reporter Olivia Howard Dunbar singled out "Mrs. Vladimir Simkhovitch," head worker at Greenwich House, as a "woman of great civic influence in a hundred directions."[34] In a long list of her "good works," Dubar cited investigation of the housing problem, establishment of a handicraft school for unskilled women, a public gym and bath for the neighborhood, and a public library at Hudson Park. Her health agenda included a tuberculosis exhibit, an open-air school for pretubercular children, and summer street flushing. Activities ranged from broad-based street festivals to opening a school for "backward children."

That record of achievement had little to do with Vladimir, who kept an official residence at Jones Street but applied his expertise over a wide swath of the city. His upward climb at Columbia had started slowly, but it was solid, and he had impressed a lot of people, even while only a poorly paid library worker. William M. Ivins, curator of prints at the Metropolitan Museum of Art from 1916 until 1946, remembered their meeting in the autumn of 1904 when V. G. was setting up a rare book room in the Columbia Library and Ivins was "truanting" from law school classes: "How we used to laugh together! And how the stuffed shirts used to avoid us...for we were no respecters of 'persons.' And how delightful and infectious [Vladimir's] twinkling naughtiness was—a lot of it camouflage for most serious thought. He was one of the most charming and interesting men I have ever known."[35]

Ivins was the sort of cultivated, well-connected person that Vladimir sought out, and he constantly looked for ways to enlarge his circle. By 1906, he had joined the Arkwright Club of the City of New York, a favorite of powerful men, especially those with significant social standing.[36] While still on the library staff, he joined the American Economic Association, and although he professed to hate travel, he made his way to the association's annual convention in New Orleans in 1903 to join the president of the association, Edwin R. A. Seligman, (who also chaired Greenwich House's Committee on Social Investigations), and Ernest Bogart, a friend from Halle-Wittenberg and best man at his wedding. The postcard Vladimir sent his father-in-law, whom he always addressed as "Colonel," showed his English retained a touch of foreign syntax: "I have here a fine time."[37]

The New Orleans trip, taken just days before the Simkhovitches' fourth wedding anniversary, set an early example of what became a pattern. The couple did not travel together. Whether going to a speaking engagement or professional conference (when it would have been expected each would go on his/her own) or a pleasure trip to Central America or Europe, husband and wife either went solo (as was almost always the case when Vladimir took one of his rare trips) or with someone other than the spouse. Mary, who chalked up many more miles than her husband, usually traveled with Ida Ripley, the friend from high school who remained through life a close confidante.

Since Vladimir published in academic journals in polished English, it is safe to conclude he received help from someone. In fact, he credited his wife in one book, expressing in unusually humble terms (for him) his "deep gratitude...to Mrs. Simkhovitch, who, I fear, has taken time from her much more important work to lend me assistance."[38] But a comparison of his writing with hers shows such a difference in vocabulary, sentence length, and style that it seems likely any influence she had exerted pertained more to content than to style.

Regardless of who edited him, Vladimir produced a lengthy publication list, while his wife received recognition elsewhere. His articles on the educational system and economic history of his native country turned him into Columbia's house expert on Russia. In the May 1907 issue of *Education Review*, he traced the development of Russia's schools over three centuries and offered his own list of what needed to change before these institutions could spread "some knowledge."[39] *World's Work* published his article "People's Uprising in Russia," *Bookman* carried "Symbolism of the Russian Revolution," and *International* included his views on "Terrorism in Russia."[40] Columbia's *Political Science Quarterly* continued to publish his book reviews, along with his essays, including a seven-piece series that began in 1908 and culminated in a book, *Marxism Versus Socialism*, in 1913.[41] One reviewer praised its "clear insight into Marx's doctrines" and its analysis of how subsequent theories deviated from them. Other reviews, more measured, judged the book, which was later translated into German, Russian, and French, "well done" (*New York Times*) and an "important study" (*Boston Transcript*).

Vladimir had another life that had little to do with academia or the settlement house. It centered on art, starting with rare books and illuminated manuscripts, then widening to include textiles, sculpture, paintings, works on paper, and jewelry. How he acquired his expertise remains a mystery. His daughter credited his "marvelous eye" and implied he had been born with expertise or acquired it at a young age.[42] Whatever the source, his article in the March 1907 issue of the prestigious *Burlington Magazine* positioned him as an authority. Titled "A Predecessor of the Grimani Breviary," it made the argument that a breviary in the collection of "Mr. J. Pierpont Morgan" equaled the highly prized fifteenth-century Belgian religious book dubbed "the Grimani" and owned by Venice's Marciana Library. In detail, Vladimir explained how Morgan's centuries-old book of more than one thousand pages had the very same subjects and workmanship as the far better-known Grimani volume. In fact, he argued, the Morgan breviary was older. Besides supporting his claim with illustrations, he made comparisons with other breviaries in Vienna and in private collections, thus underlining his authority to judge. That he managed to get his piece published in a periodical that billed itself "for art connoisseurs" suggests he was taken seriously.

According to his daughter, Vladimir figured in J. P. Morgan's acquisition of the breviary for what was still a private collection.[43] Morgan Library records show that the magnate bought manuscripts from V. G., and in 1912 conferred with him on how best to exhibit the growing collection.[44] The two men had met through J. P.'s nephew, Junius Morgan, who also collected rare books and became an associate librarian at Princeton.

Vladimir's connection with Junius Morgan gave him the opportunity to know Belle da Costa Greene, J. P. Morgan's trusted curator and agent, who was African American but passed as white. Her career shares a lot with Vladimir's. Like him, she managed a quick entry into New York's art world without great wealth or family connections to clear the way.[45] With only a short summer course in library science, she began working in Princeton University's library, where she had access to old books and art and to the professors and donors who could enlighten her on their provenance and quality.[46] She soon gained the attention of the same Morgan nephew who had helped Vladimir, and in 1905, when Greene was only twenty-one, J. P. Morgan hired her to catalog his private art collection designated for the neo-Renaissance mansion he was building at Madison Avenue and 36th Street. Fashionable dresser and sophisticated woman-about-town, Greene caught the eye of older, established connoisseurs. She learned from them, and then applied what she knew to make shrewd purchases for Morgan.

The quick ascension of both Vladimir Simkhovitch and Belle da Costa Greene in Gotham's art world suggests cataloging in a library may be an excellent route for the socially ambitious, especially if they are quick learners. In 1907 V. G. became a member of the Century Association, a male bonding group formed in 1847 by one hundred of the city's preeminent men in arts and letters. After the Century Association moved to an imposing new building at 7 West 43rd Street in 1899, it added members while preserving its elitism. Its constitution required that all newcomers be of "similar social standing or shared interests" and be proposed by two current members, then wait a year for admission. Vladimir's sponsors were his wife's Episcopalian rector, Percy Stickney Grant, and Columbia Professor Frederick J. E. Woodbridge.[47] Not surprisingly, Vladimir used the Century's stationery when he answered queries about who owned the best collection of antique brooches or Chinese scrolls.

Two experts on the same subject, operating only a few blocks from each other, Belle da Costa Greene and Vladimir Simkhovitch exchanged views. After she returned from a lengthy buying trip in Europe, Vladimir wrote her one of his rare self-deprecating letters to explain why he had not called on her: "I understand that you have seen such famous people in London that you would not even look at plain common mortals like myself."[48] The "famous people" may have been a reference to the noted art connoisseur Bernard Berenson, a friend of Vladimir's and the man with whom Greene was romantically involved at the time.

Press coverage underscores the high level of Vladimir's early art collecting, including illuminated manuscripts and prized tapestries. In 1915 the *New York Tribune* reported he had purchased a "fine woven Seley Kermanshah palace carpet from Silo's Fifth Avenue Art Gallery for $385."[49]

At the very same time Vladimir was conversing with art connoisseurs and collectors in uptown mansions, Mary Simkhovitch continued to focus on dilapidated, congested tenements downtown. The Committee on Congestion of Population (CCP), which she had formed in 1907 with Lillian Wald and Florence Kelley, had its headquarters at Greenwich House and acquired the funding for research. After hiring Benjamin C. Marsh as executive secretary, the CCP sent him to Europe to assess how Germany, France, and Britain dealt with their housing problems.[50] Armed with Marsh's conclusions, the CCP joined with other New York organizations (including the Municipal Art Society) to mount an exhibit showing uptown New Yorkers the horrid conditions tenement dwellers endured. Full-scale models of tiny, crowded rooms, photos of ill-clad, hungry-looking families, and charts illustrating appallingly high death rates shocked viewers who flocked to the Museum of

Natural History to see the exhibit extending over three weeks in March 1908.[51] The images of cramped, dark quarters, with children huddling and laundry hanging made such an impression that the editorial board of the *New York Times* labeled the exhibition a "remarkable work" and predicted lasting results: "It is impossible to come away from even a cursory visit, without a new understanding of the problem, and the typical middle class viewer shudders at the proofs he sees of the hopeless sanitary conditions that excessive crowding compels, the poisoned air, the lack of life giving light, the inevitable uncleanliness."[52] The newspaper's prediction proved accurate when New York State named a Commission on Congestion of the Population soon afterwards.[53]

When financing the 1908 Congestion exhibition proved difficult, Mary turned to a young heiress for funds. Carola Woerishoffer came from a family that made a fortune publishing New York's leading German newspaper, the *Staats-Zeitung*, but showed little interest either in pursuing the lavish lifestyle her inheritance permitted or making a career in journalism. After graduating from Bryn Mawr in 1907, she defined her objective as "to learn and to help," and she pursued her goals with the same energy and determination that had marked her female ancestors.[54]

Coming from a family known for its strong women and benevolent works, Woerishoffer soon found a way to use her talent and money in a project of Simkhovitch's, and she became a regular at Greenwich House. How much Vladimir figured in Woerishoffer's attraction to the settlement is not clear, but a close relationship developed between the two. He dedicated his first book to his attractive, young "friend" and called her a "realistic genius."[55] She had helped him shape chapters of his book, *Marxism Versus Socialism*, at the same time she was financing his wife's exhibition on housing. Although Woerishoffer continued to sleep at her family's spacious Midtown apartment, she spent time with young Stephen and Helena in the country, and when her family's apartment closed for the summer, she moved into whatever tiny, sparsely furnished room was available at 26 Jones Street.

Woerishoffer refused to act the part of an uptown society woman only peripherally engaged in downtown problems. In the summer of 1909, to get an accurate picture of what the job entailed, she worked full shifts alongside immigrant women in a laundry where temperatures rose well into the nineties and steam became so thick she could not distinguish the shapes of those around her. When shirtwaist workers went out on strike that fall and many were arrested, Carola and her mother posted bond to get them out of jail. The Woerishoffers preferred acting anonymously, but word quickly spread that they stood ready in time of need, and women in trouble learned to call on them. Their money turned out to be a life changer for the Simkhovitches.

While Vladimir was placing his articles in academic and art journals, Mary published how-to pieces in a range of magazines. Her "Settlement Organization" appeared in *Charities* in September 1906, "Handicrafts in the City" in *Craftsman* in December 1906, and "Settlement's Relation to Religion" in *Annals of the American Academy* in November 1907. *Survey* published "Consulting Housekeepers" in December 1910, and then "Lincoln's Birthday" a few months later. Although "Mary K. Simkhovitch" was her typical author line, she sometimes identified herself as "Mrs. V. G. Simkhovitch," as she did when she published "Standards and Tests of Efficiency in Settlement Work" in *Conference of Charities and Corrections*.[56]

As her work expanded, she needed more space, and in 1909, the Cooperative Social Settlement Society purchased three more buildings on Jones Street (16, 18, and 20) for $42,000 (equivalent to about $15 million in current dollars).[57] Multiple edifices increased operating expenses, however, and board members began making a case for a single, large structure to accommodate under one roof all settlement house activities: auditorium, gymnasium, classrooms, medical facilities, and living quarters for staff. The question was whether to convert an existing multistory building or construct something new.

Much of her work continued to focus on problems beyond the walls of her settlement—problems affecting the entire state, even the nation.

New York's Republican governor, Charles Evans Hughes, named her to represent New York at the National Conference of Charities in St. Louis in 1910.[58] The two were already collaborating on obtaining the vote for women, a campaign she entered enthusiastically by hosting meetings of the Equal Franchise Society at Greenwich House. She admitted she came late to the suffrage movement. While speaking in Albany to a committee of the New York State Legislature in March 1910, she noted she had been there before—to push for child labor laws and, later, as a member of the Committee of Fourteen founded to eliminate hotels operating as brothels. This time, she spoke with even more vigor, having concluded that any serious attempt "to improve living conditions, we need the aroused, conscious, responsible vote of women." To those who worried that letting women vote would bring them into the unseemly world of politics, she assured them that women were already there: "Gentlemen! The bringing up of children, housekeeping and the earning and spending of money *is* politics."[59] She joined the New York Woman Suffrage Party and marched in their parades alongside V. G. and their daughter.[60] When William Thomas Manning, the rector of Trinity Episcopal Church, demeaned the Episcopal Suffrage Association, which Simkhovitch helped form, she wrote in some sarcasm that she would be glad to enlighten him on how important the vote was to working women "if [he had] time to spare."[61]

To her Greenwich House board, she explained that her enthusiasm for extending suffrage came from the realization that women were key to change: "Every day teaches me that if we are serious in our attempt to improve living conditions we need the aroused, conscious responsible vote of women to effect the ends in view."[62] This became her standard argument, repeated in speeches on many stages, as she joined the campaign to hold a referendum in New York State on the subject.[63] When a "suffrage shop" opened at 663 Fifth Avenue in New York in October, 1914, she was a featured speaker.[64] National leaders came to Greenwich House on November 16, 1914, for an event billed as the "Opening of the Suffrage Campaign," and several months later, members of the Woman's Suffrage Party held their spring tea at Greenwich House.[65] Whether speaking to a friendly crowd at the Equal Franchise Society or a more skeptical one of Italian immigrants at Greenwich House, her message remained the same: Women had a right to vote as part of their housekeeping for the community, and they would use their vote to gain improvements for all.

Speaking from a public podium had started early for Simkhovitch, and her confidence dated back to student days. After facing a prestigious gathering in Berlin, she was "much in evidence" at a meeting of the Federation of Graduate Clubs of American Universities, held at Johns Hopkins in 1896.[66] The following year she had gained mention as the "most interesting speaker" at a meeting of the Denison Settlement House.[67] When the New York Charity Organization Society convened a few months later, "Miss Mary Kingsbury" sat on the dais, alongside Bishop Henry Potter, the seventh Episcopal Bishop of New York and one of the city's most prominent clergyman.[68]

This long record of impressive public speaking served her well as her agenda widened. A few weeks after she spoke on suffrage to a joint committee of the New York State Legislature, a factory fire a few blocks from Greenwich House propelled her into the forefront of public protests. The Triangle Shirtwaist fire on Saturday afternoon, March 25, 1911, ended the lives of 146 workers, mostly women, trapped on a high floor because exits had been locked, and investigators soon pinned the blame on factory owners and lax inspectors. Adding to outrage over the tragic loss of life was the fact that police had a record of arresting women who complained about unsafe factory conditions.

The Triangle disaster may well have influenced Carola Woerishoffer to investigate working conditions across the state for the Bureau of Industries and Immigration. As part of her assignment to inspect day camps of migrant workers, she drove herself from one site to the next in her own "machine," and it was on one of these missions that she had a fatal accident. On a rainy September night in 1911, she skidded off a slick road near Cannonsville, about 150 miles north of New York City, slid over an embankment, and was so seriously injured that she died the following day.[69]

Her mother, grieving the death of her daughter, acknowledged the important role the Simkhovitches had played in Carola's life. In a handwritten note to them just weeks after the tragic accident, she reminded "My dear friends, Carola loved you and your children dearly and I know I am doing what she would have liked me to do today. I have just signed a deed for Helena and Stephen, giving each of them the sum of twenty-five thousand dollars, [about $735,000 in current dollars] so arranged that they may have the income for their maintenance and education as you please."[70] The bereaved mother regretted she could not express fully her gratitude "for all Professor Simkhovitch did until [Carola's] last moment, but believe me, I shall always cherish it in my heart, wherever I am. Yours with much love, Anna Woerishoffer."

Woerishoffer's largest contribution, however, went to Greenwich House. She signed over $125,000 of city bonds, yielding $5,000 annually, and she specified that the principal remain intact and be known as the Carola Woerishoffer Fund.[71] Later, remembering her daughter's enthusiasm for the work at Greenwich House, she gave another $125,000 outright toward a new building. On January 11, 1914, Simkhovitch wrote her father on Orlanova stationery that she had decided on the architect for her new settlement house, and "I do hope the House will be up by a year from now."[72] When war broke out in Europe the following summer, Vladimir and others suggested putting the new building on hold. This was not the time to engage in a major expansion, they argued, but Mary insisted on proceeding, albeit with major delays.

Indeed, the Great War of 1914–1918 exacted a price on many. Long friendships broke over whether the United States should enter the fighting, changing needs for manpower and materiel caused a geographical realignment and reassignment of family responsibilities, women took the jobs of men who went to war, and questions rose about loyalty and treason.

The Simkhovitches changed, too. Mary and Vladimir still appeared to be a team, although he was keeping a separate apartment a few blocks away.[73] Satisfaction with Orlanova had dimmed, and teenaged Stephen and Helena raised concerns as they moved toward adulthood. Greenwich

House still provided Mary's major identification, though she was now defining her "neighborhood" more broadly. Her debut on the national stage, at the 1909 City Planning Convention in Washington, underlined her priorities. Knowing full well that most Americans opposed public funding of housing as "socialistic," she remained determined. That had not changed.

8

Conflicts and Critics

Greenwich House's move in late 1917 from cramped quarters on Jones Street to an elegant, Federalist structure a few blocks away might have served as a culminating triumph for Mary Simkhovitch. Besides celebrating her fiftieth birthday that year, she published her first book, adding to a long list of achievements noted by both colleagues and national media. All the festivity coincided, however, with a slew of changes resulting from US entry into war in April, with enormous consequences for her neighborhood, especially in housing. As inflation spiked across the country, workers flocked to sites where jobs paid best—especially in port cities like New York. Although immigration dropped to a tenth of its previous level, American-born laborers from across the continent, including Blacks as part of the Great Migration from south to north, arrived to replace them. Urgent need for war materiel turned formerly poorly remunerated jobs requiring little skill into moneymakers, and landlords took advantage of the competition for their space by raising rents and cutting back on service and maintenance. With little to stop them, they could evict renters on whim and install others at a higher price tag. Even with the armistice in November 1918, residential construction continued to lag, and affordable housing remained a dream for many.

The situation in New York, where five out of six persons lived in rented quarters, was particularly grave. If anyone stopped to think about the origin of "landlord," it certainly fit here. "Lords of the land" acted like the name implies, and the most avaricious imposed rent increases repeatedly during a single year, often as much as 25 percent. Occupants could either pay up or face eviction, and if they resorted to the latter, they faced retribution in the form of bullying and threats to shut off water and heat.

Some fought back. Resistance often took shape in organized defiance. Dozens of tenants leagues formed throughout the five boroughs, and they invited sympathetic Socialist Assembly members to support their claims and propose solutions. Rent strikes in 1904–1905 and 1907–1908 had proven hard to organize, and they concluded without significant gains. When the city set up committees to mediate between renters and landlords, the process became long and complicated, with results not entirely satisfactory for either side.[1]

A law on any level—city, state, or national—that limited what a landlord could charge struck many Americans as "Socialistic" and "Un-American," and only the emergencies of wartime cracked that perception a bit. In March 1918, Congress passed the Soldiers' and Sailors' Civil Relief Act, barring eviction of families of servicemen in the nation's capital. Recognizing that the housing shorting affected more than military personnel, Congress went further, to ban evictions generally if they resulted from failure to pay newly increased rents. Groundbreaking as these two measures were, bringing the government into what had been an entirely private province, they were only temporary, mandated to end with the war.

Vigorous opposition immediately rose to any such measures becoming permanent. New York's Real Estate Board argued that construction would pick up when the fighting stopped and the supply problem would right itself. Others claimed constitutional protection. The president of New York's Board of Aldermen maintained that the city could do nothing about the housing shortage because property owners had free rein: "The Constitution of the U.S. provides that a man is able to do within the law what he sees fit to do with his property."[2]

On the other side were professionals like Dr. Royal S. Copeland, a Michigan native who became New York City's health commissioner in 1918. He promptly noted the connection between poor housing and poor health. "It may be socialistic or communistic or idealistic," he argued, "but I say that if we cannot get houses any other way they must be built with public funds."[3] John V. Van Pelt, an architect and professor at Cooper Union, joined ranks with Copeland: "I have always been intensely conservative," he admitted, "but if providing houses, schools, [and] recreation buildings for the needs of [working] men and women, the sinews of our country, is Socialism, then up to this point I am ready to be called a Socialist."[4]

Faced with angry tenant organizations and an upcoming election, New York's state legislature passed a spate of bills in 1920 to limit what landlords could do. All were temporary, and many would be contested because they dealt with abstract terms such as "reasonable rent," "property value," "fair taxation," and "acceptable reasons for (and timing of) evictions." As landlords and renters waited for court decisions on these laws, their termination date approached, and it was clear that a permanent solution was needed.

Most of Simkhovitch's contemporaries continued to favor regulations and restrictions on landlords—on what they could build and how they administered them. Rather than limit their profits, these laws would regulate size of rooms, amount of natural light, sanitary facilities, and day-to-day maintenance. Lawrence Veiller, active in tenement house reform since 1894, had solidified his stand on the subject after working with Simkhovitch on the 1900 exhibition. His message now was loud and clear. He deplored filthy tenements as strongly as anyone yet insisted private investors could meet the need. Government should stick to setting standards and let builders do the building. He became such a dominant voice in housing reform that some have dubbed his decades of activism as the "Age of Veiller."[5]

Simkhovitch and her allies made a different argument: Safe, affordable housing was a human right, like water and air, and government had to provide it since private investors could not. In those pre–New Deal years, public investment and surveillance in some areas (roadways, water supply, food quality) went largely unquestioned, but platforms for labor protections, wage guarantees, and slum clearance—all geared to help the less advantaged—met stiff challenge. None made the case for housing better than Edith Elmer Wood. Unlike Simkhovitch, Wood came late to what became her life's major achievement. Born in New Hampshire in 1871, she graduated from Smith College, married, had four children, and then moved with them and her naval officer husband to his various assignments around the world. To occupy her active mind, she started writing fiction and then, while living comfortably with her family in Puerto Rico in 1906, her eyes were opened to the problems of substandard housing. By this time in her forties, she signed up for a graduate degree and earned a Ph.D. with a dissertation on housing that became her first book.[6] Other books followed, and Wood collected multiple accolades, although she gained little serious attention from historians until decades later.[7]

Slums would inevitably result if housing was left to the private sector, Wood insisted, and in her 1919 book, *The Housing of the Unskilled Wage Earner: America's Next Problem*, she underlined the urgency to act. New York's governor was the progressive Al Smith, and while he would not go so far as to commit public money, he did set up an agency to deal with the postwar housing shortage. He established the State Reconstruction Commission, with Clarence S. Stein, a trained architect and anti-slum activist, serving as secretary of its Housing Committee. The committee came up with two significant proposals, one to empower a state agency to make loans and the other to permit local housing boards to buy land and build. Governor Smith was amenable, but the state legislature was not, and the bill that passed did nothing to fund new housing (although it exempted new apartment houses from property taxes until 1932.)[8]

As Simkhovitch battled for housing for others, her own living quarters became more spacious with her family's move into the settlement's new building on Barrow Street in 1917. She always credited her husband for finding the funds to build new quarters, and indeed it was his friend Anna Woerishoffer who provided much of the money. V. G.'s bond with Carola's mother was both authentic and deep. Following her relocation to Switzerland, he went out of his way to visit her whenever he traveled to Europe. Mary's exchanges with Woerishoffer tended to be perfunctory and practical, but Vladimir's were warm and caring, and they continued until her death in 1931.

This was one more example of how Mary and Vladimir complemented each other's achievements. People who found her too "good" and too organized were drawn to the unpredictable, impulsive, temperamental Vladimir. Their friends divided into "his" and "her" camps, the former relishing an invitation to his apartment, where he served paté and fine wines, in striking contrast to the meat and potatoes at Greenwich House.[9] When the British artist and journalist Clare Sheridan came to New York and, as she wrote in her memoirs, "dined with poets in Greenwich Village," she marveled at the collection of Chinese paintings Vladimir showed her at his apartment. "He is a great authority on Oriental art and loves his things," she wrote, "and we are going back again."[10]

Rather than Chinese paintings, Mary's new settlement house displayed local talent behind its large, elegant façade, and hosted a range of activities and services. After Vincent Pepe, a local real estate agent and member of her board, located three contiguous twenty-five-foot plots on Barrow Street for the Cooperative Social Settlement Society to buy, she chose Delano and Aldrich, an architectural firm known for its stately structures.[11] The relatively young partnership of William Adams Delano and Charles Holmes Aldrich had designed Georgian/Federal style homes and private clubs on the Upper East Side for wealthy clients, including Rockefellers, Vanderbilts, and Astors.[12] The interior of Greenwich House would obviously be very different from those magnates' mansions, and Simkhovitch outlined what she wanted: "Plenty of fireplaces, the dining room and drawing room on the second floor...and the noisy gymnasium far away from the rest of the House. And of course, a roof garden."[13]

Although pedimented windows and marble framed doors were common uptown, they struck a jarring note in bohemian downtown, and when the new Greenwich House opened (quietly, given that the war made any big celebration inappropriate), the response was not entirely positive.[14] Neighbors found it intimidating and uninviting, more like a bank or museum where they never felt entirely welcome. Young men claimed to be "a bit afraid" of the imposing front door and outsized drawing room.[15] Such grandeur emphasized the distance they sensed between them and the woman in charge, whom they called "Mrs. Sim" or simply "The Lady."

The additional space provided for activities unthinkable in the low-ceilinged tenements on Jones Street. A gymnasium on the top floor functioned both as dance hall and athletic arena. The floor below accommodated various boys' activities, with a pool table, a meeting room, and six separate clubrooms. Quarters for ten women residents took up the fourth floor, while the floor below served as kindergarten, meeting rooms for girls' clubs, (one called the "Mary K" club), and an apartment for the director.[16] Every level had its own kitchenette, but the main refectory and drawing room (for use by residents as well as visitors) filled the second floor. An auditorium, the "central feature of the House," took up a major part of the ground floor, leaving cubicles along the entrance hall for a clinic and several small offices to be assigned according to current needs.[17] In 1917 most of those offices were dedicated to war work, with the Red Cross and Liberty Loan Campaign sharing space with volunteers helping families obtain information about their soldier kin.

However fine the new building at 27 Barrow Street looked to "Mrs. Sim," many of her neighbors preferred the old Greenwich House, and since her Cooperative Social Settlement Society retained ownership of the buildings on Jones Street, she continued to schedule some activities there. Extra club meetings and classes fit easily into the cozy old quarters, and street dancing on Jones Street was especially popular. She had encouraged the "open air" or "pavilion" dances as a place for young people to socialize, and narrow Jones Street was much more congenial to having fun than the institutional-looking top floor of 27 Barrow Street. Even though facilities at the original site were often makeshift, with sound and seating thrown together in haste, the dancers enjoyed themselves. As one resident reported, "The music was awful, the dancing was awful, and the floor was awful...but somehow there was a very fine, friendly, joyous feeling to the thing that redeemed it from the writhing."[18]

Space at 26 Jones Street no longer needed for clubs or classes was sold in what was becoming a new method of home ownership in the nation's largest city. Conflicting accounts leave unclear who can claim to be the first cooperative housing in the nation, but several buildings in New York merit mention. When middle-class families could not afford a brownstone of their own, they teamed up with others of similar circumstances to buy a building with dedicated space for each family. The "co-op" resulted, and by the early twentieth century, several addresses in Manhattan reported multiple shareowners, each paying for upkeep according to the number of shares assigned to the unit they occupied.

Given Simkhovitch's commitment to affordable housing, it is not surprising that she signed on early to cooperative ownership. The apartment at 26 Jones Street that she sold as part of a co-op in 1920 was occupied by the same family for decades. Charles Woolley later explained how he came to live there as a child. His midwestern parents were on their way to Europe with him in 1917, but during their stop in New York his father died in the flu epidemic, and his mother was left to fend for herself and young Charles. In services at the Church of the Ascension on 10th Street, she met Mary Simkhovitch, a fellow worshiper, and with her help the young widow purchased shares in 26 Jones Street and moved into one of the apartments with her son. Although Charles Woolley eventually left New York to pursue a writing career in Los Angeles, his mother retained ownership of her shares in the building, and he inherited them at her death. They provided him a place to live whenever he wanted to spend time in New York, and he was living there at the time of his death in 1986. In an interview four years earlier, he had only praise for "Mrs. Sim" for her aid to the neighborhood and for helping introduce co-ops to New Yorkers.[19]

Woolley remembered that in his early years at 26 Jones Street, the top floor remained the property of Greenwich House. Male settlement house workers slept there, and when they went to 27 Barrow Street for dinner, he sometimes joined them. He retained vivid memories of those gatherings when Mary and Vladimir presided from opposite ends of the long table, and everyone talked about politics and art and community problems. For holidays, such as the annual "birthday" dinner on Thanksgiving Day, the number of diners sometimes climbed as high as forty. Woolley's recollections underlined those of others who reported that neither Vladimir nor Mary liked to dwell on the past or reveal personal details. "They never talked about themselves," one longtime resident said, "or what they had done. They only talked about the present or about what ought to be done in the future."[20]

Among the Italian community, the largest ethnic group in her neighborhood at the time, Simkhovitch had admirers as well as critics. Theodore Barbato, who rose to a profitable career in leadership at Union Carbide, remembered how much she helped him. After emigrating from Brazil in 1895 with his Italian-speaking parents, he enrolled in local schools but found a congenial refuge at Greenwich House, where talk of doing better than one's parents was not viewed as disrespectful. A leader in the Stoic Club, a discussion group consisting of young, ambitious men like himself, he became such a fixture at 26 Jones Street that he used it for his mailing address. He even felt free to spend the night at Greenwich House, sleeping in a spare bed in the residents' quarters if weather or work complicated his commute. A lifetime fan of Simkhovitch, he credited her with helping him reach a level of success rare among his boyhood friends.[21]

Other Italians felt differently, partly because her pushing their sons up the social-economic ladder threatened family solidarity. Although Simkhovitch talked about the need to preserve ethnic differences, she sometimes failed to incorporate them into her policies and projects. For example, she continued to advocate the vote for women (and hold debates on the subject), even though the concept of a woman entering an election booth was entirely alien to the Italian experience.[22] In spite of Italian men's insistence that their wives and daughters be always chaperoned (preferably by a male relative), Greenwich House programmed cooking classes, English instruction, and union meetings for females only. When these events were scheduled for evening hours, so that those with jobs outside the home could participate, women often met such strong resistance from their menfolk that they just gave up and stayed home.²³

Most of those who walked in and out of Greenwich House had never encountered a "career" woman. Yet here they met Simkhovitch, the epitome of a successful, professional female, running the place. One advice book for young women, titled *Girls Who Did: Stories of Real Girls and Their Careers*, featured her as a model to emulate. That book was not one that every parent in her neighborhood wanted their daughters to read.²⁴

Diet was another sore point. Mediterranean-style meals, heavy on grains, fresh fruits, and vegetables, admittedly nutritious and healthful, did not fit with what Simkhovitch and her co-workers thought appropriate or economical. Italians typically began the day with only a skimpy roll and then consumed a large bowl of pasta at midday. An Italian child attending the Greenwich House kindergarten confronted a big serving of cold cereal early in the morning—and then got reprimanded for refusing to eat it. This seemed grossly unfair, both to the parents and the children who thought cold cereal about as tempting as Mrs. Sim would have found a morning bowl of spaghetti.

Simkhovitch's demeanor also distanced her from some of her Italian neighbors. Often described by her contemporaries as "Boston Brahmin," she did not look or dress or act like any of the women whom *contadini* knew—not the nun or the aristocrat or the neighbor—and this gave reason to distrust her.

Given the scale of problems she was trying to solve, she exposed herself to condemnation, and in her reports to her board acknowledged as much. One account (of many) told of an Italian family who ended up worse off than before because of her well-intentioned effort to help them. The Italian household she described had come to depend on the earnings of two teenaged daughters after their father, "a gambler and drunkard," failed to support them. The wife, "a sturdy and well-meaning Italian," saw nothing wrong with keeping their daughters home from school to work long hours making artificial flowers. Spurred by talk they heard at Greenwich House about the evils of child labor, the young women refused to make more flowers. Rather than return to school, however, they "wandered around the streets," because they couldn't keep up with the teacher's assignments after so much time lost. Their truancy caught the eye of law enforcement, and they ended up in a female reformatory.[25] It didn't take a degree in social work to see that intervention had fallen woefully short of improving their lot, and that the girls had been better off making flowers in the family kitchen than serving time in a reformatory.

Such failures were not unique to Greenwich House. In 1920 there were four hundred settlement houses operating in the United States, with a wide variety of programs and mediations. Not one of them could solve all the problems presented to it, and with its mix of conflicting ethnic groups in ever more densely populated space, New York's Ninth Ward was especially challenging.

In its 1918 evaluation of social welfare institutions, the Carnegie Foundation concluded that Greenwich House fell short on two counts.[26] Its health department performed poorly, failing to coordinate personal service, such as home visits to assess hygiene and health. Simkhovitch quickly turned for guidance to the Henry Street settlement, where Lillian Wald's visiting nurse service had gained wide recognition for its efficiency and outreach.

The Carnegie Foundation's second criticism hit harder. It faulted Simkhovitch's management. She held the reins of control too tightly, according to the Carnegie investigation, and ought to give more responsibility to those who worked for her and to those who came to Greenwich House for help. This flaw proved more difficult to counter. Although she began delegating more authority to the various clubs and organizations under her aegis, such as young Barbato and his fellow officers of the Stoic Club, she found it hard to relinquish control. Like many leaders, she trusted herself most.

The Carnegie Foundation's objections paled in comparison to a criticism leveled at Simkhovitch more than a year earlier. She had seen it coming and had reported to her board in 1916: "Some fear that the House may be a propagandist agency of some sort, religious or political."[27]

Unfortunately, the debate over entering the war in Europe had divided the country, and she suffered the acrimony of those who disagreed with her.

The criticism resulted partly from her association with pacifists. Jane Addams, a mentor and friend for years, had visited Greenwich House when Helena was young enough to sit on her lap. In 1912, when Addams worked with Simkhovitch in Theodore Roosevelt's Bull Moose campaign, the Chicago settlement founder enjoyed a nearly "saintly" image and was hailed as one of the most admired women in America. Her halo quickly dimmed, however, after she, along with other colleagues and friends of Simkhovitch (including Berlin classmate Emily Balch, Henry Street director Lillian Wald, and Wellesley professor Vida Scudder) attended the Hague peace conference in 1915. Addams later charged that soldiers were drugged before being sent into battle—a comment that infuriated Roosevelt, who despite her earlier support of him, denounced her as "poor bleeding Jane," a "Bull *Mouse*," and one of the "hysterical pacifists."[28]

When Addams continued to advocate mediation as the best way to end the war, she was vilified as "Slippery Jane," and even dubbed a "traitor." As president of the Woman's Peace Party, she attended the Women's Conference in Zurich in April 1919 and then accompanied her pacifist allies (Balch, Alice Hamilton, Wald, and Florence Kelley) on a tour through war-torn Europe. The taint of "traitor" followed them all. Addams and Balch eventually resurrected their reputations by continuing their social reform work and promoting alternatives to war. Both won the Nobel Prize for Peace. But for several years, they remained villains, and anyone who associated with them came under suspicion.

With some bravado, Simkhovitch dedicated her first book to Addams. In *The City Worker's World in America*, she professed "admiration and affection [for Addams] who, more poignantly than any other in this generation, has sounded the depths of life in the industrial centers of America."[29] The book placed blame for city problems—congestion, inadequate schools, unsafe food supplies, and insufficient medical facilities—on public officials, not on the people who lived there.[30]

Such an interpretation struck many readers—particularly those who used poor people and immigrants as scapegoats for social woes—as misplaced indignation.

Simkhovitch could hardly be described as pro-war, but she refused to line up with those who opposed the war. She argued that the United States could not continue to stand aloof and unengaged, especially after 1915, when the torpedoing of the *Lusitania* cost so many lives. This was one case, she argued, when some Americans must be willing to fight in order that all could live freer, safer lives.

Instead of pacifism, she talked of preparedness, though not the usual kind that focuses on equipping for battle. When invited to speak at her alma mater, Boston University, in June 1916, she chose as her topic "true preparedness," which meant educating a civilian population in the widest sense rather than simply stocking up on military hardware. Eliminating illiteracy was high on her list, along with acceptance of new immigrants and respect for their language and traditions. To "Americanize" did not mean to "New Englandize or Old Colonialize," she reminded her audience. "We ought to welcome and conserve variety in our newcomers." The implementation of "a national educational efficiency as a basis of all true preparedness" would be costly, she acknowledged, before reiterating her firm belief about who should pay for it: "[W]hen the states fail to come up to the standard set, the Federal government should give financial aid to realize the program."[31]

After the United States entered the war in April 1917, Simkhovitch focused the settlement's agenda on helping those engaged in fighting and the families they had left behind. Greenwich House sponsored activities for young people to steer them away from delinquency, supported enforcement of labor laws to protect workers from exploitation during a national emergency, monitored compensation of soldiers so that their families would not have to turn to charity, and opened nursery schools for the children of women who went out to work on war materiel.[32] When critics nonetheless later attacked her settlement as a "center of pacifism," she responded that this was no center of pacifism but rather an important part of the war effort, although not centered on the battlefield.

Progressive thinkers and antigovernment voices had found a warm welcome in Greenwich Village, but at war's end the welcome weakened. The Bolshevik Revolution in Russia in 1917 and the changes it promised in transforming society attracted attention from discontented Americans, and more than a few went to investigate for themselves. As fears multiplied of a similar revolution in the United States, a counter movement mobilized to deal with what came to be known as the Great Red Scare—a series of repressive measures taken throughout the United States and especially on the East Coast to identify and prosecute persons seeking to overthrow the American government. The New York State Legislature formed a committee in early 1919, under the chairmanship of State Senator Clayton Lusk, "to investigate the scope, tendencies, and ramifications of . . . seditious activities and report the result of its investigations to the Legislature."[33] Universities and settlement houses came in for special scrutiny after headlines appeared about "Professors who teach Bolshevism," and "Revolutionary Ideas in United Neighborhood Houses."[34] As a founding member of United Neighborhood Houses, Simkhovitch remained closely associated with it.

Senator Lusk had intended to start hearings in July but moved up the date after a burst of hysteria engulfed the country following bombings directed at prominent business and government leaders. Feelings ran particularly high in New York City after post office workers discovered sixteen packages containing bombs and addressed to public figures, including John D. Rockefeller. In Washington, DC, a domestic employee of Georgia Senator Thomas W. Hartwick suffered serious injury after opening a package addressed to her employer. The name of Supreme Court Justice Oliver Wendell Homes Jr. turned up on a similar package.

Prompted to move more quickly, Senator Lusk opened his inquiry in May 1919 and proceeded with his mission to ferret out suspicious activity in New York City. In the process, he arranged for raiding the offices of the Russian Soviet Bureau, the Rand School, and the International Workers of the World, popularly referred to as the "Wobblies." Lusk did not order raids of settlement houses, but he summoned their directors for interrogation.

When asked by the Lusk Committee what Greenwich House did for the "education and Americanization of adult illiterate foreigners," Simkhovitch dutifully forwarded the materials requested but made no attempt to mask her indignation. She explained that "foreigners do not enjoy going to the night schools [because] . . . they are tired out from their work and also the schools have not that hospitable, warm cordial atmosphere which is necessary if people are to take advantage of the opportunities opened to them." As for imposing English on foreigners, that made no sense at all. "I think it ridiculous to prevent people speaking their own language in social centers of any kind," she wrote, "and I believe also that suppression of foreign newspapers is foolish and would mean, if carried out, elimination of a great opportunity to bring foreigners in close touch with American life."[35]

Rather than blotting out "foreignness," she preferred to emphasize American values. "We should not fear public discussion," she continued, in a letter to the legal counsel of the Lusk Committee, "but should see to it that American traditions and ideals dominate these public discussions. Suppression never leads anywhere, but permeation with American ideals does."[36]

If the Lusk Committee remained intent on stamping out un-Americanism, she suggested, it should start by taking a good look at the local police headquarters. Five Russians had recently been rounded up and held there in one small cell for four days, in a space so constricting that three of them had to stand. Such an experience would "make for discontent with our government more rapidly than does any theory."[37]

Simkhovitch had no intention of letting zealous state legislators muzzle her, and she spoke up in defense of five Socialists who found themselves barred from seats in the New York State Assembly after being duly elected in November 1919. They were among the rare voices supporting the idea of publicly funded housing, and she didn't want to see them denied the offices they had been elected to. With other prominent New Yorkers who called themselves "a committee of seven," she signed a public statement against their suspension, because it was "inconsistent with the principles of representative government...

[and to bar men] because of their beliefs, opinions, or political affiliations [would] establish a precedent for the exclusion of any minority at the will of the majority."[38]

Opposed to so much of what the Lusk Committee stood for, Simkhovitch was incensed when it came up with specific proposals to limit freedom of speech and punish those holding certain views. The "Lusk laws" passed by the legislature required teachers to submit to a loyalty test and gave the state board of regents the right to license private schools and revoke licenses where "courses and conduct of private schools did not conform with rules and regulations established by the Regents."[39] An angry Simkhovitch appealed to her friend, State Senator Jimmy Walker, to fight against passage of these repugnant restrictions. It wasn't just the money they cost. If enacted, they would block innovations in education, stifle informed discussion of important questions, and create an atmosphere of suspicion. The proposed laws would put all organizations involved in education, including settlement houses, on the defensive, "requiring them to justify what they taught."[40]

When the bill passed the legislature despite her protests, Simkhovitch urged Governor Al Smith to veto it on the grounds that it gave excessive authority to the board of regents. If allowed to decide what is "detrimental to the interests of the state," the board would pose "a menace to American institutions."[41] Smith did veto, but his successor Nathan Miller signed it into law a few months later, leaving it up to Smith to put his seal of approval on the repeal of those laws after he returned to the governor's mansion in 1923.

Simkhovitch saw the attack on individual freedoms as just one more in a long line reaching back to the earliest days of European settlement in North America. "From the beginning of our history," she wrote in her memo to Governor Smith, "it has been a struggle to maintain the liberty our forefathers came here to secure. The Baptists in Rhode Island, the Catholics in Maryland, and many other groups, from time to time, have had to struggle against bigotry to maintain their right to freedom." Now it was urban dwellers who came under attack for their lack of patriotism, and she argued that New York City residents were as loyal to their country as "anybody to be found in [upstate] Oswego or St. Lawrence Counties."[42]

A woman with the surname "Simkhovitch" was especially suspect and vulnerable at a time when the Russian revolution had made headlines around the world and "bolshevism" was the bad B word. When Simkhovitch went to speak at the Women's Club of Forest Hills Gardens, an upscale section of Queens, in March 1921, news releases took time to emphasize her "American roots" by including Kingsbury in her name and noting she had been born and educated in Boston. Her audience apparently needed evidence for why they would want to hear a woman named "Simkhovitch" talk about citizenship. Although Vladimir was rarely mentioned in connection with her work, he was identified in the Forest Hills Garden Bulletin as the husband who helped found Greenwich House, the "settlement which has done so much with the Irish and Italian people" in Greenwich Village.[43]

Calm and measured in her delivery and choice of words, Simkhovitch made her own views on American citizenship very clear to the women in Forest Hills Gardens. In any analysis of the subject, consideration must be given, she argued, to "what our country is and how it is made up." It would be "invidious to pick out our own grandfathers as the only ones expressing ideals." She encouraged her audience to "respect and look with toleration upon the different viewpoints" of those who "come to us." They had every right to discuss politics and economics freely, without fear of repercussion. "American citizenship is not an idea, not a motto, not a flag, not a symbol; but it is hard, cooperative work on the part of us all."[44]

Her methods of supporting elected officials who shared her thinking sometimes got her into trouble. Continuing to judge candidates against one yardstick—what they would do for the most vulnerable members of society—she backed Al Smith for governor of New York in 1918. He was, she argued, the candidate most likely to "protect and safeguard women and children."[45] That premise seemed reasonable enough to her male

Italian neighbors, but the pro-Smith rally held at Cooper Union a few days before the election struck them as much too radical in its all-female program. Women in New York State would be voting for the first time in this election (a result of the 1917 referendum), and the entire evening centered on them. Only women were invited to attend. Everyone on the dais (except Smith) was female, and the police department called in two hundred members of the women's police reserves so that all those on duty that night were female.[46] To the Italian American men who frequented Greenwich House, this was too much. Supporting a candidate was one thing—parading hundreds of women in a public venue was something else. Simkhovitch refused to back down. She had campaigned for women's suffrage throughout New York State during the referendum and even appealed to church leaders to take a position alongside her. She understood that there was a strong sentiment for keeping the church out of politics, "but when great questions of public policy come up," she admonished, "churchmen have not felt it was necessary to be silent."[47] When the referendum went her way, she helped stage a victory party at St. Mark's in the Bowery.[48]

Deep ties to a candidate's family did not suffice to win Simkhovitch's support. In 1920, when the Democrats nominated Ohio Governor James M. Cox to head their presidential ticket and Franklin D. Roosevelt as his running mate, she gave merely lukewarm support, although she had had a friendly relationship with Franklin and his family for decades. Al Smith's re-election as governor of New York was far more important to her agenda, and she praised his capacity for hard work, his unusual intelligence, and his advocacy of progressive measures. The fact that Smith had appointed her, along with such notables as Bernard Baruch and Samuel Gompers, to the state labor board, to monitor workers' rights, compensation, and safety issues, showed the respect was mutual.

Whatever problems she encountered, Simkhovitch had her religious faith to sustain her. However progressive her ideas and open her attitude toward those of different creeds, religion remained a pronounced element in her life. Almost every morning of her adult life, no matter how crowded her schedule, she stopped at the closest Episcopal church for a few minutes of meditation and prayer. In the early years at Greenwich House, that meant the Church of the Ascension at Fifth Avenue and 10th Street, whose rector, Percy Stickney Grant, became a close friend.[49] In 1909, when the young Reverend Edward Henry Schlueter became rector at St. Luke's Parish, she transferred her membership to that church, and over time Schlueter became a trusted confidant.

Church time was private, however, and she never tried to force her beliefs on others. People who knew her well could not recall a single instance in which she had made them feel uncomfortable for not sharing her faith or declining to join her at worship service. Not that she ever invited them; she left it up to them. Vladimir, despite his Jewish roots and upbringing, accompanied her on the most important holidays, such as Christmas and Easter, explaining to his daughter, "I have faith. I'm a little short on piety."[50]

As a young woman, Simkhovitch had once considered the cloistered life of a nun but had decided against it for herself, she wrote, because it was not the "American way." Later, as a married woman, she joined the Society of the Companions of the Holy Cross, the group of Episcopal women who met for study and companionate exchange of ideas. It offered a religious retreat of sorts. For a few days each year, Society members gathered at a property they owned in western Massachusetts to debate and discuss topics ranging from world peace to neighborhood poverty.[51]

It was a diverse and highly accomplished group. Several lesbian couples participated in the retreat, including Wellesley professor Vida Scudder and her young protégée Florence Converse, as did wives who used the community as a respite from problematic marriages. Frances Perkins, one of the most famous members after FDR named her secretary of labor, was married to a man who supported her work but suffered crippling mental illness and was eventually institutionalized. Although she visited him regularly, she formed emotional attachments elsewhere and became a lifelong member of the Society of the Companions of the Holy Cross. For Simkhovitch, those few weeks spent at the retreat each year offered time away from Vladimir and her children and the challenges of running a settlement house while pursuing a range of reforms. They gave her the chance to stretch her thinking.

That retreat was not her only one. In 1918 the Simkhovitches acquired an additional property, to serve as escape, especially in summer, when the New Jersey farm was not enough. This time, it was not a loan from Mary's parents but Vladimir's money that made it possible. He had just completed his first significant sale of Chinese paintings and scrolls to the Metropolitan Museum of Art when he found a summer home just north of the town of Robbinston, Maine, that he wanted to buy.[52] Named "Mansion House" by previous owners, the Greek Revival structure dated to 1785, and its glass-enclosed cupola gained attention in the War of 1812 when it was reportedly used by a local militia leader for spying on the enemy. It was a grand house, eventually listed in the National Register of Historic Places, and went "dirt cheap," according to Vladimir's grandson, Paul Didisheim, because the owner, a German American, wanted to flee anti-German feelings connected with the war.[53]

For the rest of their lives, the Simkhovitches made Mansion House their summer home. The journey from New York required multiple means (train, bus, boat, and local conveyance) and long hours, but the end justified the effort. The main house, with its multiple drawing rooms and spacious lawn, resembled a small hotel; outbuildings provided offices and accommodation for guests and the associates they brought with them. Vladimir refused to have a telephone installed in the main house, and despite Mary's objection about the inconvenience of going to another building whenever she wanted to make or receive a call, he held firm. In one of her rare rebellions, she took advantage of an extended absence of his to have a phone installed in the main house. When he came back, he was furious. "Now it will be just like New York."[54]

Mansion House also provided the Simkhovitch children with some of their best memories. In their late teens by the time Vladimir acquired the Maine property, they relished the remoteness and recreation (especially boating) it offered. Stephen, who had his own apartment in Greenwich Village by the time he was twenty, barely spoke to his father, whom he found overbearing and unsupportive, but he was willing to put animosities aside to spend time in Maine. He liked to sail in Vladimir's boat *Chaika* (meaning "seagull" in Russian, which was printed on the wrappers of the cigarettes he smoked). Stephen had already picked up his father's princely affectations but without any of the academic success that might have offset them.[55] While Vladimir, with his doctorate from Germany and reputation as an art expert, could pass as a "man of the world," accepted even by those who disliked his acting like he "had everything in his grasp," Stephen struggled to graduate from high school.[56] Helena did well at her New Jersey school, but she remained unsure about what to do after graduation. It could not have escaped their mother's attention that her two teenagers faced the same uncertainties as the youth who frequented Greenwich House.

Besides concerns over her children, Mary Simkhovitch faced a multitude of conflicts and critics in the years following World War I. Hounded by the Lusk Committee, disparaged for wanting a grandiose replacement for 26 Jones Street, panned for her management style, and condemned for failing to solve all problems her settlement faced, she remained resolute. Again, deeply felt religious beliefs and committed allies supported her, and she had piled up a long list of achievements. While focused on the underside of the world, she remained upbeat. Her daughter said that she always concentrated on the "good side" and liked to call it "pure velvet." It was an optimism that was about to be tested.

9

Keeping Reform Alive

The onset of a new decade in 1920 accompanied rapid changes, requiring reformers to fit their campaigns into an ever-shifting context. For the first time in the country's history, census takers reported urban dwellers outnumbered rural folk; adult females could finally vote in all forty-eight states. A sense of euphoria at war's end in 1918 and a pro-business Republican in the White House (from 1921 to 1933) tempered the formerly strong Progressive movement, and anyone speaking out for modification in healthcare or education or housing had to muster a strong argument. With a new emphasis on high living and hedonism, any serious talk about poverty, illness, and illiteracy sounded dull and pedantic.

Nowhere in the United States did the phrase "Roaring 20s" resonate more strongly than in New York's Greenwich Village. As it became a mecca for artists and free thinkers, a place where eccentricity flourished and convention capsized, Simkhovitch and her allies persevered as part of the "female dominion" pushing for passage of progressive legislation on the national level.[1]

Several historians credit Florence Kelley with igniting the crusade. While a temporary resident in Hull House in the early 1890s, she turned it into "an engine of social reform" by initiating surveys of poverty and publishing descriptive maps.[2] Simkhovitch followed Kelley's lead, and Greenwich House sponsored research and published the results. After Kelley relocated to New York, Simkhovitch teamed up with her, and together they accomplished a lot in record time, forming the

Mary Melinda Kingsbury Simkhovitch, 1867–1951.
Credit: Graciously provided by New York University via its Special Collections.

Mary Kingsbury, on the right, with her father (far left), brother, and mother, just before she sailed to Europe in July 1895.
Credit: Didisheim Papers, Courtesy of Andrea Didisheim

Mary Melinda Kingsbury matured into a woman her contemporaries described as the "most beautiful" they every met.
Credit: Didisheim Papers, Courtesy of Andrea Didisheim

In October 1897, while still in Germany, Vladimir Simkhovitch sent this photo of himself to "Meiner Molly" in New York.
Credit: Didisheim Papers, Courtesy of Andrea Didisheim

The small brick building on Jones Street offered plenty of space for one family but not for all the activities Greenwich House sponsored after renting it in 1902.
Credit: Graciously provided by New York University via its Special Collections

Even after 1917, when Greenwich House moved to this new, much larger building on Barrow Street, it lacked space for all the classes and other activities it sponsored.
Credit: Graciously provided by New York University via its Special Collections

Stephen and Helena Simkhovitch had many different caretakers after they became residents at the family farm in New Jersey in 1909.
Credit: Didisheim Papers, Courtesy of Andrea Didisheim

With its glass cupola, Mansion House offered a lookout as well as access to water sports after the Simkhovitches began summering there in 1919.
Credit: Didisheim Papers, Courtesy of Andrea Didisheim

Stephen Simkhovitch (on left) posed with Sonja Stockstad before the birth of their son in 1931. The man on the right is not identified.
Credit: Didisheim Papers, Courtesy of Andrea Didisheim

Vice Chairman of the New York City Housing Authority, Mary Simkhovitch spoke at the opening of the Queensbridge Community Center in 1940.
Credit: New York City Housing Authority Collection at the LaGuardia and Wagner Archives, LaGuardia Community College, City University of New York

Eleanor Roosevelt enthusiastically backed Simkhovitch's work, and she supplied crucial help in getting the 1937 housing act passed.
Credit: Graciously provided by New York University via its Special Collections

Mary and Vladimir Simkhovitch remained in their apartment at Greenwich House after she retired as director.
Credit: Didisheim Papers, Courtesy of Andrea Didisheim

Mary and Vladimir Simkhovitch celebrated fifty years of marriage with a festive party at Greenwich House in January 1949.
Credit: Graciously provided by New York University via its Special Collections

William Reid, third from right, chair of the New York City Housing Authority, joined other city leaders to break ground for Mary K. Simkhovitch Houses, June 5, 1961.
Credit: New York City Housing Authority Collection at the LaGuardia and Wagner Archives, LaGuardia Community College, City University of New York

The six white towers in drawings of Frederic Wiedersum Associates, designed to be Mary K. Simkhovitch Houses, opened in 1965 as Gouverneur Gardens.
Credit: New York City Housing Authority Collection at the LaGuardia and Wagner Archives, LaGuardia Community College, City University of New York

Sculpture of Mary Simkhovitch, by her daughter Helena, a noted artist, is currently on the garden wall at Greenwich House Music School, 46 Barrow Street.
Credit: Photo by Author

The Wonder Woman Comic book series on Diana Prince frequently carried an insert, titled Wonder Women of History. Each issue featured a real person, and Number 55, published in 1952, named Mary Simkhovitch as the woman who made Greenwich House "the most important place in Greenwich Village."
Credit: © dc comics

Committee on Congestion of the Population, mounting that major exhibition at the Museum of Natural History in 1908, and sponsoring the first national conference on housing and city planning in 1909.

The same atrocities Simkhovitch cited, when she spoke at that conference, continued to mark her neighborhood in the 1920s. She saw firsthand evidence for her claims every day. The infant mortality rate in her ward remained high, as did the many childhood diseases. The lack of ventilated sleeping spaces, sufficient toilet and bathing facilities, and adequate waste removal left a mark on older children, too, and they had high dropout rates at school.

The "female dominion" of women activists had zeroed in on children's needs, or what Kelley and her allies called—a little clinically—the "child crop," and others joined the campaign. Just before leaving the White House in 1909, Theodore Roosevelt held the first White House Conference on the Care of Dependent Children. His successor, William Howard Taft, established a Children's Bureau in the Department of Commerce in 1912 and named as director Julia Lathrop, the first woman to head a national bureau. The Children's Bureau coordinated the work of multiple organizations, including Kelley's Consumer League, to improve children's lives.

Under Lathrop's leadership, the "child crop" advocates registered their biggest success in infant care. In her 1917 annual report to the secretary of labor, Lathrop suggested creating a federal program to empower states to offer education on prenatal and infant health and to supplement the teaching with home visits by traveling nurses. She traveled the country promoting the idea, and in 1921 Congressed passed the Promotion of the Welfare and Hygiene of Maternity and Infancy Act. Commonly known as the Sheppard–Towner Act (for Texas Democrat Sheppard and Iowa Republican Towner who advanced it through Congress), it provided appropriations to states so that they could do as Lathrop advised—educate women on prenatal health and on the care of their infants.

While Kelley and her allies presented detailed arguments about how Sheppard–Towner would benefit the nation's children, opposition came from other quarters, including the American Gynecological

Society, voicing doctors' fear that educating mothers would interfere with their treatment and that such government intervention was a precursor to socialism.³ Partly to appease the opposition, Congress made state participation voluntary and put a five-year lifetime on the law. Forty-one of the forty-eight states signed up the first year, and one historian noted the effect was most noticeable in the southern and western United States, where prenatal care had been scarce. It was up to individual states to decide how to use the money, and records indicate 3,000 prenatal care clinics were established during the five-year period. Some states funded public nurse programs, sending trained medical workers into homes to help new mothers.⁴

Congress failed to renew Sheppard–Towner in 1927 (one explanation centers on the perception that women were less potent voters than expected), and after the two-year extension expired, funding stopped altogether on June 30, 1929, ending the federal government's first significant foray into the health field. It was a big loss for the "female dominion," although the provision for maternal and infant healthcare resurfaced later in Title V of the Social Security Act of 1935.⁵

The infant mortality rate in her neighborhood had long alarmed Simkhovitch, and with population changes occurring in the 1920s, she had little reason to expect much improvement. The Ninth Ward had long been home to writers and artists of national, even international, reputation, but in Simkhovitch's opinion, the influx after war's end in 1918 brought inferior types. She saw them as tasteless "imitators"—poseurs—and "foreigners to the region." "Sandals, bright colors, earrings, and the inevitable cigarette" showed that the women were part of a "Village cult." Talk of shoddy housing and children's health rarely entered their conversations. "Art, love, and freedom were the watchwords of this new Village," and she did not like its acceptance of "free love" nor the fact that "marriage was regarded as bourgeois and to be apologized for."⁶ Although she understood that some of the newcomers were "brilliant young people of great gifts. . . . Edna St. Vincent Millay, the Washington Square and Provincetown Players groups," they were surrounded by losers. These were the ones she impugned: the "young people who felt it was à la mode to drink and have affairs." Rather than question their own expertise, they blamed the publishers and galleries for refusing to accept their books and art.[7]

Along with talk about sex, prostitution became more evident, and Simkhovitch had to deal with the repercussions. The problem of brothels spreading throughout the city was not new to her. She had arrived in Manhattan shortly after New York State passed a law (sponsored by State Senator John Raines in 1896) that made prostitution far more visible—if not actually more widespread, as its critics charged. The Raines law permitted hotels to sell liquor on Sunday, while bars could not. Since the law did not define either the size or number of rooms required to qualify as a hotel, saloonkeepers quickly saw an opportunity. By adding a few sleeping cubicles, they qualified for a hotel license to sell liquor seven days a week, thus increasing their profits considerably. Before long, these "Raines hotels" became big moneymakers because, in addition to selling alcohol, they rented rooms by the hour, twenty-four hours a day.[8]

A citizens' group, calling themselves the Committee of Fourteen, formed in 1905 to combat the Raines law, with Simkhovitch, just at the beginning of her career, the only female member. Its first report charged that the Raines loophole law did enormous harm, providing "unexampled accommodations" for sex workers, with the result that New York had more prostitution than any other American city.[9] Irate residents appealed to the Committee of Fourteen to close these brothels, which they were seeing for the first time in their own neighborhoods. "I simply cannot stand it any longer," one father of "several young daughters" wrote the committee in July 1908. In a "so called hotel" near his home, he saw "women of the street go in there with different men," and on one Saturday night he counted the same young woman entering the building nine times with a different man in tow each time. He implored the committee to exert influence on the police "to do something."[10]

The Committee of Fourteen listened and then acted with what some critics judged excessive zeal. After hiring investigators to keep watch on various establishments and report back on comings and goings, the committee began applying pressure on everyone connected to Raines hotels—owners of the buildings, brewers who furnished the alcohol, and insurance companies who bonded the saloons. Then the committee added to its watch list other establishments suspected of commercialized vice, including massage parlors and tenement house brothels.

Some of Greenwich House's neighbors protested that the Committee of Fourteen was going too far. Surveillance of activities intruded on people's lives, they charged, going beyond an investigation of prostitution to delve into levels of alcohol consumption and to condemn sexual activity between consenting adults. One newspaper accused the committee of showing a zeal that exceeded reason: "With its aim of stamping out the vice of prostitution every right-minded citizen sympathized but, as so often happens in the case of organized reform, this committee... condoned and even encouraged evils of a far more demoralizing nature than the one it sought to suppress."[11] How could anyone justify an entity that engaged in entrapment, used bribery to collect information, and paid off police for making arrests?

Simkhovitch's continued prominence in the Committee of Fourteen into the 1920s marked her as a prude and a puritan to more open-minded Villagers. Those who had gathered at Mabel Dodge's literary salon at 23 Fifth Avenue had to find other meeting places after she moved to Taos in 1917, but they weren't going to turn up at Greenwich House to discuss the limits of monogamy.[12] Neith Boyce and her husband, Hutchins Hapgood, a writer and well-known personality in Greenwich Village, had frequented Dodge's salon while trying at the same time to maintain a household that combined unconventional patterns with traditional ideas about family and marriage. It was a constant struggle. To Mabel Dodge's query, "Why do we want men to be monogamous?" Boyce, a mother of four, answered with a question of her own: "Do we?—So long as they won't be, why should we want them to be? Why want anybody to be what they are not?"[13] This was not the kind of attitude the Committee of Fourteen wanted to endorse.

To offset neighborhood vice in the Village, Simkhovitch ramped up offerings at Greenwich House. Although not yet able to garner much support for public investment in slum clearance—the notion that this should be publicly funded remained unpopular—she offered temporary escape to those living in small, dark spaces. Short visits to the countryside had been part of her program from the earliest years, and now, with the addition of artists, musicians, and theater people to the neighborhood, she could increase programming. The "dean of American sculptors," Daniel Chester French, whose statue of Abraham Lincoln for the memorial in Washington was dedicated in 1922, lived on 11th Street and joined the Greenwich House Arts Committee in 1920.[14] John Sloan, master printmaker and leader in the so-called Ashcan School of painting, kept a studio near 8th Street and participated in the settlement's arts program. Both men had national reputations, and their association with Greenwich House provided a significant seal of approval for the arts program, with its classes in pottery, painting, music, dance, and theater. Some of the novice artists turned a profit with their pottery, and others generated good publicity for the music school, which was thriving, even if not what the "New Villagers"—as Simkhovitch called the chic bohemian set—liked.

Gertrude Vanderbilt Whitney was no bohemian, and she played an important role in the settlement's visual arts program from the beginning. Born in 1875, she married financier Harry Payne Whitney in 1896, and as she concentrated her own artistic talent on sculpting and collecting, she became a fixture in the downtown art community. In 1907 she opened her own studio on 8th Street. In the beginning, she directed her money to promoting the works of others, whether children still in school or adults embarked on art careers. An original member of Greenwich House's board on Jones Street, Whitney made sure the new building at 27 Barrow included art facilities, and enrollment spiraled from 120 to 500 after it opened in 1917.[15] Under the tutelage of no fewer than fourteen instructors, the students needed even more space, and the Cooperative Social Settlement Society turned over the entire building at 18 Jones Street to arts and crafts programs.[16]

Music merited even bigger headlines. Most settlement houses offered some training in music—lessons for string players and opportunities to join a chorus. Greenwich House went much further, and after starting a small music program in 1905, gradually began teaching a wide selection of instruments (woodwinds, the Irish harp) and subjects (piano accompaniment and how to teach music). The justification came straight from Mary's Grandmother Kingsbury, who insisted that every child has a right to music education, not to become a professional but to enjoy a richer cultural life and greater personal pleasure.

Greenwich House's music program would not have thrived without the abundance of teachers available in the immediate area. Musicians at uptown venues could augment their incomes, and newcomers still looking for jobs could earn precious dollars teaching there. As the school's reputation grew, a separate brownstone at 46 Barrow Street was purchased in 1913 to serve specifically as a music school. It provided small rooms for individual instruction and a concert hall large enough to accommodate chamber ensembles. Full-sized orchestras used an uptown hall or (after 1917) the auditorium at 27 Barrow Street. In 1927 the Settlement Society purchased an adjoining brownstone on Barrow Street, thus doubling its space for music lessons and performances.

With its attractive venue, Greenwich House's music program stood out as the leader among the city's many settlements, drawing students from outside the area and attracting praise from professional musicians. After Marion Rous, an acclaimed pianist, became director, the forty-member student orchestra gained special recognition, winning prizes in competitions. When the Detroit Symphony performed in Carnegie Hall in April 1928, it donated proceeds from a portion of ticket sales to the Greenwich House Orchestra. A few months later, the internationally renowned violinist Ossip Gabrilowitsch played a concert at the Biltmore Hotel to benefit the music school.

Simkhovitch's satisfaction in seeing her settlement associated with celebrities extended to headliners outside the arts. Gene Tunney, a neighborhood boy who had taken his first boxing lessons at Greenwich House, dominated the boxing world in the early 1920s.[17] In 1928 he married a wealthy socialite and retired to Connecticut to raise their four children in luxury. In nearly all his accounts of how he rose to wealth and recognition, Greenwich House merits mention, and Simkhovitch included him in her 1938 book, *Neighborhood*.[18]

Stephen Simkhovitch, only four years younger than Tunney, could have profited from the same lessons at Greenwich House, but he showed no interest. Instead, he acted more like the sandal-wearing, unproductive vagabonds his mother belittled. Resolved to change his outlook, she took him on a lengthy trip to the American Southwest in 1921. Far away from the temptations of Greenwich Village, she introduced him to tourist sights and to Kingsbury relatives who had made successful business careers in California. Mary relished her first look at the nation's West, and she described Arizona as better "than anything I have ever seen."[19]

Stephen remained much less impressed and as aimless as before. After returning briefly to school in the East, he was soon back on the West Coast with a job at Standard Oil of California, headed at the time by his mother's cousin, Kenneth Kingsbury.[20] Although admitted to the freshman class at Princeton in 1922, Stephen boasted to his grandmother that he didn't plan to enroll anywhere.[21] Confident he could make it "to the top of the oil business" without a college education, he planned to keep his distance from professors.[22] He shamelessly directed her to send any birthday or Christmas gifts "in the form of a check—I have everything I want except—checks." Flattering her, he requested a photo, "which I would like immensely as I have none in my room." He preferred to see her in person, he wrote but was waiting for "next year" when he would "come of age...and have enough money that I can come back and quite a little more besides."[23]

The job at Standard Oil did not last long, and Stephen announced he was going to Cuba. His Grandmother Kingsbury confided in her diary that she feared for his future. She had come to appreciate the lovable side of him, and she treasured his visits, especially after she was widowed in 1919. When in New York, he would make the trip to Hartford just to have lunch with her or take her to church. Although always grateful to see him, she could not rid herself of the fear that he would meet a tragic end. At age 22, the enormous contradictions in his personality stood out: "Still Stephen! Optimistic and boyish," she wrote in her diary.

"A clean boy but only half awake as yet. God bless him! And keep him from evil."[24]

Mary had done most of her children's parenting up to that time, and with Vladimir taking little interest in their son, she resolved to double her efforts. As a result of the generosity of Anna Woerishoffer, Stephen had a sizeable trust fund, and having his own apartment gave him a sense of independence and augmented a stubborn insistence to do as he pleased. After his mother realized he needed help, she enlisted Dr. Thomas Salmon, one of the top doctors in the field of "mental and nerve" diseases, to see him. Salmon's enormous reputation derived from his successful treatment of shell-shocked soldiers and for connecting their physical illnesses after the war to emotional origins. After accepting a professorship at Columbia in 1921, Salmon turned his attention to truancy and delinquency in young people, a subject of special interest to Mary.[25] Holding little faith in psychoanalysis, an increasingly popular form of therapy at the time, he reported that few of his patients had profited from it, and he recommended instead that they engage in discussion with others to discover more about themselves. That commonsense approach appealed to Mary, and Salmon's optimism encouraged her.

How much effect Salmon had on Stephen in the four years he saw him is difficult to say, but when the doctor died in a Long Island boating accident in 1927, Vladimir, writing from Europe, admitted to Mary that he was "terribly sorry" to hear about Salmon's death.[26] As Vladimir and others could see, Stephen still had plenty of problems. Brief stints at both Princeton and Columbia ended without completion of two semesters at either of them.[27] He began identifying himself as a playwright, although he was doing "more playing than writing."[28] Like the would-be authors his mother ridiculed, he did not get published. In a place rife with outsized career dreams, he encountered many actors and painters no more successful than him, but that did not relieve his mother's worries.

Stephen had his father's eye for attractive women, and the "beautiful and shapely young blonde" actress Sonja Stockstad was a perfect candidate for his attention.[29] He may very well have met her when Greenwich House opened a tearoom at 20 Jones Street in 1929. Named "Charles and

Kitty," for the settlement's popular cook and butler, it offered training in culinary skills and waitressing while providing a salubrious meeting place for young men and women. In a well-lit tearoom, they could converse with others and widen their circle of friends. The Greenwich House board apparently expected the tearoom to show a profit while also offering guidance on the preparation and serving of food.[30]

Sonja Stockstad was one of the early employees, and any account of her life up to that time reads like a movie script. Born Gudren Stockstad in 1898 to Norwegian immigrants in North Dakota, she returned with her parents to their native country before learning much English. She recrossed the Atlantic in 1921, without any intention to return to the rural Dakotas and work as a "domestic" as the ship's manifest listed her. She dreamed of becoming an actress, and after dropping Gudren from her name, found success on stage and in silent movies. The acting company Stockstad joined gave her the chance to see much of the United States on tours from New York to California. Her hopes for a movie career were cut short, however, because the "talkies" that became popular in the late 1920s could not accommodate her heavy Norwegian accent.

That accent was no detriment to popularity in Greenwich Village, however, and Stockstad rented a room at 116 Washington Place, took a job in the tearoom nearby, and met Stephen Simkhovitch.[31] A photo taken about 1930 shows a handsome couple, smiling broadly, with arms linked tightly as they pose with a friend in a rural setting. It's autumn, with the trees nearly bare of leaves, and it may be one of the very few photos of them together.

By February 1931, his grandmother believed Stephen was headed to Brazil, and she implored Mary to pass on any information she had. Laura Kingsbury had been following her grandson vicariously and contributing financially to his ventures. "I live in Rio at present," she wrote her daughter, "studying atlas, encyclopedia."[32] She hoped the check she had mailed to his bank's address reached him and worried that bad habits would do him in: "He is sure everybody is his friend! And so easily somebody's dupe." Dangers he might encounter in a foreign country had to be balanced against the advantages of starting anew, however, and his grandmother remained optimistic: "I'm sure his intentions are to go straight...in every way....I hope he finds real friends soon, and may be very happy, even successful in fresh fields and pastures."[33]

Three months after Laura wrote that letter, Sonja Stockstad gave birth to a son in New York, and she claimed the father was Stephen Simkhovitch, whereabouts unknown.[34] He refused to have anything to do with Sonja or the baby, either then or later, and continued with vague plans to write. It was his mother who looked for ways to provide for the child. She would soon be drawn into a lawsuit, reported in local newspapers, and struggle with maintaining responsibility toward that grandson for the rest of her life.

Had Stephen really wanted to establish himself as a writer, he might have settled down in New York and looked to Greenwich House personnel for contacts and guidance. Theater productions, which had remained limited affairs in the cramped quarters on Jones Street, flourished in the new home on Barrow Street, with an auditorium seating 199. To direct the program, Simkhovitch hired Helen Murphy, who had moved to New York to study at Columbia after first meeting her while Murphy was working as a storyteller in Boston. Murphy remembered the encounter vividly, and decades later recalled that while preparing to relate one of her most popular tales, she looked out on an audience of social workers "so old and so serious" and a single face had stood out: "One stately, beautiful woman...looked so interested that I plunged into my story and felt the pleasure that comes from such a receptive listener."[35] After Murphy learned the identity of that "receptive listener," she volunteered to join Greenwich House. "I had ideas of creative work," Murphy later wrote, and Simkhovitch was all one could ask for in an advocate: "dignified, scholarly, kind, supportive."[36]

Murphy made her debut as theater director in Greenwich Village with a large outdoor performance in June 1919. The pageant, featuring a cast of 500 people of all ages, depicted the life of Joan of Arc. Staged to begin in Washington Square Park and then parade up Fifth Avenue, the event cost Greenwich House less than $500 but won wide praise. Euphoria over the war's end was still high at the time, and a peace pageant based on a popular heroine resonated with viewers. Churches, schools, and other neighborhood organizations joined in the effort, and police officers took the time to teach a fourteen-year-old Italian girl how to ride a horse so that she could lead the procession. Simkhovitch proudly pronounced it one of the most successful pageants ever undertaken by the Greenwich Village community, and very shortly afterwards she put the director on her payroll.

Murphy chose not to reside at the settlement, but went every Monday night for dinner.[37] Her insistence that the study of drama could enrich all lives, not merely prepare a few people for professional careers, made her popular, and she drew admiration for her patient and creative work with children. Although her drama classes never matched the music school's reputation, the actor and future matinee idol Kirk Douglas agreed to succeed her in the late 1930s.

None of the Greenwich House arts programs appealed to Stephen Simkhovitch. Nor did his sister want to act in any pageants. Explaining that she "always wanted to become an actress," Helena left Bryn Mawr in her sophomore year to perform on Broadway.[38] By December 1923, she was living in a tiny rented room at 414 West 20th Street in what she called the "shabby" Chelsea section of Manhattan and receiving favorable mention in the *Daily News* for her part in "Cyrano de Bergerac." Her role was small, the reviewer noted, but her exceptional beauty assured that two brief appearances sufficed to make a mark. The following summer Helena appeared in a Provincetown production on Cape Cod and impressed the play's author, Eugene O'Neill, who wrote her a glowing letter, remarking on her beauty and "very fine work." He promised to recommend her to others and followed up with another letter, asking a friend to give her a part "if something comes up."[39]

Acting soon lost its appeal, however, and by the fall of 1925, Helena, continuing to echo the fickleness of those her mother labeled "false Villagers," announced she was leaving for Europe.[40] While looking for a reasonable price on a good ship, she wrote her grandmother that she meant to buy no clothes "except the necessities." Then she clarified that her new fur coat was "quite a big expense," but definitely "necessary."[41]

In mid-January 1926 Helena arrived in Paris, the European capital most favored at the time by expatriate American writers and artists, and her mother visited her there the following summer. After meeting several of her daughter's new friends, Simkhovitch endorsed her decision to relocate, and in September received word that Helena intended to stay. She had decided to marry Frank Didisheim, an American-born son of Swiss parents, and had shifted her interest to writing, submitting articles for publication in the United States.[42] Frank Didisheim had moved to Paris with his parents after graduation from Massachusetts Institute of Technology, and Helena's marriage to him raised the possibility she would continue living an ocean away from her mother.

Young women with dreams even bigger than Helena Simkhovitch were still coming to volunteer and live at Greenwich House. Amelia Earhart, six years older than Helena, became the most famous. She had originally opted for a career in medicine, then altered her plans after taking her first plane ride at age twenty-three. Medicine and social work became a way to pay for what she wanted to do above all else—fly airplanes. While employed at Denison House, the Boston settlement where Simkhovitch herself had started out, Earhart also worked part-time as a sales representative for a Boston aircraft company and wrote newspaper columns on flying. Transferred to New York in 1927, she used her Denison House record as recommendation for working at Greenwich House, and in the next two years she put in enough hours to secure a room for herself when she needed it. "She used to go out quietly at night," Simkhovitch wrote, "and when she came back, she would say she had flown over New York. We always felt that we had someone from another sphere, notwithstanding the fact that she was so human and jolly."[43]

In June 1928 Earhart made international headlines by becoming the first woman to fly across the Atlantic, although not yet as pilot. Previously known around Greenwich Village as the pants-wearing mechanic who repaired her own car, Earhart was on the way to becoming a household name, and she no longer needed Greenwich House accommodations. She continued to have contact with the Simkhovitchs, however, and after her marriage in 1937 raised questions about whether a woman should continue to work after marriage, she cited Simkhovitch as her model of a "career woman who runs home and business with success."[44]

After Earhart's disappearance in the Pacific in July 1937, Simkhovitch wrote a condolence note to Earhart's widower, George Putnam, recalling that she had seen her at a party the previous year. As in so many of her references to young attractive women at Greenwich House, she noted that Vladimir "knew Amelia better" than she did, and since "I think they enjoyed each other's society very much," he would be a better source than she on Earhart's early years.[45] It was Vladimir who had sent Earhart a telegram of "Love and Congratulations" when she made her first solo flight by a woman across the Atlantic in May 1932, and he signed it simply "Simkhovitch."[46]

Although not on Earhart's level as a household name, Marion Tanner added an equally colorful personality to the Greenwich House circle. In 1927 when she was thirty-four years old, Tanner bought a house in the heart of the West Village at 72 Bank Street and turned it into a refuge for whoever wanted to stop by—extending an invitation that drew, according to her disapproving neighbors, drunks and derelicts.[47] Tanner's antics made her the model for Auntie Mame in Patrick Dennis's bestselling book (later movie) of the same name, and since her generosity fit with Simkhovitch's agenda, the two began to work together.

By Tanner's time in Greenwich Village, volunteering to live and work in a settlement house was losing its appeal. Social work was becoming professionalized, with case studies and graduate degrees.[48] Men and women who finished an academic program expected to be paid for their work, and they wanted to live independently, not in dormitories. Gone were the days when Greenwich House had more applicants than it could possibly accommodate.

Male workers were particularly scarce because they had so many other opportunities. This loss hit Greenwich House especially hard, and Mary mounted a campaign to win male workers back. Boys in the neighborhood needed models, she insisted, "men of broader contacts" to set an example for what they could become, and the benefits ran both ways.

Evoking what she had first heard at Toynbee Hall in 1896, she labeled settlement house work a valuable apprenticeship for college-educated men because it gave them the chance to learn "the point of view of people whose leadership they hope to assume in the field of business and politics."[49] That reasoning may have resonated with her neighbors struggling with delinquency and gangs, but did little to change the course of men with other career plans.

Male mentors were not the only ones missing at Greenwich House. A significant change in immigration laws in the 1920s meant fewer Italians entered the United States each year. Italians still constituted the settlement's largest ethnic group, but these were families who had been in the city for a while, and they looked for services different from those needed by new arrivals. The programs at Greenwich House had to adjust to that change.[50] Instead of lessons in basic English and help in gaining citizenship, the settlement scheduled debates on current topics and offered chances to socialize.[51] A population with more second-generation Italian Americans stood ready to participate in decisions affecting them, and with conservative ideas about family, religion, and politics, they constituted a counterweight to their free-thinking neighbors.

Neither the Italian component nor the "New Villagers" provided adequate funding to keep Greenwich House afloat (although attendees at events paid a few cents), and Simkhovitch looked to affluent New Yorkers, not only in the Ninth Ward but throughout the city. With government contributing a measly 1 percent of GNP to social welfare, private donations remained critical. In 1923 the situation was so bleak that the director and several staff members risked losing their salaries in order that their work with baby clinics, Italian clubs, and lobbying could continue.[52] At a special meeting called to discuss finances, Simkhovitch volunteered to raise one-quarter of the $12,000 needed, and she suggested that board members come up with the rest.[53] Her secretary had already appealed to local real estate agent, Vincent Pepe, for a list of any "wealthy, new tenants" in the vicinity.[54]

Vladimir was apparently not on that list, although he was earning significant income from art sales. In January 1922 the *New York Tribune* announced that "selections" from his "Egyptian, Greek and Roman, Indian, Chinese, and European" collection would go on sale.[55] The *Tribune* followed up with an announcement that the Art Institute of Chicago had purchased some of the most prized items for a total of $12,225.50 (more than $200,000 in current dollars), though offered no details on what he did with the money.[56]

Rather than rely on her husband or any other single benefactor, Simkhovitch looked to her roster of donors. While Jacob Schiff, the banker/businessman continued to subsidize Lillian Wald's Henry Street and even paid for Wald's extensive travel in both Europe and Asia, Simkhovitch had to scramble for multiple donors of more modest means. Gerard Swope, president of General Electric, although not in the same financial stratum as Schiff, became one of her loyal supporters. He had a soft spot for settlements because he had met his wife at Hull House, and by the 1920s, he had the financial resources and personal commitment to make a difference at Greenwich House. Simkhovitch looked to him to bring other rich folk her way. "I appreciate your going over to see Mr. Leffingwell," referring to Russell Leffingwell, a banker, partner at J. P. Morgan, and trustee of the Carnegie Corporation, she wrote Swope in early 1924. "I have written him another note this morning (not mentioning your visit, of course) and if you could clinch him now, I think it would really be very fine." Typically reticent about compliments directed to her, Simkhovitch knew how to hand them out. "See how effective you are whatever you undertake," she wrote Swope.[57] A few months later, she invited him and his wife to dinner, along with the Leffingwells and the Marshall Fields.[58]

Such careful tending of contacts paid off, and by early 1925 Simkhovitch had a well-heeled board lined up. Gerard Swope agreed to take on the presidency, Mrs. Marshall Field accepted the vice presidency, and Russell Leffingwell joined the board.[59] Simkhovitch reached out to former board members, encouraging them to increase their contributions. To Fulton Cutting, one of the original founders of Greenwich House, she suggested he might "see [his] way clear...to becoming a life member and in that way lead the way for others." This honor carried a price tag, however, and it "involves a payment of $1,000."⁶⁰

The biggest and recurring donations came from people with long ties to Vladimir and Mary. Until her death in 1931, Anna Woerishoffer remained a regular contributor, with annual donations of $9,000. Mrs. Marshall Field was also generous, giving $5,000 or so at a time, and Gertrude Whitney supported several art students and turned over her studio on 8th Street for their exhibits.⁶¹

As the money situation eased at Greenwich House, Simkhovitch found her personal finances in better shape. She sold the New Jersey farm in 1925, finding less use for it with both children on their own, and she had more cash than usual. Rather than asking Swope for a donation, she turned to him for advice on how to invest $2,000, half in her name and half in Vladimir's. With little regulation of stock trading at the time, speculation was popular and tips from insiders highly valued. She confessed that as a "social worker" she had little understanding "in this field" and hoped Swope would enlighten her.⁶²

Vladimir showed little interest in stocks—he continued to trade art. In a typical operation, he exchanged one piece for another or bought a "lot" [batch] of items, retaining one or two of the most valuable pieces and getting rid of the rest. By March 1929, he felt flush enough to offer to match donations to Greenwich House, up to $10,000, but imposed conditions. The entire amount raised had to be designated seed money for what would become a total endowment of $200,000 that would yield income of "ten or 12,000 a year."⁶³

Besides rethinking her financial support and personnel shortages, Simkhovitch tightened ties with academia. Both Columbia Teachers' College and Fordham University had sent graduate students to work at Greenwich House in its early years, and now she wanted to formalize the arrangement. Her short stint on the Barnard faculty (1907–1910) and Vladimir's much longer connection with Columbia helped pull them both into that university's orbit rather than into a partnership with neighboring New York University.

In 1929 the Cooperative Social Settlement Society and the Trustees of Columbia signed papers to "secure the maximum of intellectual intercourse between the two groups."[64] Columbia secured the right to appoint four members of the Greenwich House board and be the "residuary legatee of [Greenwich House] property in case of the dissolution of the work of the Society." No direct financial assistance was promised, although the Rockefeller Foundation provided Columbia with $15,000 to fund research. Two economists, a husband-and-wife team, took part-time offices at the settlement, signaling serious purpose, and in a period when Greenwich Village was known for bohemian excesses, Greenwich House reasserted its dedication to hard-nosed research. The cooperation with Columbia endured, although not always smoothly, until officially terminated in 1944.

Among the first graduate students sent by Columbia to do research was Caroline Ware, who later served on President Franklin Roosevelt's Consumers Advisory Board.[65] With funding from a Rockefeller grant, the thirty-year-old Ware began her investigation in 1929, and six years later published a book that became a classic on that part of Manhattan: *Greenwich Village, 1920–1930*.[66] Although it did not purport to be a study of Greenwich House, it could hardly avoid mentioning its founder and director, and Ware's initial assessment of Simkhovitch was fairly damning. She charged her with not understanding the various components of the population in her area, specifically how the "bohemians" interacted with newly arrived immigrants, how Irish and Italians had different priorities, and how the second generation of any immigrant group did not conform to patterns of their parents. As a result, "Greenwich House facilities were used by a few Villagers."[67]

After reading a copy of Ware's manuscript, Simkhovitch sent an angry letter to the author's supervising professor, Robert M. MacIver, outlining her objections to its publication. She found nothing new, she wrote, and although the book was "readable," it was "misleading and untruthful" and showed a "lack of generosity." Too "psychological" and "destructive," the book gave too much prominence to the "villager" and treated sex "from a somewhat pathological angle." Simkhovitch speculated that the book's weaknesses resulted from the fact that the author was a woman—specifically one who disapproved of Italian males and their traditional views of women—and placed little value on what Greenwich House had achieved.[68]

As chair of the Columbia University Social Science Research Council, MacIver had the uncomfortable task of mediating between Simkhovitch and Ware, and he tried to persuade the author to treat the settlement's founder more sympathetically. "For example," he advised Ware, "you dwell on the point that [the area around Greenwich House] purports to be a neighborhood while in reality there is no corresponding neighborhood." The annual reports of Greenwich House would show, he pointed out, that "the Director and staff are quite well aware that it is no longer a neighborhood in the old sense and that they have sought to adapt their work to the changing neighborhood character."[69]

Ware subsequently toned down her criticism of Greenwich House, and she included praise for its programs, especially the workshops for boys to learn cabinetmaking, but she did not change her personal assessment that Simkhovitch had never bridged the chasm between herself and the Italian community. Nor did Ware think that Italians really understood the "lady" they called "Mrs. Sim." More than fifty years after publishing the book (and after Simkhovitch's death), Ware explained the split between the two camps by highlighting a social center that drew young people away from Greenwich House. The Italian director at the competing center had a ready explanation. "My people understand two things, force and kindness. At Greenwich House they talk about fair play which seems to my people like weakness or not caring."[70] Ware's recounting that conversation indicates she believed Greenwich House offered too little direction. A tighter hand would have done better.

Without mentioning Simkhovitch, Ware credited Greenwich House for its "performance of certain neighborhood functions, primarily those which fell in the category of social work." Any university offering a degree in social work took note of Ware's account of assistance provided at Greenwich House. In addition to a nursing service, an "agency for the care of cripples," and a place where probation officers met with "juvenile delinquents," the settlement sponsored art and music activities that "became widely known and drew from all over the city."[71]

Ware devoted an entire chapter of her book to "Social Welfare," which, she argued, entered a new stage in the United States after the war's end in 1918. Starting out as a moralist concept of the virtue of helping others, social welfare entered a second phase in the late nineteenth century, she posited, by adopting social gospel thinking that the entire community shared responsibility for the poor and disadvantaged. According to Ware, this second "attitude," which most readers would identify with Mary Simkhovitch, had failed, and "after thirty years, both settlements and churches were on the defensive" for not doing what they had promised. The professionally trained social workers who replaced them in the third stage judged their predecessors inefficient and set on much too broad objectives. Rather than trying to solve all the world's problems, social welfare workers needed to focus on treating "the maladjusted individual" as they had been trained to diagnose and heal.[72]

It isn't surprising that Ware disagreed with Simkhovitch on what her book should contain. She came to the subject of Greenwich Village with different priorities than Simkhovitch. Born in 1899, Ware was a full generation younger than Simkhovitch, and she had earned a Ph.D. in economic history and taken a teaching position at Vassar before she was thirty. Both women remained active through the New Deal. They came from well-established New England families, with ties to Harvard and progressive branches of Protestantism (MKS was Episcopalian and Ware was Unitarian). But as Ware emphasized, ideas on social service had changed, and neither the bohemian Villagers nor any of the immigrant enclaves qualified as homogenous. To treat them as such was a mistake, and to speak of Greenwich Village as a "neighborhood" was grossly misleading.

Ware did not identify how members of Simkhovitch's own family fit in with the freethinking villagers that she, Simkhovitch, disparaged.

Besides Stephen, there was Vladimir, who could have been a poster boy for libertine imbibers. With the 18th "Prohibition" Amendment in effect, he insisted on serving his guests the best vodka he could obtain. Although a tenured professor at Columbia University, he maintained friendships with those who championed radical causes and unconventional living arrangements, including Polly Porter, an heiress to family money and holder of decidedly communist views. Her associates insisted the stance was mostly a reflection of her need to create independence from her life partner, the feminist/reformer Molly Dewson, but Porter made no attempt to conceal her radical views. Porter's family wealth permitted the two women to buy a cooperative apartment at 171 West 12th Street, where other unmarried professional women, both single and in couples, lived.[73] Historian Susan Ware (not related to Caroline Ware) notes that this "homosocial" enclave was "far from anti-male," and Vladimir Simkhovitch was a "close friend."[74]

Helena resembled her father in many ways, and she shared his interest in the visual arts. After spending time with him during one of his rare visits to Paris in 1927, she wrote her mother, "V. G. impresses me more than ever, a really unusual intelligence and with a very wide scope of knowledge." She recognized his limitations, however: "As a *man* I can't say I can *compliment* him. He has no gentleness in him, has he?" Yet she found him "fascinating."[75] Before meeting his new son-in-law on that trip, Vladimir went to Warsaw to visit his own birth family, whom he had not seen since leaving for the United States in 1898. To Mary, who never met them, he wrote a postcard in September 1927, giving a brief but favorable description: "Am having an extraordinarily good time. My folks are fine folks and are glad to see me. Much love, Vladimir."[76] A longer letter revealed more: "My parents are old and of course sick. I promised to see them next year, if my salary is increased, so that I can come over for a week. They will hardly live very long. [T]hey of course lost everything in the war and revolution, but my bro[ther]—He has a large practice and is taking care of them, they [are] living together. But they are proud people used to give & not to receive so it is hard for them. Of course they were terribly happy to see me and terribly sad to see me go."[77]

Vladimir's letters to Mary during that trip underline the unpredictable, wide-ranging, rather reckless nature of his personality. Showing a modicum of concern for Mary, who was not well when he left New York, he assured her that he was "glad" her leg "was better," but most of what he wrote was about himself. Overspending as usual, he confessed, "God knows I will need money. The journey is ruining me."[78] As for bills that had been forwarded to him in Paris, he promised to "pay some day."[79] From Hotel Saint Regis, where he was staying, Vladimir wrote far more about the art dealers his daughter had lined up for him to see than he did about his infant grandson, to whom he gifted a chess set and called a "nice kid."[80]

While husband, son, and daughter cavorted with the "Village cult," Mary Simkhovitch continued the serious business of getting public support for safe, affordable housing. Edith Elmer Wood remained her most visible and effective ally, and together they pulled sympathetic women's groups into the campaign. The suffrage cause had spawned many women's associations, with the Women's City Club, founded in New York in 1916, boasting a prominent membership that included Eleanor Roosevelt and Belle Moskowitz, a key advisor to New York Governor Al Smith.[81] Other support came from various mothers' clubs, who saw decent housing as a parental responsibility. The United Neighborhood Houses, the umbrella group of settlement workers that Simkhovitch had started, named its own committee to work specifically on housing and particularly public funding.

With that kind of backing, Simkhovitch pressed Governor Smith to deliver, and the 1926 State Housing Act brought government into the housing picture in new ways. Rather than simply setting standards for new and inspecting the old, the law recognized the legitimacy of using eminent domain to acquire property for new construction. A state housing board (with Edith Elmer Wood as adviser) was appointed to oversee acquisitions by eminent domain and the new twenty-year tax exemption for builders of low-cost housing.[82]

The State Housing Act was a major innovation, and this provision for a state to take such a decisive role in providing housing occurred in the middle of a decade often written off as centered on hedonism and personal pleasure. The milestone in affordable housing should be credited, according to many historians, to the "indefatigable reformer" Mary Simkhovitch.[83] More than a breakthrough, it served as marker for far more significant housing reform in the following decade, when New Deal legislation finally put the federal government into the supply chain.

10

Gains and Losses

Career and family rarely meld seamlessly for even the most diligent and gifted women, and for Simkhovitch, the 1930s brought both public success and private heartbreak. The same size font fits headlines on losses as well as wins, and the Simkhovitch name showed up in both.

The fact that she made headlines was by this point no surprise. She had been laying the groundwork her entire adult life. Her founding of Greenwich House, then directing its activities over decades, and her work to improve health, education, and labor conditions had put her name in print. She wanted to do much more—to expand her reach—but had to wait for the nation's thinking to change.

Providing decent, safe housing for those who couldn't afford the going rate had preoccupied Simkhovitch from her first years in New York, and she made sure Greenwich House programs included tactics to help. Classes in housekeeping and family budgets offered strategies for dealing with inadequate space and income; kindergartens and baby clinics helped equalize opportunities for children from the poorest homes. The Congestion Committee had its headquarters at Greenwich House, and her 1917 book and her speeches across the nation outlined ways others could help.

Although early to enter the cause, she also knew she wasn't the first. Others had come up with multiple proposals to expose slum conditions, increase the supply of units available, and regulate what landlords did. One briefly popular idea in both England and the United States focused on limiting investors' profits—a solution dubbed "philanthropy plus 5%."

Alfred Tredway White, a wealthy banker, signed on to the idea in his native Brooklyn in the 1870s.[1] Introduced to congested housing in his youth when he taught at the settlement school of his Unitarian Church, he began in his thirties building apartment complexes and renting the units below market price. Unfortunately, few of his fellow New Yorkers liked the idea of only 5 percent return on their investments, and White's renters grumbled about what they got. They liked neither the "institutional" look of his buildings nor the "strict house rules" enforced inside them.[2] Philanthropy yielding a small return didn't work.[3] The editors of the *New York Times* summed up the matter succinctly: "Philanthropy, pure and simple, will never greatly improve the housing of the people. The problem is too vast."[4]

Legislation to set minimum requirements hadn't worked either, and by 1930, Simkhovitch lamented that more than 1.5 million New Yorkers lived in quarters lacking adequate light, access to outer air, and sanitary conveniences."[5] The national picture was equally grim. Little had changed since Edith Elmer Wood used census reports in her 1919 book to show that fully one-third of Americans lived "under subnormal housing conditions," and one in ten confronted housing harmful to himself and others.[6]

Yet opposition to government funding of new housing remained adamant. Lawrence Veiller, who dedicated his life to the problem of housing, continued to argue that laws would work and that government funding could go to slum clearance but not to construction of new buildings on the site. Most Americans continued to agree with him that such use of public funds would be "socialistic."[7] Rather than socialism, Simkhovitch maintained that decent housing was a basic right, like access to air and water. Even the lowest-paid urban workers deserved safe shelter "in just the sense and for precisely the same reason" as they were entitled to a "cubic air space standard."[8]

The Great Depression of the 1930s accomplished what all the exhibits, books, and speeches could not. It changed people's minds. Shocked by the extent of homelessness and joblessness that exacerbated it, Americans began questioning old ideas about the role of government. Simkhovitch, whom her co-worker Coleman Woodbury described as a "Boston Brahmin who was a superb politician able to manipulate and persuade," perceived that change and took advantage of it.[9] Susan Ware claimed that Simkhovitch was "about thirty years ahead of her time," and her achievements during the 1930s bear that out.[10]

As the economic downturn put more families out on the sidewalks, the director of Greenwich House convened a small group of like-minded New Yorkers in late 1931 to consider the best strategy for pushing the national government to act.[11] Initially named Public Housing Conference, the group soon widened its scope and became the National Public Housing Conference (NPHC), with a membership that included Norman Thomas, head of the Socialist Party and former presidential candidate, Henry Street Settlement founder Lillian Wald, and Mayor Fiorello LaGuardia.[12]

By January 1932, Simkhovitch's cofounders agreed that she should head the NPHC, although she was not the unanimous first choice. When Paul Blanshard wrote her to offer the job, he noted that other names had met with some objection, but hers had been "favorably received by everybody."[13] She accepted. The NPHC stood for exactly what she wanted, and its stationery touted its purpose very clearly: "to promote low-cost housing for workers through public construction and with the aid of government funds."[14]

As head of the NPHC, Simkhovitch immediately advanced her view that long-held values no longer served. The rugged individualism popular in rural America failed miserably in crowded cities, where even the most conscientious, hard-working men or women could not dig a well or build a house or provide recreation space for their children. These services were a "public responsibility." Much remained open to discussion—where to build and whether government's role should be direct or indirect. But one fact was clear: "Private capital and effort cannot make drastic improvements on a large scale in housing for the lowest income groups and this must be a function of the community."[15]

President Herbert Hoover had already taken note of a looming housing crisis, and in August 1930 he convened a Conference on Home

Building and Home Ownership, the first federally sponsored housing conference ever held.[16] Attended mostly by real estate and construction people, it adhered to Veiller's line of thinking rather than to Simkhovitch's. He had not budged from his earlier views, and he sounded a lot like Hoover when he proclaimed, "It is an American principle that the People should support the Government, not that government should support the People."[17] The most significant accomplishment of that conference laid the groundwork for the Federal Home Loan Bank Act, passed in July 1932. But as Simkhovitch and her associates knew well, the people most in need of help could hardly use a loan, even a low-cost loan—not in a city where single family homes housed only the rich, and residential buildings in working class neighborhoods were pressed to take in an ever increasing number of renters who had no hopes of buying real estate.

As economic conditions worsened across the nation, New York was particularly hard hit. Around the corner from Greenwich House, bread lines snaked around the block, and crudely constructed tents and huts sheltered families with no other place to go. Many of Simkhovitch's neighbors had eked out only a precarious living in the best of times. Now, in the worst depression the nation had ever experienced, with nearly a quarter of the workforce unemployed, people were desperate.

By mid-1932, families in New York were receiving dispossess notices at the rate of more than 5,000 per week, and it became commonplace in poorer neighborhoods to see a family's entire possessions deposited on the sidewalk in front of the building where they had lived.[18] Teachers and social workers listened as school children related their latest nightmare about returning home in the evening to find they no longer had a home.

In these dire conditions, Edith Elmer Wood's 1931 book, *Recent Trends in American Housing*, found a more receptive audience than her earlier book. Both fully supported Simkhovitch's call for government-funded housing. To those who favored raising wages as the best way to get workers into better living quarters, Wood responded: "It is easier in practice to lessen the cost of housing than it is to change the distribution of income in favor of the lower groups."[19] This put the available options in blunt contrast, and housing activists cited Wood's book as their "bible."[20]

While Mary's new prominence as head of the NPHC put her in headlines, the Simkhovitch name also appeared in less rosy contexts. The *New York Times* reported in November 1934 a dispute that had been brewing for some time: "V. G. Simkhovitch of Columbia Accused of Misrepresenting Old Painting He Sold." This was the newspaper that her friends and associates read, and the same month it reported the charge against Vladimir, it announced that both Eleanor Roosevelt and Mayor LaGuardia would attend a dinner in honor of Mrs. Simkhovitch. A companion article reported a sizeable contribution ($26,000) to Greenwich House, but not from Vladimir. Mary Simkhovitch left little record of how she viewed the charge against her husband, though she wrote her daughter that she hoped it the would be resolved quickly when "the Armenian"—referring to Hagop Kevorkian, who had filed the charges against Vladimir, returned from Europe.[21]

Details of the business deal are complex and extend over nearly a decade. Kevorkian enjoyed a reputation as a prominent antique dealer in New York, and his name later marked significant collections at the Metropolitan Museum of Art and buildings at New York University. In his lawsuit, he contested an agreement made with Vladimir a decade earlier when he agreed to buy a Chinese painting, *Red Robed Man*, for $37,500, a high figure at the time. Vladimir collected $20,000, part in artwork and part in cash, in early 1924, with the remainder due later that year. Kevorkian never paid up. When Vladimir subsequently decided to put his entire Chinese collection up for sale, the Philadelphia Museum of Art wanted to buy it, *Red Robed Man* included, but attorneys wanted the matter with Kevorkian settled before proceeding. After multiple attempts to reach Kevorkian, Vladimir sold *Red Robed Man* to the Pennsylvania Museum of Fine Arts in November 1930 for $20,000.[22]

Kevorkian's lawsuit apparently aimed to retrieve the $20,000 ("with interest") he had turned over in 1924, but since he had failed to pay the remainder due, his only recourse was to charge the seller with misrepresentation, thus making the agreement invalid.

It was a weak argument, and Kevorkian backed off. A notarized court document dated January 2, 1935, only two months after the *New York Times* article appeared, survives in Vladimir's papers. It relieved him "[a]nd all his heirs from any debts or obligations whatsoever from the beginning of the world."[23] Of course that news did not make headlines, and he continued to barter and trade as he had always done, relying on his own judgment to single out the one valuable piece in a collection of junk.[24]

Mary's name did not appear in the *New York Times* coverage of the Kevorkian/Simkhovitch dispute, but readers had little trouble connecting *that* Simkhovitch with the one whose name made a headline in the same newspaper multiple times that year.[25] Some of those readers encountered her often at Greenwich House; others learned of her work with the National Public Housing Conference. Still others heard her radio speeches and read Eleanor Roosevelt's praise of her in "My Day" columns.

While her husband battled over art, Simkhovitch continued her long fight to bring city government in on her side. In March 1932 she appealed to her friend Jimmy Walker, New York City's mayor (he would resign on September 1), to "go in for housing, either by the creation of special city housing authority or through a Housing Department."[26] She had already been successful, she explained, in having two bills introduced in the state legislature, one a first step toward changing the constitution to permit municipal housing and the other an enabling act. Neither had a "ghost of a show" in the last session, she realized, but she had inserted a wedge. "The New York tenement still stands as a disgrace to the richest city in the world," she reminded the mayor. The time to act had come. As a result of the currently depressed economy and the hardships caused, she believed the public will "stand for the idea of municipal housing now, where even five years ago it was unthinkable."[27]

In June 1932, while FDR campaigned for the presidency against Hoover, Simkhovitch continued to argue in the *New York Times* that thinking on housing had not kept pace with changed attitudes on other subjects, such as child welfare and old-age security, provisions for public parks and playgrounds, and the realization that art and music are a "necessity for a civilized people." Housing, especially for the "lower income" or the "poorest classes," continued to be ignored, and while some experiments with cooperatives and model tenements had been made, they were directed to middle-income workers. She urged *Times* readers to recognize that "health and decency demand a recognized minimum standard of shelter, just as there is a public demand for a minimum standard of education."[28]

More articles and speeches on the same subject followed, and to her critics who charged her with holding "socialistic" views, she repeated her old claim, "If this is 'socialism' so is a public water supply and so are public schools and health centers." Besides, residents who occupied federally funded apartments would not be the only ones to gain. Jobs would be created for construction workers, and a new "standard of public housing decency" would result.[29]

After FDR's victory in November 1932 and his inauguration in March 1933, Simkhovitch used her national platform to reach more people. In Detroit, she reminded her audience that poor Americans lacked any power over their own housing—except the power to vote.[30] She reminded people that other countries had done better at solving housing shortages. England stood as prime example. Despite political differences and many problems, the British had shown "admirable evidence of clear thinking, sympathetic understanding and sustained effort [in the field of] working class housing." That movement had the support, she noted, of churches and organized labor.[31]

By the time the Great Depression made its full bite felt across the nation, a wide range of reformers had entered the housing movement, including some who were not even born when Simkhovitch began her crusade. The most prominent of these was Catherine Bauer, born in 1905, and a graduate of Vassar and Cornell. Daughter of wealthy, conservative New Englanders, she became interested in housing through her study of architecture and close association with Lewis Mumford. As a protégée of Mumford, she proposed that new housing be architecturally exciting, a view she explored in *Modern Housing*, a book she published in 1934 when she was only twenty-nine.[32] The ever-practical Simkhovitch did not put design high on her list of priorities.

Bauer, who would leave a large footprint on housing reform in America, was four years younger than Stephen Simkhovitch, but they could not have been more different. In the summer of 1935, while readers were still comparing points in Bauer's book, Stephen made headlines of an entirely different sort. In its science section, *Time* magazine featured an article titled "Jekal & Mr. Simkhovitch," which explored the attempts of a "burly, brooding scenario writer named Stephen Simkhovitch" to get himself frozen to death as part of an experiment by a young physician in Hollywood.[33] Dr. Ralph Willard had already managed to asphyxiate a twenty-pound rhesus monkey (named Jekal) and then bring it back to life with a variety of injections. Now he proposed learning whether prolonged freezing could cure diseases, such as cancer and syphilis, in human beings. The results with the monkey were encouraging. Jekal, diagnosed tubercular, tested negative on resuscitation, and that was enough to encourage Dr. Willard to proceed.

From the 180 persons who volunteered for Dr. Willard's trial with human beings, he chose one whose parents he identified fully for *Time* readers: "Dr. Vladimir Gregorievitch Simkhovitch, professor of economic history at Columbia University" and "bustling, pompadoured Mrs. Mary Melinda Kingsbury Simkhovitch, founder and head of Manhattan's Greenwich House (social welfare), president of the National Public Housing Conference."

Newspapers flashed the bizarre story across the nation, and many carried photos of Stephen. The Associated Press account included details of the liquid diet he had started in preparation for entering a frozen state.[34] According to the front page of the *San Francisco Examiner*, Stephen had flippantly advised his parents to "sit tight and wait for my letter."[35] The *Boston Globe* put Mary Simkhovitch's photo, captioned "Mother of Stephen," alongside its story.[36] The *Richland-Times Dispatch* noted that both Stephen's parents were well known, and his mother had just been named by First Lady Eleanor Roosevelt as one of the ten outstanding women in the United States.[37]

Press reports did not agree on the parents' reaction. Contradictory accounts had Mary supporting the experiment ("Mother Approves Son's Offer to Become 'Icicle'").[38] And opposing it ("Woman Objects to Son Being an Icicle").[39] Fuller accounts revealed that after first dismissing Stephen's "publicity venture" as a misguided attempt to boost his faltering career, she determined to prevent the experiment. The telegram she sent to Los Angeles authorities requested that they block Dr. Willard from proceeding with his "human guinea pig idea."[40] Whether due to the request of a distraught mother or other considerations, Los Angeles officials stopped Dr. Willard's experiment.

Stymied temporarily in his self-destructiveness, Stephen exposed his mother to public embarrassment. It wasn't the first time. Three years earlier, Sonja Stockstad, the mother of his child, had made headlines with her complaint against Simkhovitch. According to the *New York Daily News*, in an article titled "Unwed Mother Wants to Quiz Society Woman," the "blue-blooded Stephen Kingsbury Simkhovitch" had fathered Stockstad's child, and Mary Simkhovitch had tricked Stockstad into dropping her "heart balm [breach of promise] suit" against him."[41] Stockstad claimed that "the dignified founder of Greenwich House" had sought her out and persuaded her to abandon her suit because Stephen was "forging checks" and risked going to jail if she proceeded with her case against him. The *Daily News*'s unflattering description of Simkhovitch battling an "unwed mother" contrasted sharply with her reputation as champion of the poor and powerless.

A few weeks after the flurry of attention over the cryogenics experiment, Stephen married a woman named Dorothy Cowan and took up residence with her on a few acres of land with several small buildings on the edge of Los Angeles.[42] It was not a happy setup, and in the summer of 1937, Dorothy appealed to her mother-in-law for help. Stephen was drinking heavily, and if he didn't get some control over his life, the necessary renovations on the property, to make it income- producing, could not proceed. Stephen had finally agreed to go to Patton, a local institution that treated alcoholics, if his mother paid.

Simkhovitch came up with the money, but, as in most of Stephen's undertakings, he soon dropped out. Against the advice of his wife and friends, he insisted on leaving Patton before the treatment concluded. The superintendent sent his mother a refund for the "overpaid board of Stephen K. Simkhovitch," along with the explanation that Stephen could not be detained against his will.[43] "We believe he should be able to work," the superintendent wrote, "if he will refrain from drinking."[44]

Drink was not Stephen's only problem. He continued to spend excessively, apparently unconcerned about the burden this imposed on others. When he defaulted on loans made or guaranteed by his friends, they appealed to his mother. She had already dipped into the "tiny capital left me by my mother," she wrote one of her son's creditors, but she did not intend to "otherwise touch" that money.[45] She pointed one of the disappointed lenders to Stephen's "very tiny trust fund from which legal assignments have...been made," but pronounced herself "unable to pay his debts."[46] She admitted to a problem: "My son is mentally quite unadjusted, I think, and although I am always hoping for his recovery, I cannot look forward to any fortunate outcome with any degree of assurance."[47]

Requests from others could not be dismissed so easily. Margaret Boynge wrote Simkhovitch that she had put up some of her most prized possessions and funds when she countersigned loans for Stephen, and now she learned he had defaulted on repaying. Dorothy pled repeatedly for help, not only in satisfying Boynge but also in paying the workers who were upgrading Stephen's property. Three different couples had applied to farm the land, but they would not go to work until repairs were made to the chicken coop and other outbuildings.

With Dorothy's help, Simkhovitch came up with a plan to pay her son's debts without his ever touching the money. His grocer in Los Angeles would serve as middleman, receiving her checks, then paying those persons Stephen owed and the workers on his property. Dorothy, continuing in the enabler role, explained to his mother why Stephen could not do more. He is "working each day from 10-4 in Hollywood," she wrote. "[He] is writing—and I believe [this]will be a grand thing....[It] is a book that should be done—[and he] is very serious about it all."[48]

While Mary continued to scrounge for money to pull Stephen out of his recurring stumbles, Vladimir kept his distance. He had not taken a stand on Dr. Willard's cryogenic experiment, saying only that Stephen was an adult and had the right to do as he chose, and now Vladimir was not about to pay any of his son's debts, at least knowingly. He may have unwittingly contributed, because when Stephen begged his mother to wire "one hundred by Saturday" because he had "payroll to meet," she sent the money, and that coincided with a letter from her lawyer, noting receipt of check "of Dr. Simkhovitch for $75.00, which was endorsed by you."[49]

Stephen had not lost his wily charm, and in his "Dearest Mother" letter on Labor Day 1937, he teased her about lacking interest in details of his drying-out treatment at Patton. Then, in contradiction to what his wife had written, he explained that he wasn't writing at all but concentrating entirely on the renovation project: "I haven't tried to get an outside job as I haven't been able to afford one." Claiming to be fully engaged in making repairs to the "front house" and the garage, he sounded almost boastful in reporting progress: "Reroofed also second house, weeded the whole place and took down irrigation pipes, moved one of the little chicken houses…remodeled the lily pool, renovated wiring in both houses." After four handwritten pages about himself, he ended with a birthday wish for his mother on her seventieth, and signed off, "with all my love, Stephen."[50]

Big talk and small achievement continued to mark Stephen's communications as his mother proceeded to give speeches across the country, travel to the nation's capital to lobby members of Congress, and direct one of New York's most successful settlement houses. To the public she showed a woman committed to helping others, but her troubled son was never far from her thoughts. After divorcing Dorothy, he married Ruth O'Brien in February 1939, but his financial situation remained precarious. While Vladimir may have registered the severity of Stephen's problems but showed no intention to intervene or help him, his mother wrestled with one catastrophe after another. He remained the adorable son she loved, and she had no way of knowing that his world was about to come crashing down.

The phone call came on Saturday morning, July 1, 1939, when Simkhovitch was having breakfast in bed at Mansion House in Maine. Paul, her twelve-year-old grandson, answered the phone, then relayed the tragic news to her: Stephen had taken his life, by drinking Lysol. It was the most devastating news a mother could receive, and in announcing the death, the *New York Times* put her name below his, in slightly smaller letters:

Stephen K. Simkhovitch
His Mother, Mary Simkhovitch, Director of Greenwich House

Paul Didisheim later observed that his grandparents reacted in different ways to the news. While Mary was visibly upset and immediately started making plans to go to Los Angeles for the funeral on Monday, July 3, Vladimir held back, both in demeanor and action. He didn't try to block her going, but he didn't help either. Since the news arrived on Saturday, when banks were closed, Simkhovitch turned to her brother (who was summering nearby) for cash so that she could purchase a plane ticket for the 3,200-mile trip. And it was her brother who drove her to Bangor, Maine, 140 miles away, so she could board the first leg of her twenty-four-hour journey.

At a time when most Americans would not go near an airplane and First Lady Eleanor Roosevelt gamely made the case that air travel was safe, Simkhovitch determined to fly. It was the only way to get to the West Coast in time for Stephen's funeral, and neither the prospect of a bumpy ride nor multiple stops for refueling could change her mind. She got airsick but consoled herself that the male passengers did too.

In Los Angeles, it was Stephen's wife, Ruth, who met Mary at the airport and gave an account of what happened. Stephen had not had a drink for two months, according to Ruth, but the consequences of his debts and legal problems proved too much. He kept talking about how "his place was mortgaged and about to be foreclosed, that he couldn't get a job and didn't think he could hold one even if he could get it. That as he had no money and no job and was in danger of being held in one institution or another that there was only one way out."[51] Ruth had been with him on that evening of June 30 when he went into the bathroom and staggered out a few minutes later. Recognizing that he needed help, she ran into the street to hail a car. By the time she returned to the house, he was unconscious, and he died before arriving at the hospital. No "one thing...provoked it," Ruth explained.

The same evening his mother arrived in Los Angeles, she went to the mortuary to see her "darling." In writing to Helena later, she acknowledged that death had not destroyed what she loved so much about him, "his true nature." While admitting she would never have wanted to lose him "in that way," she found some consolation in the fact that he had not "sunk to unfriendliness and true hardness like the businessmen's faces" she saw on her trip.[52]

Because it was a holiday weekend, many of Stephen's friends were still out of town on Monday, but Mary insisted on talking to everyone who showed up for the funeral. To them, as to her, Stephen "was not a problem but a person—one to love."[53] Ruth had planned for burial in Los Angeles, but his mother insisted on cremating the body and taking the ashes with her.

By the following Friday morning, Simkhovitch had completed her cross-continent train journey and was back in New York, less than a week after leaving Maine. Son-in-law Frank Didisheim met her at the station and thought she looked "tired" but seemed comforted by the "general sweetness" of Stephen's friends, who "all spoke affectionately of him."[54] One act of Stephen's struck Frank as particularly kind: He had left a will designating one-quarter of his estate for the Didisheims's son, Paul, whom he had met only "one or two times." The rest went to Ruth. "There probably won't be anything after all the claims are paid," Frank added, "but isn't it touching that he should have done that." The deceased Stephen's biological son, eight-year-old Steve, got no mention at all in the will, and it is unclear when he and his mother learned of the death.

Following her return from Los Angeles, Simkhovitch spent one night in New York and then left for Maine with her son's ashes. The Reverend Schleuter, who had been her minister at St. Luke's for twenty-six years, accompanied her. After a short service, Stephen's ashes were buried in the Brewer Cemetery, just down the road from the family's summer home.[55]

Although Helena had relocated to the United States with her family a few years earlier, she was back in France that summer pursuing the study and practice of sculpture. Her determination to be a writer had shifted, and she was eager to work alongside sculptors she admired, as she shaped pieces for an upcoming exhibition. This was just the beginning of what would become an outstanding career, with major museums acquiring her work, but even at this stage, her mother enthusiastically backed her.[56] The letter Mary wrote, describing the trip to California for Stephen's funeral, emphasized that Helena's career came first and she should not alter her plans and cut short her stay. The upcoming exhibit was too important to sacrifice for a family reunion. Vladimir would need her, Mary explained: "You alone can revive him after the years & years he has had of despair about Steve." But Helena ought to think of her own future: "[C]ertainly don't come now. It is better for you to finish your work." Much as she would like to see her daughter's sculptures, she knew "of course it would be very expensive." In the meantime, she reported that young Paul was doing well at Mansion House, happy and "plump & rosy, & he works for V.G. in the field." Even if V. G. had occasionally "called [his grandson] Stephen by mistake," everything was "settled & delightful here [in Maine]."[57]

Those were strange adjectives to describe a grieving household, where Mary found herself nearly paralyzed by the tragedy. It took days before she was able to put words on paper to her daughter in France. How to contemplate, she wrote Helena, "[to] what a pass had he come...to the lonely night—where he could do this thing. God help us all & all the suffering world....I feel that he did right. He could not cope with anything. Yet he lived....God loves him so...far more than you or I."[58]

She rarely referred to the tragedy, and her explanation to an editor that she had failed to meet a deadline because "of my son's death" is terse. "I am now starting to work again," she wrote on July 17, promising to "send...an outline shortly."[59]

As the decade ended a few months later, Mary Simkhovitch's reputation as one of the country's most influential advocates for housing reform was secure. She had finally managed to get public housing on the nation's agenda and win attention as "mother of public housing." But on another kind of mothering, the record was murkier.

II

National Breakthrough

Franklin Roosevelt played a key role in Mary Simkhovitch's achieving her goal to put housing supply on the nation's agenda in the 1930s. Her job would have been incalculably more difficult without the buttress of the decades-long friendship between their families. The teenager with a sailboat she knew from summers with her parents in Maine was now president of the United States, and his family's vacation home Campobello was even closer to the Simkhovitches' Mansion House than it had been to the Kingsburys' home in North Perry. During warm weather, shared picnics and sailings brought the two families together, and even when they were all back at winter jobs, they exchanged books and views on multiple subjects.

Opportunities to socialize diminished after Franklin's mobility was compromised by polio in 1921, but the mutual respect endured, and one of Simkhovitch's fondest memories of him was a trip he made to Campobello as president. She joined the local crowd who turned out to welcome him, and then was invited as part of a small group to join him and Eleanor at the Roosevelt compound.

That long amity did not guarantee access to the highest levels of government during his presidency, but it helped pave the way. Both Eleanor and Franklin made clear they valued Simkhovitch's opinions. Eleanor Roosevelt lauded her in a radio talk as one of the eleven American women who have been "a constant inspiration and help to me."[1] At a dinner in Simkhovitch's honor, Eleanor praised her "very human courage, which makes everybody her supporter and friend."[2] Drew Pearson's nationally syndicated column, "Washington Merry Go-Round," identified Simkhovitch as a "good friend of Eleanor Roosevelt".[3] The First Lady's "My Day" columns repeatedly expressed admiration for the founder of Greenwich House.[4]

Getting a major housing proposal into law required more than connections, however, and Simkhovitch used her platform as head of the National Public Housing Conference (NPHC) to gain support. Immediately after FDR's inauguration in March 1933, when the administration was formulating a huge economic boost to counteract the Depression, she saw a chance to have housing included and took a train to Washington to present her case to a special caucus of congressional Democrats.[5] Ever pragmatic, she argued that even a "token" mention in the bill would help because it would help set the stage for bigger changes later.[6]

Simkhovitch and her NPHC settled on New York's Senator Robert Wagner as their designated spokesman in the housing fight. They could not have made a better choice.[7] Born in Germany in 1877, Wagner had personally experienced poverty, having immigrated to New York with his family when he was nine. As the youngest of nine children, Wagner knew all about overcrowded housing, and while working at various jobs, including assisting a janitor and selling newspapers, he managed to get himself through high school and City College. Then he turned his talents to enlarging opportunities for others. Soon after earning a law degree at New York University, he entered politics, and in 1914 he won his first elected office, as assemblyman from the 30th District on New York's Upper East Side. Four years later, he went to the state senate, where he gained a reputation as a reformer. He eventually introduced bills to enfranchise women, limit child labor, establish a minimum wage, and inspect factories. Elected to the US Senate in 1927, he was prepared to introduce some of the most progressive legislation Congress ever passed.

Senator Wagner was the face of getting housing into the public works section of the 1933 National Industrial Recovery Act, but he relied on Simkhovitch and her NPHC for the wording and backing.[8] Helen Alfred, her administrative assistant, practically gloated about what a difference the two of them had made. After passage of the act, which would have profound effects, she wrote to Edith Elmer Wood: "What do you think of the Public Works Bill? Pretty interesting, eh?"[9] Alfred explained just how she and Simkhovitch operated and why what they did was so essential to the cause: "Immediately upon reading the detailed news of [the early draft], we communicated with the President and a number of key people in Washington." Alfred underlined the short phrase that they had written that made all the difference: "*Construction by public bodies*" meant federal funding for housing.

Bureaucracy slowed results, however, and staff hired for the housing division sat and waited while members of Congress argued about how much money to appropriate and who would get it. By the end of 1933, nine months after FDR had assumed office, only seven applications had won approval, and Public Works Administrator (PWA) Harold Ickes took what was for him an unusually bold stand and decided to parcel out loans to municipalities rather than limit them to private companies.[10] Cities enjoyed one huge advantage over private companies—they could invoke the right of eminent domain to obtain land.

With the federal government now willing to work directly with municipalities, the picture changed radically. In January 1934, $25 million became available to New York City, with the condition that a housing agency be in place to spend the money. Although Simkhovitch considered the amount about one-tenth of what was needed, she noted, "[W]e are not complaining. We propose to do what we can and must do with the money at hand."[11]

Adamant about local control, she insisted that decisions remain with the community. She had no trouble with the "S word" and sometimes voted for Socialists, but in housing, she thought decisions should be made on the local level. Her equally zealous friend, Edith Elmer Wood, concurred. After trying to work with the New Jersey State Housing Authority, Wood quit in disgust. The experience confirmed her belief that only the people most directly affected should be making the decisions.[12]

New York is touted as the place where public housing was born because it was the first city to set up its own housing board. Its ebullient new mayor, Fiorello La Guardia, had been talking about municipally owned apartment houses for a dozen years before he took office in 1934, and the talk came directly from his heart. Although he grew up in the open spaces of Arizona, he blamed "filthy tenements" for harboring dangerous diseases such as the tuberculosis that killed his young wife and baby in 1921. In February 1934 he appointed five informed activists to the New York City Housing Authority (NYCHA). Simkhovitch, the only female, was immediately elected vice chairman, and she served alongside Chairman Langdon Post, the city's tenement commissioner; Louis Heaton Pink, a member of New York State Housing Board; Charney Vladeck, labor leader and founder of the Jewish Labor Committee; and the Reverend E. Roberts Moore, director of charities for the Catholic Archdiocese of New York. Simkhovitch was finally able to help spend millions of federal dollars to tear down slums and erect new housing. Her dream was being realized.

Questions arose immediately about site selection and how to use eminent domain for slum clearance.[13] Louis Pink explained that the "most difficult problem" he faced as a member of the Housing Authority was deciding where to build, since land in the slum districts, home to half of Manhattan's population, had a very high price tag.[14] Albert Mayer, a member of the Slum Clearance Committee, insisted on building in the outer boroughs, where land was cheaper than in Manhattan.[15] This disagreement persisted, dividing the NYCHA for years. Going to the fringes of the city to build looked good because land cost less there; building in the center dislocated large numbers of people. But the periphery required transportation lines and other services that could not be provided quickly or cheaply. Simkhovitch, who had previously looked more favorably on building in less-populated areas, now sided with Pink and Chairman Post. They all argued that slums had to be eradicated because of the dangers they posed to health and safety. Labor leader Charney Vladeck, whose priority was jobs, defended going to less-crowded areas.

Federal authorities had to be placated, too, and some balked at acquiring high-priced real estate.[16]

Even with their differences, members of the NYCHA moved ahead. Within six weeks of their first meeting, they had chosen two sites for federal approval, and one of them, Williamsburg, in Brooklyn, won an immediate nod from the PWA. The other, in Harlem (sometimes called the twin of Williamsburg), ran into more difficulty. Simkhovitch had by this point become a champion at settling for what she could get, and she was energized and encouraged by the progress. After some research of her own, she announced in early May 1934 that housing could be developed in New York to rent for about half the going rate, thus putting it within the reach of most workers.[17]

In all her planning, Simkhovitch had failed to factor in one big obstacle: bureaucracy. She never had much use for officialdom, and the formation of the Federal Housing Administration (FHA) in June 1934 meant cumbersome regulations for her work. Projects stagnated. Negotiations for acquiring land dragged on through the summer. By the time she returned from a short vacation in Europe, where she checked out public housing in London, Simkhovitch was so disappointed by the lack of progress that she appealed directly to Eleanor Roosevelt.

The two women had a history of turning to each other for support and advice. Simkhovitch would appeal to Eleanor to speak at a housing conference and lend her name to events that benefited Greenwich House; she also used Eleanor as a conduit to the president.[18] Eleanor relied on Simkhovitch to investigate claims of hardship.[19] They both treasured memories of those summer visits, and Mary ended one letter, "I looked across at Campobello yesterday when we were at Quoddy Head and thought of you."[20] Even with extremely busy schedules, the two women exchanged pleasantries about whose "front lawn" they would meet on. Simkhovitch had no qualms about being frank with the First Lady.[21]

That camaraderie served as Simkhovitch confronted obstacles to her plans for housing. She was shocked to find, she wrote the president's wife, that the "housing situation here in New York has received a big setback."[22] Placing the blame squarely on Washington, she defended the NYCHA by noting it had been "anything but slow," and she listed its accomplishments. "But we have met with the most extraordinary difficulties in our dealings with Washington," she complained. If federal authorities continued to insist on controlling every little detail, it "would put our local authority in the position of being nothing more than a managerial body." "That was not at all the intent of the law, the purpose being, as you know, to establish local authorities who would, when the 'emergency' is over, be embedded in the social structure." While she needed the government's help, it was key that projects be guided by local authorities, those who best knew the situation.[23]

After admitting that new projects often encounter mix-ups, she noted that what she was encountering went beyond anything she had ever confronted: "A calendar of our dealings with Washington would be a comedy if it were not at the same time a tragedy. Somebody is sent, whom we have never heard of, to take charge of something. He is then, in a day or so, withdrawn. We are told to hurry up, and then we are told we must wait until this and that and the other decision is made." With apologies for "pouring out all my troubles on you," Simkhovitch made a final appeal to be allowed to " take the money and go ahead," so that new housing construction could finally begin.[24]

How much that letter, dated July 2, 1934, figured is not clear, but the next eighteen months brought enormous progress, and by December 3, 1935, the NYCHA opened its first completed project on the Lower East Side. Formerly known as the "Astor Project," it became "First Houses," because it could claim title to the first publicly financed housing development in the United States.

Two plaques currently mark the spot at Avenue A and 3rd Street. Simkhovitch's name is on neither. The "designated landmark" stone placed in 1989, which salutes Frederick L. Ackerman for designing the building and the artists from the WPA who contributed the sculpture for the paved courtyard, is weathered and barely readable. A larger, more legible plaque marks the date (November 21, 1934) that the "city began its battle against the slums when the newly-formed New York City Housing

Authority obtained the right to demolish and rebuild the tenements on this site." The buildings remain "a fitting monument to the beginning of the public housing program in the United States of America." The names attached are not those of the men and women responsible for this innovation but those who added the plaque in 1974: Mayor Abraham Beame and Joseph J. Christian, chair of the NYCHA at the time.

The relatively quick completion of First Houses resulted partly from the fact that the project did not involve complete clearing of the site. An arrangement had been worked out so that some of the buildings in the designated area could be razed, providing more open space for playgrounds and outdoor use, and the remaining structures were gutted and renovated.

Once they were finished, the apartments in First Houses struck many New Yorkers as "miraculous." Instead of cheap linoleum, these units had oak floors and shiny brass light fixtures. Each apartment had its own toilet and hot running water; a landscaped courtyard provided outdoor space. In a *New York Times* interview in 1995, Frank LiCausi, an early resident, called First Houses "an oasis in the desert, a jewel."[25] Word spread, and as a sign of how badly this project was needed, 11,000 applications were filed for the 123 apartments available.[26]

The very same day that families started moving into First Houses, the NPHC met at New York's Commodore Hotel to celebrate this milestone and outline future projects. Speakers constituted a roster of prime movers: Mayor La Guardia, Eleanor Roosevelt, Senator Wagner, and Mary K. Simkhovitch.[27] All of them recognized First Houses as a major achievement, though they knew much more needed to be done to ensure that government funding continued beyond the exigencies of the current economic crisis.

While construction on First Houses was underway, Simkhovitch campaigned vigorously for a long-range public housing program. In a radio speech on February 19, 1934, she warned her listeners that the funds already allocated would be quickly exhausted and immediate action was needed to make housing a "permanent municipal service." Instead of thinking of it as a handout, she explained, it would be an improvement "both economically and socially to the city as a whole."[28] That was a plus for everyone. In her Easter message a few weeks later, she called on churches to help. Anglicans had "blazed the way for England's improved housing," she noted, and US churchgoers could have a similar impact, resulting in "permanent program" for "municipal services...all over the country."[29]

Rather than blame either occupants or landlords for slums, she considered them an inevitable result of the industrialization and urbanization that necessitated workers live close to their jobs. In an undated manuscript titled "What a Slum Is—What a Slum Does," she examined a dictionary definition and found it deeply flawed: "A foul back street of a city, especially with a slovenly and often vicious population; a low or squalid neighborhood." That wrongly shamed the "population" and unfairly blamed occupants for their circumstances. Rather than equating "viciousness" with slums, she observed that crime occurred "on Park Avenue and Riverside Drive" as well as on college campuses, and yet no one labeled them "slums." Poverty should not be equated with dirt, she argued, and vice was not limited to one kind of housing.[30] That admonition against equating poverty with crime and dirt became a common theme of her speeches and writing.[31]

Working with Helen Alfred, Louis Pink, and Ira Robbins, who was especially proficient at drafting legislation, Simkhovitch had a housing bill ready for Senator Wagner in late January 1935. It made the federal government a major player in a permanent way, by providing funds for slum clearance and designating the Department of Interior responsible for acquiring land for new construction and operating the low-rental units built.[32] After altering the bill and its title to emphasize that housing construction would stimulate employment and boost economic recovery, Wagner introduced the bill in the Senate on March 26, 1935. Representative Reuben T. Wood of Missouri handled the matter in the House.[33]

Newspapers reported how Simkhovitch kept pushing for public support of the bill. When she spoke, which was often, she reminded her audiences that First Houses had been part of a temporary response to dire economic conditions and that it was of "the utmost importance" to make such projects part of a "permanent governmental structure." The problem of insufficient housing at affordable rents had existed long before the Depression began and would continue afterward, she noted. While other nations had already embraced the problem, and the "concept of public housing has long been accepted, most notably in England and Holland," the United States kept hanging back. The nation's blindness was inexplicable, she noted, and though "slums confronted us at every turn in our cities, we persisted in the belief...that the situation would automatically right itself, that housing of acceptable standards would somehow be provided."[34]

Neither her words nor those of her allies, Wagner and Wood, gained the necessary traction, however, and Congress adjourned August 26, 1935, without taking any action on housing. Prospects looked grim in early 1936 for getting the kind of legislation she wanted. The *New York Times* put it bluntly in a front page article titled "Government to End Housing Subsidies," noting that it had been "learned on high authority" that the government will "turn its back upon further federally subsidized slum clearance and low-cost housing, either eliminating it or reducing it to a relatively negligible quantity."[35] Simkhovitch immediately fired off a telegram to President Roosevelt, asking for clarification of his stand and urging him to favor the measure sponsored by Senator Wagner.[36]

That same issue of the *New York Times* reported a speech Simkhovitch had just delivered to over two thousand members of the Federation of Jewish Women's Organizations. In a talk at New York's Hotel Astor titled "Better Homes Through Better Housing," she explained why audience members with comfortable residences of their own should favor government subsidies to house others. She noted that two million New Yorkers lived in structures that should be replaced, but because they earned less than $1,500 a year, they could not afford the rents asked for apartments on the market. This wasn't just a New York problem. One-third of the nation lived in substandard quarters.[37] Her appeals consistently featured facts—statistics and examples of how getting rid of poor housing was more than a matter of what was right—it was a matter of national security, of protecting everyone from the ills spread in congested, dwellings.

Simkhovitch and her NPHC recruited new members and published a bulletin, "Public Housing Progress," which regularly updated what was happening. Even President Roosevelt's retreat to Warm Springs, Georgia, did not insulate him from NPHC appeals. Alfred sent him a petition signed by attendees at a New York convention on housing, and Simkhovitch wrote a long telegram requesting him to speak out on "the importance of a government subsidy to ensure low rent housing initiated and carried forth by local authorities."[38]

Splits within the ranks of housing reformers retarded progress. Although no less zealous than Simkhovitch in their desire to improve city dwellings, some housing activists continued to stress new, innovative, architecturally notable building on the outskirts of cities. Others worried about how the money was being distributed. Catherine Bauer, who had taken a job as head of the AFL's housing division, helped write her own housing bill and got Pennsylvania Congressman Henry Ellenbogen to introduce it.[39] More radical and far reaching than the NPHC bill, it called for uniting all housing agencies into one department (with cabinet rank) and allocating $500 million for slum clearance and construction of housing.[40]

Simkhovitch's long personal relationship with the president and First Lady meant she got attention that Bauer lacked, and it was her version that defined the bill. On October 28, 1935, FDR wrote to Senator Wagner, "After...I get back from Warm Springs, I should much like to have a talk with you in regard to the more permanent aspects of slum clearance and low-cost housing." In the margins of that message, a handwritten note to the First Lady clarified that the president was referring to "Mrs. Simkhovitch's request."[41]

When Senator Wagner prepared to present the housing bill that the NPHC had drawn up in 1936, Simkhovitch went again to Washington to speak to a congressional committee. This bill reached wider than the previous one, she argued, because it had support "country wide" from churches and organized labor. Americans had finally accepted the fact, she believed, that "the major social need of the country is decent dwellings for all," and that "public housing for low-income groups is not competitive with commercial housing" because it is not possible to make a profit in that field. If the congressmen had any doubts, she assured them that President Roosevelt agreed with her: "He has it as far as public housing is concerned."[42]

As Senator Wagner's bill proceeded, she went on radio station WEVD to proclaim, "At last the American people are making a definite attack on slums." Wagner's housing bill provided for a "permanent U.S. Housing Authority to set housing standards and cooperate with state and local public housing agencies in financing slum clearance and low-rent re-housing projects." This was no small change, and it was historic: "It represents the first attempt in American history to make the housing of our citizens a public concern and to provide machinery for bringing it up to a decent standard where private enterprise has consistently, indeed necessarily, failed to do so." Governments routinely spent lavishly on parks, streets, roads, and bridges, she reminded her listeners, and "now is the crucial hour in the war on slums."[43]

That optimism proved unfounded. Wagner's bill failed to get congressional approval. Roosevelt wrote Simkhovitch, promising to do better: "I am sorry that the housing bill did not pass the House.... I did all I could. Next winter I am confident we will get a good housing bill."[44] By October, with his campaign for re-election in full swing, the president attracted huge crowds in New York as he combined campaign promises with acknowledgment of the fiftieth anniversary of the Statue of Liberty. Speaking to residents of the congested Lower East Side, he tied success on a new housing law to his audience—if only they would elect the right people in November.[45]

After winning a second term, the president became preoccupied with other matters, including the public outcry against his plan to "pack" the Supreme Court. It was left to the housing troops to carry on, and they doggedly persisted. Edith Elmer Wood published another book, *Slums and Blighted Areas in the U.S.*, in which she used once again the same figure she had introduced nearly two decades earlier. It was still true, she argued, that "one third of the nation's total population" was living under conditions detrimental to their health and to public safety.[46]

Buoyed by what seemed like a change in the wind, both houses of Congress passed a compromise housing bill, which the president signed on September 1, 1937. He simply penned his name, without any ceremony. There were no photo opportunities, and no pens passed out to those who had worked so hard for passage. In fact, the president put his name on the bill at the same time he signed several others, and he did this hurriedly at Hyde Park just before leaving on a five-day cruise. It was an anticlimactic ending to a long fight, a scant nod to the multitude of lives it would change.

Unlike earlier bills, this one put the United States Housing Authority (USHA) in the Department of the Interior and gave it responsibility for setting standards for slum clearance and construction of public housing to be done by local authorities. With the prospect of hundreds of millions of dollars becoming available, work could begin on a level that even Simkhovitch approved.

While the Housing Act of 1937 provided funds, its authors had trouble clarifying who qualified to live in the new units. After considerable debate, lawmakers finally agreed that applicants for public housing units should constitute "a natural family," live in an "emergency" situation, and lack the means to pay for standard housing.[47] Deciding exactly what percentage of their income should be designated for housing proved difficult, and in the end the USHA took Edith Elmer Wood's advice and used a system of graded rents, so that not all tenants paid the same amount for equivalent space.

Just who in the large pool of qualified applicants should get the apartments was left up to local authorities, and Simkhovitch, as a member of NYCHA, quickly came face to face with a question that was more than academic. Harlem Houses, a project initiated at the same time as the Williamsburg project, finally opened in upper Manhattan in 1939. Although approved four years earlier (partly as a measure to placate the Black community after the Harlem riot in March 1935), high land costs in Upper Manhattan delayed action. Discrimination had forced African

Americans into a confined space above 110th Street, sending land prices spiraling. Any attempt to dislocate people would inevitably cause more discontent. Finally, a vacant area was found, adjacent to the Harlem River, and when the Rockefellers, who owned the land, protested the sale, it was taken by eminent domain.[48]

In November 1939, while Simkhovitch was still trying to recover equilibrium after Stephen's death in the summer, she got called to Harlem Houses for a discussion of how tenants and building employees were to be selected. Since the NYCHA was between chairmen at the time, Simkhovitch, as vice chair, had the task of conducting the meeting. Although not outspoken on racial inequality, she had not been silent and currently served on the executive committee of the National Urban League. When African Americans were excluded from jobs on public projects, including some very close to Greenwich House, she protested.[49] For the meeting in Harlem, she evidently felt in need of a little extra support and invited the Reverend E. Roberts Moore to accompany her. His experience at the Catholic Charities would presumably make him a sympathetic listener and guarantee deferential treatment as he and Simkhovitch listened to complaints about what was happening at the Harlem Houses.

As the meeting began, tempers stayed cool, and everyone was very polite, but when members of the Harlem committee questioned how tenants were selected and Simkhovitch answered by "a regular procedure" set down by the USHA, frustration surfaced. Harlem Houses, with its 576 units, dwarfed First Houses, but the line to get in was much longer, and her explanation, "We just follow the law," was not what people wanted to hear.[50] To make matters worse, the Williamsburg Houses, which opened in 1938, had clearly been designated for whites. When one angry man at the Harlem meeting charged, "[O]nly one Negro family got in each," Simkhovitch could only counter, weakly, that there were two, and ten more were being considered. She then started using statistics to make what was essentially a weak argument for the NYCHA's fairness. About 18 percent of the units already constructed had gone into "predominantly colored sections," she pointed out, even though

"Negroes make up less than 5% of the population." Although her argument clearly ignored a point that experts agreed on—that a higher percentage of Blacks than whites lived in substandard shelter—she concluded that a "fair ratio of Negro to white tenancy in the projects" would be about 6 percent, "which, I think, is a very sound way of presenting that."[51]

When reminded that census figures understated the Black population, she refused to budge, saying: "I think you will find these figures correct." As for mixing races within one project, she reacted much as she had decades earlier when the question came up at Greenwich House events: It would not work. She had visited Charleston, South Carolina, and seen racial mixing in the "same area but not in the same houses," she reported, and "I would rather object to that arrangement for the north." Besides, she pointed out, the NYCHA was the only housing authority in the nation that funded projects for "whites and colored" (although some other cities had done so in the old PWA projects). As for hiring Blacks in the new buildings, she noted that among 467 employees, 32 (6.8 percent) were Black "which is really high for the basis of population."[52]

At this point, tempers evidently flared, and when Simkhovitch was challenged to explain why "only the Negroes" were assigned to work in Harlem while white porters got their pick of locations, she replied that she didn't "know anything about it." Then, in a kind of desperation move, she announced she would "like to start this meeting over again." After reiterating her interest in fairness, she admonished them all to remember that the people of New York had not yet arrived "at that condition of social justice that we should." Although it was well and good to say that whites should be able to live in Harlem and Blacks in Williamsburg, the fact was that people would not accept the mixture, and "we don't want to kick over the whole business of housing. We have to think... of housing first and second of these other points." She insisted that she herself had no problem with racial mixing, but "you and I know that if we had an equal number of colored and white," it wouldn't work.

Simkhovitch's reluctance to integrate housing through resident selection was not unique to her. National policy dictated observing existing community patterns while selecting tenants. Even Black activists shied away from using public housing as a tool of integration. Robert C. Weaver, a Harvard Ph.D. and the first African American to sit on a president's cabinet when he headed the new Department of Housing and Urban Affairs in 1966, was an assistant to Secretary of the Interior Ickes in 1940 when he wrote, "Negroes Need Housing" for *The Crisis* magazine. He understood that restricting Blacks to certain areas meant that "all colored persons, regardless of income, will face a grave housing problem," with excessively high rents and less to spend on "the other essentials of a decent standard of living."[53] Low-income Blacks, both rural and urban, suffered disproportionately, he argued, and he documented this claim with statistics on the death rates from tuberculosis and other diseases. Well before the economic crisis of the 1930s, he noted, it was evident that "private industry could not provide decent homes at rents within reach of great masses of low-income families...confining the vast majority of Negro families to the slums."

Weaver stopped short, however, of attacking neighborhood covenants or endorsing mixed-race housing in public projects, leaving readers with the impression that simply increasing the number of units built by federal funding would solve the problem. In another article that same year, 1940, he continued to endorse the status quo rather than calling for integration. "Public housing should not establish racial patterns less democratic than those which now exist in any given community," he wrote, leaving everything up to the local community.[54] Even the National Urban League directed its integration efforts at jobs, as if acknowledging that integrating housing required more time. Or would take care of itself. It is one more example of how social rights differed from political or economic rights, in the minds of most people.[55] It is easier to champion the vote and fair pay than offer a seat at one's table.

Protest came from other ethnic groups, especially those displaced by the clearing of substandard housing. After Italian Americans in East Harlem teamed with Puerto Ricans to form a housing committee and call for improvements in shelter, they welcomed the news of an enormous low-rent project to be built between 102nd and 105th Streets near the East

River Drive. It would house 1,326 families at an affordable $5 per room. Their victory celebration in October 1939 proved hollow when tenant selection began, favoring lower-income Puerto Ricans and Blacks. Italian Americans, with their relatively higher earnings, had to look elsewhere.[56]

In addition to the matter of racial integration in the selection of tenants and hiring of building employees, Simkhovitch faced more criticism about her work on public housing. Both she and Wood had approved a British model, introduced by Octavia Hill, that put a female manager in charge of each building. In a PWA-funded study in 1933, both women endorsed the idea of posting a female assistant to look after the "[p]rotection of tenant health and morals" in each public housing project. The female assistant was charged with making weekly visits to each unit to collect the rent, observe living conditions, and advise on matters of health, diet, and childcare. Only after tenant protests about surveillance mounted did the visits stop at the end of World War II.[57] Renters could then pay at another location, although community centers for socializing and recreation continued to operate in the projects, and they provided some opportunity for observing tenants' lifestyles. Catherine Lansing, who worked for the NYCHA, warned rent collectors against meddling in renters' lives, but told them it was their duty to direct persons in need to the appropriate agency for help.[58]

Rent collection was only one of many problems still to be worked out on public housing in the United States, and debate would continue to this day on site selection, choosing tenants, design of units, and much more. But the important step had been taken: The federal government had entered the field, and recent scholars of housing reform have singled out Simkhovitch as a prime player, noting that she formulated "the only way to achieve truly equitable, and durable, housing outcomes."[59]

The 1937 Housing Act marked a major change in American thinking. One historian recently underlined Mary Simkhovitch's significance in that change, noting that she "played a key role over half a century of activism (ca. 1900–1950), transforming the Progressive Era movement for settlement houses and tenement regulation into a local and national movement for tenement destruction and public housing construction."[60] Her radio speech in 1934 had made a clear demand, and now it had been answered. She had argued: "Government credit at low interest and amortization rates should be made available for public housing wherever it is most needed, not only now in the emergency, but as a permanent public policy."[61]

12

"Woman-Made America"

Simkhovitch never claimed she had acted alone in changing her nation's thinking so that public aid to housing no longer sounded "un-American" or unacceptably "socialistic." An army of allies, many of them women, helped define the form that publicly financed housing should take, and an article titled "Woman-Made America" highlights the significant role women played.[1] These activists had not only argued that shelter was a human right. They also spelled out minimum standards for that shelter. A towering brick rectangle, with identical units tightly positioned against each other, leaving no space for recreation or green grass, would not suffice.

Edith Elmer Wood stated the case emphatically in her 1931 book, *Recent Trends in American Housing*. A minimum standard for public housing did not mean the "existing standard, nor minimum legal standard, nor minimum attainable-under-existing-conditions standard, but minimum health-and-decency standard."[2] This included enough space per person to permit privacy, accessible toilets and bathing facilities, adequate light and ventilation."[3]

That level of housing should be available to "every self-supporting family, rich or poor, large or small, white or black, American born or foreign-born, throughout our land," Wood continued, and it should be reasonably close to their jobs, with a rental price not more than 20 percent of their earnings.[4] For the non-self-supporting, she recommended public assistance be provided. Crucial as her standard was to "safeguarding life, health, morals and economic solvency," she noted that many Americans could not afford it. A full "95% of farm homes and 80% of village homes" fell short on toilet facilities and running water.

Women also made the case for including aesthetic considerations in public housing, a subject that New York's Museum of Modern Art (MoMA) explored in 1932.[5] Titled "Exhibition of Modern Architecture," the show garnered immediate attention when it opened on February 10. The architectural critic Lewis Mumford, writing in the *New Yorker*, called it an exhibition not to be missed, and an estimated 33,000 followed his advice.[6] Although the main gallery featured sleek, unornamented creations of international giants Le Corbusier, Walter Gropius, and Mies van der Rohe, a smaller section, titled "Housing," showed homegrown, low-rental apartment complexes for workers. Mumford judged the latter "much more convincing" than some of the flamboyant skyscrapers nearby.

Men put together the show of International Style, with architect Philip Johnson and historian Henry Russell Hitchcock officially credited, but it was the young, ambitious Catherine Bauer who captured the essence of the exhibition. Bauer came to the housing cause from a different path than Simkhovitch and operated in a different social milieu. After majoring in art at Vassar, she went to live in Paris in the 1920s, where, as she later wrote, she "moved in avant-garde circles (once dancing the Charleston with Adolf Loos)" and became a fan of the "new architecture."[7] In 1928, when she was twenty-three years old, she wrote in the *New York Times* that Americans could learn a lot from Europeans about home building. Titled "Machine-Age Mansions for Ultra Moderns," the piece praised Europeans for declining to copy the past, with its "rosy ideals of homelike atmosphere," and opted instead for a "new domestic architecture," featuring reinforced concrete and steel, "suitable in every way to house the best of modern furniture."[8] After noting that French architects had been inspired by US skyscrapers and modern machinery, she questioned why most Americans stuck to old ideas and did not apply the same principles to their own homes. In answer to the question "What is a house?" she wrote, quoting Le Corbusier, whose book *Vers Une Architecture* had come out in 1924: A house is "a machine for living."

That definition failed to resonate in the United States, where white clapboard and dark mahogany, like that in the house where Simkhovitch grew up, still dominated home design.

In MoMA's 1932 exhibition, Bauer zeroed in on a low-rent project from Germany. Some might view it as "opposite" the spacious, beautifully designed structure nearby, but the two had much in common, she argued. Each resulted from thoughtful planning and consideration for people's needs.[9] With recent advances in construction, low-cost housing using prefabricated elements could have the same amenities as high-priced models: "Light, air,... Color... No meaningless clutter." Bauer recommended low-lying buildings (maximum four floors) of quality construction, with wide green strips of communal space for outdoor enjoyment and recreation. Europeans were already producing attractive low-cost units that met standards for health and leisure, but Americans lagged. She hoped the exhibition's three-year tour of the country would change some minds.

Bauer's 1934 book, *Modern Housing*, explored the same themes in more detail. With graphs and charts, she showed how eleven European countries had, since World War I, built 4.5 million dwellings, sufficient to house nearly one-sixth of their people.[10] This was not a free-market development. About two-thirds of the new housing came from "official aid," she wrote, either local governments building on land owned by municipalities or public utility housing societies. The final third came from private enterprise but had to measure up to standards set and be subject to restrictions on rental and resale.[11]

MoMA followed the 1932 show with one in 1934 that gave more exposure to what Bauer and Simkhovitch were saying, if in different ways. "Housing Exhibition of the City of New York" focused on the deplorable condition of local tenements. Rather than tout the beauty and ingenuity of the "new architecture," such as that being produced by Frank Lloyd Wright, this exhibition showed photographs of currently overcrowded, under-serviced apartments alongside pictures of what was possible: pristine, light-filled model rooms (supplied by Macy's.) Co-sponsored by the New York City Housing Authority (NYCHA, where Simkhovitch served as vice chairman), the 1934 exhibition made a case that dramatic change was needed, and the catalog, edited by the Romanian-born social reformer Carol Aronovici, was provocatively titled "Americans Can't Have Housing."

Elisabeth Coit's photographs for the 1934 exhibition showed that conditions documented in Jacob Riis's 1890 book, *How the Other Half Lives*, had not merely persisted in America in the following four decades, they had worsened. In the densest sections of American cities, cluttered apartments, with laundry hanging above kitchen tables where hungry-looking children did their homework, were common.

Like Bauer, Coit's enlistment in the housing cause came through art. She dropped art study at Radcliffe to earn a degree in architecture from the Massachusetts Institute of Technology in 1918. Licensed in New York State in 1926, she opened her own firm in New York City in 1930 but turned from designing private residences for the well-to-do and took up housing for workers. After a stint as adviser to Simkhovitch's National Public Housing Conference (NPHC), she enlisted fully in the cause. Her 1941 book, *Design and Construction of the Dwelling Unit for the Low-Income Family*, showed her new direction, and she took that thinking to the NYCHA as principal planner and to the US Housing Authority (USHA) in Washington, DC, where she worked from 1942 to 1947. Her biographer credits her with making public housing units more livable, with larger rooms than originally projected.[12]

With a slightly different focus, Catherine Fox Lansing also contributed to "Americans Can't Have Housing." Born in 1901, Lansing, like Coit, came to densely populated New York from a small-town youth. Her Dutch ancestors were early settlers in the Hudson Valley, and she could document her relation to two US presidents and one secretary of state. When her father died in 1910, leaving a widow with five children, Catherine, the eldest, resolved to take charge. As soon as she reached adulthood, she moved them all—her mother, three sisters, and one brother—from Little Falls, New York (population 10,000), to Manhattan. While supervising her siblings' schooling and career choices, she directed her own future to social work and joined the Christodora House on Manhattan's Lower East Side in 1925.

Although Christodora founders announced in their opening statement that they meant to make their settlement house a place of religious work, an arrangement Simkhovitch did not endorse, Lansing's path soon crossed with Greenwich House, and she became the founder's fan.[13] An early member of the NPHC, Lansing attended a month-long seminar it sponsored in Washington, DC, over the Christmas holidays in 1934. By 1935, she had a job in the Management Division of the NYCHA, where she worked directly with Simkhovitch to promote her own ideas about how tenants should be chosen and how rooms in public housing should be sized.

Lansing criticized architects who failed to consider tenants' needs and preferences when designing units for low-income families. Kitchen size was a special sore point, and while planners typically called for a one-person workspace that looked like a science lab, Lansing noted many families made the kitchen table their central gathering point. "Whether architects realize it or not," she wrote, "people who do not have servants enjoy sitting in a cheerful kitchen and will continue to do so wherever there is room to put down a chair."[14] She also pointed out that while architects planned for a typical family unit—two parents and their children—apartments had to serve a variety of occupants: a widowed mother with young children and adult boarders; three generations rather than two; a single person.

Lansing used the *New York Times* to promote her views, although she often found her pieces on serious topics like childcare and the need for public parks relegated to the society pages.[15] A certified member of Hudson Valley aristocracy, she made a point of writing on the need for greater acceptance of public housing tenants by their better-off neighbors.[16] Mum on many subjects, including her family relationship to Eleanor Roosevelt, she never wrote a memoir about her work on housing, including the years of her association with Simkhovitch, and she left her papers to family members. Frances Lansing, a niece who inherited two large boxes, remembers how central the subject of affordable housing was to her aunt's life. Catherine Lansing spoke of Simkhovitch with "a kind of reverence," her niece remembered, and she enjoyed pointing out housing experiments that worked, like the span of neat brick buildings and gently curving, tree-lined streets near Penn Station sponsored by the International Ladies Garment Workers Union.[17] Like Simkhovitch, Catherine Lansing never received the scholarly attention she deserved.[18]

Lansing and Coit are only two of a large cadre of housing activists, most of them women, whose names have been forgotten. Black women suffered the equivalent (or worse) cancellation from history. Lugenia Burns Hope, founder in 1908 of the social service agency Neighborhood Union in Atlanta, went on the national stage after her husband's death in 1936.[19] As assistant to Mary McLeod Bethune, director of Negro Division of the National Youth Administration (NYA), Hope traveled across the continent investigating branches of the NYA.[20] When her failing health dictated curtailing travel, she continued working with the National Association for the Advancement of Colored People (NAACP) and other organizations seeking equality for Blacks in housing and education. Yet a major reference work ignores those years on her own, reporting only that she "fell ill and spent the remainder of her life in New York City, Chicago and Nashville."[21]

While Simkhovitch remained on the East Coast, Hope and others across the continent contributed to "Woman-Made America." Albion Fellows Bacon, a housewife living in Evansville, Indiana, played a major part in changing that state's housing laws. Born the daughter of a Methodist minister in 1865, she had only a high school education when she took a job as secretary and then married banker Hilary E. Bacon in 1888.[22] Following the birth of four children and a serious illness, Bacon turned her energies to charitable work in Evansville and quickly zeroed in on squalid housing as the cause of illness, delinquency, and multiple other problems.

Evansville's population had exploded after the Civil War, growing from fewer than 12,000 in 1860 to nearly five times that by 1900, as Black migrants from the South and immigrants from Europe came looking for jobs and a better life. With only poorly financed public schools open to them, Blacks had little occupational mobility. Only one in ten African American households owned a home by 1900, compared with four in ten white households.[23] As renters confined to segregated areas, Blacks were at the mercy of landlords who could raise rents anytime they chose. When families doubled up to get by, their overcrowded, underserviced quarters became disease incubators.

Bacon observed the appalling situation and in 1908 vowed to change it. The first step was exposing the problem and then getting a law passed on the state level. When she spoke to the General Assembly, she used photos of "Cocaine Alley" to show how it was a breeding place for crime, and how the same beds served both "day shifts and night shifts." She warned assembly members that they had a personal stake in improving housing because their sons and daughters were "elbow companions" of children from disease-ridden tenements. When William Jennings Bryan, a three-time nominee for president, came through Indiana, she enlisted him to talk about the housing problem. The law the Indiana legislature passed in 1909 fell far short of what Bacon wanted because it applied only to the state's two largest cities. With renewed vigor, she proposed a revised bill, which was defeated in 1911 when landlords mounted a campaign against it, calling it a scheme to raise rents on the poor. More hard work and the enlistment of women's clubs and prominent individuals to apply pressure finally led to success in 1913. Bacon's disgust with the "death trap" mentality of male legislators who made her fight so hard turned her into a suffragist. Edith Elmer Wood pointed to Bacon as an example of what "single-hearted devotion to an idea" could achieve, and she identified Indiana's housing law as the "work of one woman."[24]

While Bacon was battling slums in Indiana, Grace Vawter Bicknell had a similar mission in Washington, DC. A member of the National Civic Federation, Bicknell chaired its housing committee, which ran a sizeable project at a 5 percent profit. When newly elected Woodrow Wilson became president in March 1913, Bickford and her friends moved to engage his wife, Ellen Axson Wilson, in their campaign for more projects like theirs. A plan to take Mrs. Wilson on a tour of squalid alley homes, scheduled for three weeks after the inauguration, had to be revised because of an outbreak of smallpox, but the First Lady, who was suffering from a kidney disease, agreed to go to the Home of the

Incurables, shake hands with every resident, and then drive past the row of model two-family houses that Bicknell's committee ran. Each of the 109 units had its own bath and two to four rooms, and the rents were affordable, at $7.50 to $12.50 per month.

Then Bicknell and her co-workers drove Ellen Wilson through congested alleys, not far from the Capitol, where families were crowded into run-down quarters not seen from the streets. Wilson felt such deep empathy for the alley dwellers that she immediately resolved to join Bickford's group. She invited members of Congress and their wives to the White House for discussion of the topic, and Bicknell noted that soon "no one could move in polite society" without a thorough understanding of the housing problem.[25] One Black domestic worker was so encouraged by the First Lady's dedication that she told her daughter "an angel lived in the White House. . . . [She is] talking about helping the poor and improving housing."[26] Ellen Wilson's engagement in reform contrasts sharply with her husband's actions. While she observed that alley dwellers were predominantly Black and that she had long felt responsibility to improve racial equality, the president was extending racial segregation in government offices and cafeterias.

After only a year in the White House, Ellen Wilson's kidney disease worsened, and she was unable to participate in Bicknell's shepherding legislation through Congress to permit condemnation of the alley properties and their replacement. Dubbed the "Alley Bill" or "Mrs. Wilson's bill," it ran into opposition in congressional committees, and just before Ellen Wilson died, on August 6, 1914, she said, according to Bicknell, "I would be happier if I knew the alley bill had passed."[27]

Bicknell, the First Lady, and most of Simkhovitch's female allies could afford to contribute their time. They had family money or a part-time job or husbands who maintained the household. Simkhovitch's time-consuming work for the NYCHA paid nothing, and she had a payroll to meet at Greenwich House, a responsibility that weighed more heavily during the 1930s when deep-pocketed donors disappeared. As breadlines grew longer and eviction orders piled up, Frances Perkins, a longtime friend, lamented to Simkhovitch that the "romantic old-fashioned fortunes" were no longer available for tapping. With a touch of nostalgia, Perkins continued, "The surplus that couldn't with taste go into diamonds and old masters often went to [charity]," but with diminished portfolios, many of the usual benefactors cut back on donations.[28] Emily Sweetser Alford, a member of the uptown Fortnightly club, noted that Simkhovitch had a knack for charming "cash out of people to keep her downtown enterprises solvent." She "rarely failed to recognize and quicken whatever humanity might be hidden under age or youth, dirt and stink, mink and scent."[29]

Some money came from those who benefitted from settlement house programs, and in 1930, the Settlement Society had funds to acquire ninety acres in Dutchess County for a sleep-away retreat.[30] Named Camp Herbert Parsons to honor an early supporter, it accommodated 150 in the early years, and when that number doubled with the addition of more cabins, participants found ways to chip in.[31] At the Greenwich House pottery studio on Jones Street, students paid for instruction, and after the pottery shop attained a world-class reputation under its dynamic director Maude Robinson, its products attracted buyers. Half of the proceeds from sales to European collectors and the Metropolitan Museum of Art went to Greenwich House.

Although these contributions helped, major fundraising remained Simkhovitch's responsibility, and at the same time she was watching every penny, both in her personal spending and at Greenwich House, Vladimir continued to splurge on art. He had followed his original sale of Chinese scrolls to the Metropolitan Museum in 1918 with smaller deals with galleries and individual collectors, some of whom questioned his expertise.[32] His subsequent collecting in Chinese art centered on paintings, coming from a range of dynasties, and after he failed to sell the collection in Europe, he kept refining and augmenting his holdings, to fetch a higher offer from the Philadelphia Museum. in the United States.[33]

While Mary rarely claimed credit for her achievements, Vladimir basked in the publicity he received. "It is now generally admitted," he wrote his daughter, "that there are no more important ancient paintings in China or elsewhere to be had except very occasionally at fabulous prices and that the most important paintings are in my possession."[34] Intent on preserving his premier position, he acquired another painting, although admitting it would "ruin" him financially, because he could not fathom having "a really important painting on the market outside of my collection."

Vladimir was not alone in crediting his collection. An article in *Art and Archaeology* reported: "Curators of museums yearn to hoard [Vladimir Simkhovitch's] treasures, while aesthetes, artists and collectors, scholars from all over the world, admire, compare and speculate on their relative merits."[35] Abigail Aldrich Rockefeller, a founder of MoMA, requested a look at his Chinese paintings after hearing them described as the "most beautiful" in this country.[36]

When the Philadelphia Museum of Art paid $225,000 for the collection in 1930, Mary thought it was "probably worth more," but she admitted this was "quite a residuum" for "more collecting" by her husband.[37] She expected nothing for herself or Greenwich House. "I do not think he will give me anything outright (except a small check for my journey)," she wrote her daughter, "but that is his way."[38] In three decades of marriage, she had come to accept that her priorities did not fit his, and that he might credit her work with words, but he wasn't about to fund it.

With all her responsibilities—vice chair of the NYCHA, head of a major settlement house, and lobbyist in Washington—it is surprising that Simkhovitch, at age seventy, agreed to run for political office in 1937. She had always shunned close affiliation with any major political party, preferring to direct her energy to supporting the individual whose agenda matched hers. Mayor Fiorello LaGuardia paralleled her thinking on most issues. She understood that not everyone approved of this ebullient, independent-minded man, but she admired his many talents. Having grown up in Arizona, he brought an outsider's enthusiasm to New York and seemed to understand the city's problems better than most of his critics. He spoke several languages and could competently conduct an orchestra and get along with people from all economic strata. He had his faults, and she admitted he could be bossy and exasperating, but his honesty and dedication knew no equal. She could think of no better leader for the city.

La Guardia reciprocated her warm regard by appointing her to committees and sending hearty congratulations whenever Greenwich House celebrated a milestone. His 1937 invitation for her to run for city council coincided with her re-evaluation of political parties. As she explained to her friends at that year's annual conference of the Society of the Companions of the Holy Cross, she had "voted the [D]emocratic ticket, sprinkled with frequent votes for socialist candidates" but she believed "the Socialist Party is too remote from any possible success [and the] Communist Party is too alien to the American tradition and current opinion to be of practical use."[39] Putting her name up for election without a party label would suit.

And that is what the 1937 New York City Council election called for. In a system new to them, voters were instructed to indicate their preferences by ranking the candidates, and then the votes were tallied repeatedly. In each round, the lowest-ranking name was dropped, and the counting proceeded until one candidate was the choice of more than 50 percent of the voters.

In a crowded field of candidates vying for one of the twenty-six seats on the city council, name recognition was important, and Simkhovitch should have had an edge. In her three years as vice chair of the NYCHA, her photo appeared frequently in newspapers, and several highly respected groups and individuals backed her. The Citizens Nonpartisan Committee, chaired by Judge Samuel Seabury, famous for heading the corruption investigation of public officials in the early 1930s, endorsed her in a plea for "intelligent votes."[40] The ailing Lillian Wald came out of retirement to serve as honorary chair of her election committee. The *New York Times* named the "director of Greenwich House and a national leader in housing reform" to its list of well qualified.[41] Harlem's *New York Age* joined her supporters, noting her long record of achievements.[42] Some of Greenwich House's old friends, including Marshall Field and Gerald Swope, sent large checks even though they did not reside in New York and could not vote for her.[43]

Dorothy Dunbar Bromley, writing in *Harper's*, singled out two women as deserving women's votes for city council: Simkhovitch, a "tireless worker" for public housing, and Genevieve B. Earle, who had a commendable record as city researcher and advocate of civic improvements. "If we can have [Mrs. Simkhovitch] and Mrs. Earle, our sex will be ably represented," Bromley wrote.[44]

Earle won a seat on the city council, but Simkhovitch did not, although the two had equal endorsements and records of achievement. Some pointed to Simkhovitch's failure to promote herself, to claim credit for her many accomplishments. Her grandson suggested it was her "foreign sounding name" that cost her.[45] She never ran for office again.

Although she lost at the polls, Simkhovitch was winning accolades elsewhere. Honorary degrees conferred on her during the 1930s included one Doctor of Humanities from New York University, another from her alma mater, Boston University, as well as a Doctor of Social Sciences from Colby College.

Yet Simkhovitch remains virtually unknown today. Like other women activists of her time, she may have contributed to the obscurity by failing to self-promote. Jill Ker Conway observed that in their autobiographies the Progressive Era's most noteworthy women played down their worth. They portrayed themselves as "intuitive, nurturing, passive, but never—in spite of the contrary evidence of their accomplishments—managerial."[46] In *Neighborhood*, published in 1938, Simkhovitch fits that description, with emphasis on working together. "[W]hen we opened the doors of the little house on Jones Street," she wrote, "we had a definite plan of operation." She takes some credit for confronting budget deficits during the early years, standing up to criticism,' and taking an active part in the woman suffrage campaign, but always in cooperation with others.[47] She dedicated the book to her grandson, Paul Didisheim, with the admonition to study his ancestors "back to the beginnings of our country."[48]

After her long service to the NYCHA, Simkhovitch might have hoped to see her name attached to one of the new public housing projects. Lillian Wald was honored with a large project on the Lower East Side, although she played only a very minor part in solving New York's housing problems.

Jacob Riis and Charney Vladeck were both memorialized on housing projects, while Simkhovitch's name got scratched after being put forward following her death. In 1958 William Reid, chair of the NYCHA, proposed a mammoth undertaking, to be named Simkhovitch Houses, and asked Mayor Robert Wagner to authorize condemnation of a large swath of land for it on the Lower East Side. Fronting the East River, the plot, bounded by Monroe, Gouverneur, and Montgomery Streets, would accommodate an enormous complex of twenty-one-story buildings.[49] Newspaper coverage at the time suggests that Simkhovitch's work had already been forgotten, although less than a decade had passed since her death. The *New York Times* identified her as "Miss Simkhovitch [who] founded Greenwich House, a settlement in Greenwich Village".[50]

As plans for Simkhovitch Houses proceeded, the project changed significantly, and the Simkhovitch name all but disappeared.[51] Opened in 1965 as Gouverneur Gardens, the six-tower complex provided 778 housing units, available to New Yorkers who qualified under the Mitchell-Lama formula. Named for the two New York legislators who introduced it (State Senator MacNeil Mitchell and State Assembly member Alfred Lama), Mitchell-Lama attempted to meet the city's housing shortage by building units for purchase by low- and middle-income New Yorkers.[52] Rather than owning physical space, buyers acquired shares in a cooperatively managed building, with right to occupy a specific unit while paying maintenance costs commensurate with their income. This new form of "affordable housing" (with public funds used for construction and then management turned over to occupants) soon became popular in New York, and "Mitchell-Lama" was a name everyone knew. "Gouverneur Gardens," named for Abraham Gouverneur, leader in New York when it was still a colony, fit this initiative better than the immigrant-tainted "Simkhovitch." As a limited-income cooperative, Gouverneur Gardens presented an attractive option to families formerly shut out of the market, but those displaced and lacking the means to buy in found themselves worse off than before.

Of all the early female housing activists, Catherine Bauer earned the greatest recognition. After her early work publicizing public housing in Europe, she continued her campaign to alter Americans' opinions on the subject. Following a job at the USHA, she entered academia in 1940 as lecturer at Berkeley's School of Social Welfare. A string of other university appointments moved her around the country before she resettled at Berkeley's Department of Architecture in 1950. Marriage to fellow professor and architect William Wurster produced an immensely popular team, and both Bauer and her husband contributed to the establishment of Berkeley's College of Environmental Design. In 2020, long after Bauer's death from a fall in 1964, the college put her name alongside Wurster's on its main building, an acknowledgment most women activists never received.

Simkhovitch's campaign for safe, affordable housing was much longer than Bauer's. It spanned half a century. Her 1898 article calling for state intervention; the 1903 publication of *Tenants' Manual*; the formation of the Congestion Committee in 1907; her speech in Washington in 1909; her book *City Worker's World* in 1917; and lastly, the founding of the Public Housing Conference in 1931 were all prelude to the New Deal triumph. She and her cadre of activists "were so good at their business," wrote one historian, "that they managed to convince a reluctant Roosevelt administration to go along with a comparatively daring national public housing program."[53]

In her first two years as vice chairman of the NYCHA, Simkhovitch oversaw the demolition of more than a thousand tenements and the opening of the First Houses.[54] With its quality construction, diligent management, and a wide range of income groups as tenants, New York City's public housing thrived for two decades. Then a mixture of shoddy construction, lax oversight, and selecting tenants from only the poorest stratum resulted in conditions as deplorable as those they replaced. The term "public housing" carried such opprobrium that the Public Housing Conference dropped "Public" from its name and became the National Housing Conference. This failure of public housing didn't happen under Simkhovitch's watch, but it may help explain why she remains little known today.

Like many of her colleagues in the fight for decent housing for all, Simkhovitch rarely appears on lists of leaders in the Progressive Era. In a Social Welfare History Project that asked scholars to suggest names of those who should be recognized, Jane Addams was the only woman to make the cut. John E. (Jack) Hansan, who started the project and who among other roles was a director of the National Association of Social Workers, spoke up for Simkhovitch. Along with housing, Hansan wrote, she led in "the opening of public schools as social centers, National Aid for Public Education, widow's pensions, nursery schools, childcare centers, woman's suffrage,... and old age poverty."[55] Yet Hansan himself never explained why she failed to collect commensurate credit.

That lack of credit in no way diminishes what Simkhovitch accomplished. From the long list of problems and social ills that she and her allies attacked, she gave special attention to housing, equating the right to decent living space with the most basic rights. That she and her "female dominion" managed to affect not only quantity of housing but also quality confirms their significance in "Woman-Made America."

13

"Pioneers Are Always Needed"

Wonder Woman Diana Prince, star of Sensation Comic's (and later DC Comics') eponymous series, landed on American newsstands in July 1942, just as Greenwich House geared up to celebrate its sixtieth birthday. Not surprisingly, the scantily clad Amazon, brandishing wide bracelets that repulsed bullets, made a bigger splash. She quickly became enormously popular, as readers eager to follow her exploits bought half a million copies of each issue. Actual readership was estimated at five times that number by 1945.[1]

Each issue of *Wonder Woman* was accompanied by a four-page insert titled "Wonder Woman of History," featuring an actual woman deserving—at least according to the creators of Sensation Comics—of attention. One issue highlighted Simkhovitch, who "occupied an important role in the life of our country's greatest metropolis for fifty years."[2] Graphic panels summarized her life, with one noting that she had made Greenwich House "the most important place in [Greenwich] Village." Unlike Diana Prince, who vanquished her enemies with those bracelets and the Lasso of Truth, the Wonder Woman of Greenwich Village spearheaded crusades with speeches, books, and articles.

Diana Prince attacked the same real-life villains that Simkhovitch went after: milk companies that charged exorbitant prices, factory owners who maltreated workers, and landlords of filthy, rat-infested, overpriced premises. In fact, the comic book's creator, William Moulton Marston, defined his goal as "change." Known mostly as a psychologist and inventor of a lie detector test, he lived in a bigamous relationship that involved the niece of the birth-control activist Margaret Sanger and was outspoken in calling for more rights for women. He even featured a woman president of the United States in one of Diana Prince's escapades.[3] Defending his comic book series against charges that it was "moronic," he replied with an article titled "Why 100,000,000 Americans Read Comics." The popularity proved significance, he argued, and was justified, especially for young people. If parents wanted their children to be super strong adults, send them to Superman-Wonder Woman picture stores [which stimulate] the child's natural longing to battle and overcome obstacles, particularly evil ones." What better way to increase a child's chance for "self-advancement in the world"? Rather than unfit reading for America's youth, his comics were a form of feminist propaganda, he argued, because they provided young people with a model "of strong, free, courageous womanhood." They would help "combat the idea that women are inferior to men" and "inspire girls to self-confidence and achievement in athletics, occupations and professions monopolized by men."[4]

Although Greenwich House's anniversary captured far less attention than Wonder Woman Diana Prince in 1942, President Roosevelt, whose mother had died the previous year, took time to send regards to Simkhovitch and remind her of his mother's esteem for her. Sara Delano Roosevelt's acquaintance with the young Mary Kingsbury during summers at Campobello had prepared her to make regular contributions to Greenwich House from the day of its founding in 1902, and her strong support for its work continued until her death.

Secretary of Labor Frances Perkins used a radio speech to offer birthday greetings. Long before Perkins became a national figure, she lived a short walk from 26 Jones Street and remembered seeing the city "through Greenwich House." That meant understanding "a lot of things about America," she explained, and she predicted the settlement house would continue spreading the word of "what America is about."[5]

Simkhovitch celebrated her seventy-fifth birthday that year, and physical ailments, including diabetes requiring insulin injections, slowed her step. Although she tended to dismiss each malady as unimportant, her energy flagged. Vladimir retired from Columbia (while continuing to teach the occasional course as an adjunct), but Mary clung to her directorship of Greenwich House.

The war increased her workload. Within days of Pearl Harbor, Roosevelt appointed her to the Enemy Alien Hearing Board for the Southern District of New York. Together with other members, she followed instructions issued by the US attorney general to assess evidence presented on those deemed "alien enemy" and decide who should be "interned, paroled, or released unconditionally."[6] The job paid nothing beyond the symbolic $1 per year and travel expenses, but it was vindication for a woman whose own patriotism had once been questioned.[7] Her FBI records went all the way back to 1918 and included not only her membership in various liberal organizations but also her supporting statements for immigrants applying for visas. One memo concluded that while she was "a liberal in her views... [she was] not a communist."[8]

Simkhovitch's workload further increased when she became vice chair of the Manhattan Office of Civilian Defense (OCD). With headquarters at Greenwich House, OCD served the area below 14th Street and west of Broadway.[9] Here again, as in her work with the Housing Authority, she chafed at the red tape. There were too many meetings, and they were attended only by the converted.

For one pressing need in the community, she came up with a solution of her own. A young mother in the neighborhood had written the local newspaper that she was happy to answer Uncle Sam's call and take a job in a defense plant but hesitated to leave her six-year-old son alone in the apartment until she returned from work at 7 p.m. Greenwich House had responded to the needs of working mothers in World War I, and Simkhovitch saw no reason why it could not help now. The settlement's daycare typically ended at 5 p.m., but she designated a room to stay open later so that young children could await their mothers, each of whom paid $2.50 a week for the service. She also arranged for the children to receive penny milk in the afternoon and a snack of government surplus food, such as bread or crackers and peanut butter. The room remained open on Saturdays to accommodate mothers who worked weekends.[10] Since she lacked sufficient space to accommodate all the children whose mothers wanted to send them there, the *Villager* reported, "There is always a waiting list."[11]

Simkhovitch expected other neighborhoods to come up with childcare arrangements, but most lacked sufficient interest and personnel. Her other suggestion for helping working mothers also failed to attract positive reception. She advocated part-time jobs for women so they could balance family responsibilities and patriotic service.[12] Employers doggedly persisted in assigning eight-hour shifts, and harried mothers continued to struggle to please the boss and still do the shopping, meal preparation, and laundry for their families at home.

By March 1943, Simkhovitch was ready to shed one responsibility—the presidency of the National Public Housing Conference (NPHC), which had of course been the chief lobbying group behind New Deal housing laws. To succeed her, she suggested Carl Hovde, whom she described as "very capable" and particularly suited because he came from Pittsburgh and would bring a fresh perspective to the problem of housing.[13] When the NPHC offered to make her its honorary president, she declined, saying, "I've never been an honorary officer of anything." She did consent, however, to be an honorary member.[14]

During the war, Simkhovitch continued to speak out on housing, and she appealed to other women to support the cause. Just weeks after the war ended, she published an article in the *New York Herald Tribune* titled "A Woman's View of Housing," in which she noted that she had been following this issue for more than fifty years, and that as the only woman on the New York City Housing Authority (NYCHA) and the sole member who had served the entire length of time it had existed (about eleven years), she wanted to enlist other women in her ongoing campaign.[15] She urged them to vote in the upcoming election for increased state aid to housing. The hefty 25 percent increase proposed (from $5,000,000 to $6,250,000) was still inadequate, she argued (and the *Tribune's* editorial board agreed.) But any addition would help. She continued to see wives and mothers as comprising the backbone of housing reform, and she tried to enlist famous names in the cause. When she organized a committee of fifty to "discover women's views on housing needs," she put the wife of Franklin Roosevelt Jr., along with novelist Fannie Hurst, on the executive committee.[16]

Simkhovitch's work on NYCHA was soon to end. In 1947 Mayor William O'Dwyer decided to replace the five unpaid, part-time members (none of whom he had appointed) with a three-member agency of his choosing. They would report directly to him. The change required legislation in Albany, but O'Dwyer successfully maneuvered to end all terms of the current Housing Authority members on July 1, 1947. Without this intervention, Simkhovitch's term would have run only until the following February, though other NYCHA members had several years remaining in their terms.

When asked about O'Dwyer's move, Simkhovitch initially refused to comment, then changed her mind. "Isn't it all as clear as a bell to you?" The Housing Authority members with whom she served had been interested only in housing, she explained, implying that the mayor wanted a board more congenial to landlords.[17] As her colleague Nathan Straus told the *New York Times* a few months earlier, "The speculative builders of shoddy shacks...never have had a better friend in City Hall than Mayor O'Dwyer."[18]

Simkhovitch's forced resignation from the Housing Authority prodded some of her admirers to tell her how much they appreciated what she had done. The Citizens' Union proclaimed their high regard: "We want to tell you how, while along with being full of years and glory you are still possessed of the keenness of mind and nobility of spirit that have always been yours, how deeply we love you and how greatly we honor you."[19]

With no superior to relieve her of her directorship of Greenwich House, Simkhovitch hung on. The Monday night dinners, where she still presided at the head of the table, had long been "an event," according to the *New York Post*, as a gathering of residents and guests reviewed the week's accomplishments.[20] Too busy to take time out for lunch,

Simkhovitch, a self-described "cheese addict," made a quick midday meal out of cheese and fruit.[21]

Like many organizers, she struggled in finding a successor. Her preference is curious. The woman who had once defended the idea of raising a child in a settlement balked in her seventies at letting another woman try what she had done. "I would love to have you associated with our work," she wrote Mrs. Charles T. Zahn, "but I do think it is very difficult to work when one has a little baby unless compensating attention can be given, which would be difficult at Greenwich House."[22] Simkhovitch preferred hiring a man to assist her, with the idea that he would take over the directorship.

Before naming a successor, she wanted to arrange for her own financial security. Writing to Lou Molloy, a member of the Greenwich House board, on November 2, 1945, she insisted that she currently felt fine but expected her "capacity for work [to] diminish." Before making any decision on leaving, she had to settle the matter of where she would live. She wanted to stay on in the director's suite on Barrow Street, and wrote Molloy that she could not "afford to send in my resignation as Director until I have an understanding of what action the Board would take in this matter."[23] She admitted having little set aside because "[m]y salary has never allowed of my saving." She thought she and Vladimir should have the right to continue to occupy the director's apartment at 27 Barrow Street after she retired.

It seems unlikely that she and Vladimir (with his profitable art deals and pension from Columbia) did not have the means to rent an apartment for their retirement years. She therefore must have had her own reasons for wanting to remain in the director's suite. Most likely, she didn't want to leave one of the busiest places in Greenwich Village, where artists and performers passed through each day. Her argument to the board, however, centered on money and a promise, as she noted in her letter to Molloy: "My husband secured Mrs. Woerishofffer's gift of the House and it was her wish that we should have the permanent rent free use [of the apartment]."[24] To offset fears that she might meddle in management if she continued living on the premises, she clarified her intentions to the board: "You could be assured that upon my retirement, I should withdraw wholly from participation in all House activities though my interest in its welfare would never cease, and I would be glad to be classed as Director Emeritus and serve on the Board if that were thought desirable."[25]

The person chosen to take over the director's job in 1946 was a childless widow, Gertrude Sturgis Cooper, who, on Eleanor Roosevelt's recommendation, had become the first woman to serve as superintendent in the National Park Service, with an assignment at the Vanderbilt Mansion, near the Roosevelts' Hyde Park estate. Like the Simkhovitches, Gertrude Cooper and her husband had strong ties to Maine, having been year-round residents there while she worked for the Park Service. Although a competent administrator, Cooper had no experience with social work or settlement houses, and her tenure at Greenwich House was brief, lasting only until 1948.

Following Cooper came Maxwell Powers, a Cleveland-born musician, who had no experience with social work but excelled at fundraising. Married and starting a family when he began teaching music at Greenwich House in 1941, he gained Mary's approval immediately. In May 1946, she recommended him as music critic to Max Lerner, an editor of *PM*, a leftist newspaper: "He is a first-class man, a composer, a thorough musician...that unusual, in fact perhaps otherwise nonexistent combination of artist and businessman."[26]

In citing his fitness to take over Greenwich House, Simkhovitch was signaling her understanding of how Greenwich House had changed: It needed a businessman as its head. Powers and his wife, Helen insisted they did not want to raise their two daughters in a settlement house. After moving his family into an apartment on the Upper West Side, Powers underlined the importance he placed on the music program by taking an office at 46 Barrow Street, several doors away from the main settlement house at 27 Barrow Street. The music school would continue to be his primary interest, as he composed and conducted concerts, and Greenwich House became known as much for its cultural activities as for its social services.

Retirement did not mean the woman a local newspaper designated "First Lady of the Village" was going to fade into obscurity.[27] Simkhovitch continued to speak out on a variety of subjects and attend conferences when she felt able. What she really wanted to do was write, and she hoped to make some money doing that. After *Neighborhood* went out of print, she asked the publisher to reissue it. The editor at W. W. Norton who turned down her request explained that no one wanted to buy a book that had "already had its day in the sun," but if she reworked it a bit so that it could be marketed as something new, he would reconsider.[28] Simkhovitch balked at that, got the rights back, and approached other publishers.

By March 1947, she was negotiating with Harper & Brothers for a contract. After meeting with editor Ordway Tead and giving him an outline and sample chapter, she wrote in what sounds like a bargaining tactic: "People tell me I should have a contract.... Is that right? Supposing that even though I do have your nice note, you should suddenly be run over by an automobile, where would I be? On the other hand, I dare say, you might think the book was no good—then where would you be?" Tead drew up a contract for a "biographical volume" with a title yet to be decided, but with no advance on royalties and only the standard royalty on all copies sold.[29]

The resulting book, *Here Is God's Plenty*, came out in 1949, dedicated to "My Family." The title came from the English poet John Dryden, who, as Simkhovitch explained in her preface, began his retelling of Chaucer's stories, "Fables of Chaucer," with the old proverb "Here Is God's Plenty." The phrase fit equally well the American scene in 1949, she wrote, "as we look at... the vast abundance, its dramatic unfolding, its great organizing ability and its fundamental democratic faith. Truly a land of God's Plenty." Simkhovitch insisted this was not an autobiography but rather "essays, autobiographical in illustration, but to the end of adding one drop more of understanding of the themes that have been the structure of my life—the building in which I have lived, if not my life itself."[30]

Much of the text of this short volume came directly from *Neighborhood*. She justified the repetition by noting that the earlier book was no longer available. Norton had given her permission to reuse certain portions in chapters on education, housing, recreation, welfare, community organization, politics, religion, and the arts.

Although the 184 pages in *God's Plenty* did not go beyond *Neighborhood* in its revelations or interpretations, reviews were kind. *Kirkus Reviews* described it as a kind of valedictory for "the retired head of Greenwich House... memories of her parents and school, a European interlude, and graduate studies and the early days of her work with the College Settlement.... "[H]er recall is mellow and gracious in tone reflecting much of the personality so many have known."[31]

Some of what Simkhovitch wrote in her last years never made it into print. The unpublished manuscript of *Green Shoots* still lies among her papers in the Schlesinger Library at Radcliffe seventy-five years after her death. The title referred to what she considered most important in life—individual relationships. On all sides, she noted, we are being pushed to focus on large-scale goals, even though it is the little things that count the most.

The chapter on family reflected her long-held views on the subject, though without reference to the rifts in her own family. After noting reports of a rising divorce rate and of neglected children, she defined a woman's central role: "Woman remains the socializing factor, restraining violence and humanizing the life of man and children." Women were increasingly working outside the home, she wrote in 1950, and "we may as well reconcile ourselves to [it] and make what we can of it." Childcare centers were essential, she advised, because although "raising children is still [women's] function, it may be done better if it is shared with others."[32] On other subjects she remained optimistic, seeing in the fields of education, labor, religion, and government "green shoots" that gave her hope that the nation's trend toward accepting "bigger is better" could be reversed, resulting in more satisfaction for individuals.

An article she wrote in 1946 shows how far she outpaced others in thinking about distribution of income. After observing the Family Allowance program in Canada, she argued the United States should adopt something similar. At an estimated cost of $200 million annually, the Canadian program gave direct subsidies to all families who had children under age sixteen, the exact amount (varying from $5 to $8 per month), depending on the age of the child. Some argued for raising wages, she observed, but Canada's program went straight to the basic problem—how to get food and clothing to children in need, and it did so in a way that benefited large families by augmenting household income.[33]

Not all her Greenwich Village neighbors approved of Simkhovitch's stand on every issue. When the local American Legion unveiled a plaque as part of its Memorial Day observance in 1948, it listed the names of 122 neighborhood men killed in World War II and asked her to speak at the dedication ceremony. Whoever issued that invitation had evidently not conferred with James J. Kirk, commander of the local American Legion, who was among those critical of her views. Kirk wrote Simkhovitch, requesting that she bow out of the Memorial Day event. He had known her for twenty years, he reminded her, and felt entitled to state his opinion that "your activities here in the community were not for the common good of our people and especially those of the poor or low salary groups." Kirk didn't like her politics either. A month earlier, she had been honored by the leftist Citizens' Committee, and Kirk zeroed in on her association with "a protest group with known communists" as the "climax" of many unsavory connections.[34] Simkhovitch replied that she would be out of town at the time of the scheduled ceremony, but gave no indication that she meant to alter her stands or abandon like-minded friends.

Traces of her Wonder Woman energy remained, and she never lost her interest in young people. After attending a meeting of the Lower West Side Council of Social Agencies, she reported that "the speakers were all youngsters and the audience were all adults. It was a very refreshing occasion."[35] That was a remarkable observation from a woman of her years. She told the *New York Sun* in 1946, "They call me old Ginger around here."[36]

The belief in progress that had shaped so many of her life decisions remained undimmed with age, and one of her last public acts was gathering names for a petition urging resolution of conflicts without force. A speech that India's Prime Minister Nehru gave at Columbia University in October 1949, when he received an honorary degree, moved her to act. Nehru had explained in compelling detail how independence of a nation could be achieved without resorting to force. She immediately drafted a letter on the subject and asked other New York leaders to add their names. Nehru's speech should make people think, the statement began, about how "competition in the use of force has come to a dead end.... There is still a possibility that the world may not be destroyed. But there is no longer a possibility that force alone can be the means of the world's escape.... A positive program for world reconstruction is called for in these days of judgment." When the letter was published in two of New York's major newspapers, it carried the names of other notables, including civil rights leader Ralph Bunche, philosopher John Dewey, clergyman Ralph W. Sockman, General Electric President Gerard Swope, Barnard President Millicent McIntosh, and Harvard Medical School Professor Alice Hamilton.[37]

Despite increasing physical ailments, Simkhovitch continued to travel. Vladimir had not accompanied her for many decades, but her old college friend Ida Ripley was still spry enough to welcome the opportunity. In 1946, the two women, both nearing an eightieth birthday, flew to Guatemala, at a time when airplanes were not yet well pressurized. The trip was uneventful, and at the end of a five-week stay, in which the two observed the country's terrain and its people, Simkhovitch was ecstatic, declaring, "I'm in love with Guatemala, with its physical enchantments and with its great democratic promise."[38] She even wrote an article on the subject, "Guatemalan Snapshot," though failed to publish it.[39]

Just before leaving Guatemala, she developed a cold, and the lack of pressure in the plane home left her deaf for several weeks. Undaunted by the experience, she continued to fly whenever she had the opportunity and was one of the first people to arrive by plane in Red Beach, Maine.[40]

Such flashes of energy and enthusiasm came less often as Simkhovitch faced the fact that while Diana Prince might be immortal, she was not. Nor did she have the same access to power that she once had. After FDR's death in April 1945, she no longer had entrée to the White House, although she continued to see Eleanor Roosevelt, who, as US delegate to the United Nations, spent considerable time in an apartment she maintained on Washington Square West, a few blocks from Greenwich House.

Religion had always sustained Mary, and she continued to rely on it as she neared the end of her life, even though no one in her family shared her dedication. Friends and colleagues invariably mentioned, when describing Simkhovitch, her devoutness, and the fact that although she attended church nearly every day of her life, she had kept Greenwich House entirely secular so that people of all religions fit in.

Having joined the Episcopal Church as a young woman, she found aspects of its hierarchy objectionable as she aged, and she didn't shy from criticizing its misogyny. No women served at its General Convention or in parish vestries, and that was a loss, she argued, because women's common-sense approach to problems might help in solving them. As for refusing divorced persons the right to remarry in the church, she thought that wrong, saying as much when asked to serve on a national committee to consider the question. Despite her confidence in the power of group action, she resisted efforts to merge the Presbyterian Church with the Episcopalian, believing that other kinds of cooperation—such as joint meetings or sharing of buildings—provided enough togetherness.

Simkhovitch had never found it easy to describe her religious views. In a letter written in May 1947 to Dr. James Lindsay of the Berry School in Mt. Berry, Georgia (which she had just visited), she noted her belief that "a church should be something very natural and simple—a place for refuge and silence as well as a center of congregational worship. I suppose I am quite conditioned by being myself an Episcopal of a Catholic turn of mind. I think our faith ought to be impressive in everything that we do or are, but not necessarily very visible."[41]

The family's retreat in Maine also provided solace. Mansion House's solitude and wide expanse gave her a place to think and refuel. Vladimir had turned it into a botanical showplace, and after the down-home crops of chicken and pigs in New Jersey, he began raising exotic birds and prize-winning delphiniums. As with everything else he did, Vladimir got attention with his crop of poisonous, showy, short-lived flowers, and he deluged friends with plantings. Eleanor Roosevelt sent a thank you for "generous gift... [of] delphinium roots,"[42] and longtime friend William Ivins, a print curator at the Metropolitan Museum, reported on how his delphinium crop fared.[43] Vladimir became vice president of the American Delphinium Society (the photographer and gallery owner Edward Steichen was president), and the garden at Mansion House included such variety that visitors came from afar to admire it.[44] One fan wrote that he had heard V. G. described as "the great delphinium enthusiast of the East and this is reinforced by a paragraph about you in the catalogue for Lyondell Gardens."[45] Although the interest in delphiniums appears to have matured in Maine, Vladimir's interest in exotic winged creatures predates the move to Mansion House. While still at the New Jersey farm, he gained mention in a local newspaper for purchasing "a pair of Chinese geese [for] his estate."[46] Grandson Paul, who continued into his teens spending every summer at Mansion House, noted how V. G.'s interest could be passing; he enthusiastically engaged in one hobby, then moved on to another. That happened with the delphiniums, and Paul noted he just stopped tending them one summer (although the "peonies are thriving").[47]

Much as Vladimir liked to keep Mansion House a refuge from New York, he made sure to furnish it with delicacies. Paul reported his grandfather stocked up before leaving Manhattan and had, in one stop, spent $140 on groceries at Macy's, including ten Virginia hams.[48] When a newly hired cook did not show up, Paul and his grandparents turned to the stock of canned delicacies that Vladimir had bought.

Close to his grandmother, Paul often clashed with his grandfather. The summer that teenaged Paul hoped to get a driver's license, tension between the two men ran particularly high. Paul needed practice to pass the upcoming driving test, and he thought the little-traveled roads of Maine and one of V. G.'s autos offered the perfect opportunity. But V. G., who collected cars but left all driving to his chauffeur, was not about to let a novice near any steering wheel of his, and a disappointed Paul pronounced him very "narrow minded" for not helping him pass that very important test.[49]

V. G., as even his grandson referred to him, fell short in other ways. His notoriously hot temper often flared at what seemed a slight provocation to Paul, who saw the acrimonious outbursts so unlike anything his grandmother did. He remembered one occasion that illustrated the difference between his grandparents. Having taken a boat out in Maine waters farther than he had permission to go, Paul prepared for reprimand on his return. Fortunately, V. G. wasn't home, but his grandmother was, and she looked Paul in the eyes and enunciated clearly, "I thought you had more sense than that." Those few words had more effect, Paul recalled, than any amount of ranting by V. G.[50]

Politically, Vladimir and Mary held views far to the left of most of their neighbors in Maine, as noted by their grandson, who claimed that the neighbors would vote for whoever ran on the Republican ticket, even if the candidate were Hitler himself.[51] Vladimir's reputation as a scholar gained neighbors' respect, however, and the board of deacons of the First Congregational Church in Calais invited him to preach the sermon any Sunday he chose during the summer of 1951.[52]

Mary also gained respectful recognition from Maine neighbors, though not all of them. After she organized a drive to add books to the local Robbinston library, she received an irate request to mind her own business. The letter she published in New York's *Villager* resulted in so many donations that a large room had to be set aside to accommodate the books that came pouring in. One Robbinston resident, signing herself "A Maine girl," wrote to the local paper that she did not appreciate being treated like a charity case: "We from Maine have been taking care of yourselves [*sic*] a long time before the name Simkhovitch was ever in USA. So please let us take care of our people and you take care of the 'itchs'."[53]

On a happier note, Simkhovitch could point to her daughter with pride. The relationship between mother and daughter had not always been smooth, and Helena felt much closer to her father on many subjects. But her mother had repeatedly encouraged Helena's creative talents, and in the 1940s she developed a considerable reputation in sculpture. Using her maiden name, she exhibited as part of the New York Six at the Petit Palais in Paris in June 1950.[54] Grandson Paul also stood out as a bright spot in Simkhovitch's final years. After graduating from Princeton in 1950, he entered medical school and specialized in hematology. The choice resulted, he explained, from his observing the effect that diabetes had on his grandmother's blood clotting.

Simkhovitch's other grandson never saw Mansion House. When Laura died in December 1932, Stephen had been living in Los Angeles, attempting a screenwriting career, and Sonja Stockstad was living in New York City, raising his son. Both households needed money, and Mary used what she received from her mother's estate to help them both. She set up a small trust fund for Stephen but retained control over how the money was disbursed. Part went for the down payment on a plot of land for him in Los Angeles, leaving him responsible for paying off the mortgage. The rest was designated for distribution to Stockstad in small, regular payments.

It is not clear who made every decision about the trust, but by 1939, when Stephen died, William Hodson, a friend of Simkhovitch's, was in firm control. It is understandable that she turned to Hodson, a social worker from Minnesota who had started out in law (with a law degree from Harvard) but found social work more satisfying than the courtroom. He had moved to New York to work with the Russell Sage Foundation as director of its drive for legislation to benefit children. Affable and well informed, he made friends at the highest level of government, and his correspondents included FDR.

Although a generation younger than Simkhovitch, Hodson addressed his letters to "Dear Mary" and kept up with her health and family news.[55] Even after becoming commissioner of NYC's Department of Public Welfare in 1934, he found time to administer the Simkhovitch trust fund, and it was he who dealt with Sonja Stockstad's requests. After Stephen's death, she petitioned to have the entire asset, amounting to $4,000 [about $74,000 in current dollars] turned over to her. Hodson objected, citing his fear that "this might result in the mother and infant being left without security and dependent upon public authority."[56] The commissioner did, however, "sympathize with [Stockstad's] desire to leave the city," and he offered to mail the weekly payment to her "in Virginia or any city she cares to go to."[57]

Years later, after Sonja's son, Steve, grew to adulthood, he told his wife of the stormy meeting between his mother and grandmother when the details of the move to Virginia were arranged. As eight-year-old Steve waited in the entrance hall of Greenwich House, his mother talked with Simkhovitch in another room, then emerged, visibly very angry, and escorted her son from the premises. That was the closest he ever got to his grandmother, and he remained bitter toward her the rest of his life. By the time the census taker came round Opequon, Virginia, in 1940, Sonja Stockstad was living on a farm with her son and reporting she had "no income."[58] According to several people who knew her, she never uttered the name of her son's grandmother again.[59]

After moving to Virginia with his mother, Steve attended local schools and became active in Boy Scouts. In late 1945, with encouragement from the Scout leader, he falsified his age, claiming to be sixteen rather than fourteen and a half, so that he could enlist in the National Guard. He still needed his mother's consent, and she gave it, reasoning that the war was over and that he would be close to home. "He loved [military] service," according to the woman he married later, "but he soon found out that it was easy to sign up for the Army if he was already in the Guard. So that is what he did. When anyone said anything about him growing up without a father, he always said that Uncle Sam was his father and the Army raised him."[60]

By December 5, 1945, still short of his fifteenth birthday, Steve Simkhovitch was collecting regular pay from the Army Air Corps, and he married the following March. By his eighteenth birthday, he had fathered a son, Ronald, born March 8, 1948, and a daughter, Judith, born May 28, 1949.

Steve still harbored bitterness about his paternal grandmother, and when an emissary of hers approached him with a proposition, he rebuffed it. The offer was to come to New York and enroll in college. How a high school dropout, especially one with a wife and two children, could be expected to manage college in a city two hundred miles away was not spelled out, and Steve didn't want to talk about it. He told the messenger who presented the offer that he had other things to do, and when questioned whether that was all he had to say to his "Grand MAW MAW," he replied in the affirmative. It would be Simkhovitch's last effort to help Steve, and when her estate was settled two years later, his inheritance was a savings bond, which he cashed for $25.[61]

As though to compensate for years of putting his own interests ahead of hers, Vladimir was especially attentive to Mary during her last years. Helena recalled that he fussed over her, keeping track of how much she drank and what time she came in. If she failed to return home at the expected time, he would telephone Helena, who lived nearby at 96 Barrow Street, and insist that she notify the police. Helena would demur, trying to assuage him, sure that her mother would arrive soon. When he persisted, concerned that she might have fallen, always a danger because of her failing vision, or stumbled in the subway, which she insisted on taking, Helena would finally relent and call the police to ask about any accidents reported. Then her mother would inevitably turn up, sit down with Vladimir for a cup of tea, and join him for a game of rummy.[62] That picture of domestic tranquility had not always been characteristic of their relationship, but it was the one their daughter preferred to remember.

By the summer of 1951, it was clear this would likely be their last stay in Mansion House. As Simkhovitch became increasingly ill, she decided it prudent to return to New York, where doctors could monitor her condition; Vladimir stayed behind to close the house. Separated for several weeks, they communicated by mail, in which he addressed her as he had half a century earlier: "Dearest Molly."[63]

On October 23, 1951, Simkhovitch was back in New York but too ill to attend a dinner celebrating the founding of Greenwich House nearly fifty years earlier. Helena Didisheim and Vladimir listened as Eleanor

Roosevelt, Gene Tunney, and other celebrities took turns recounting anecdotes about how Simkhovitch had affected their lives. President Harry Truman, Governor Thomas Dewey, Mayor Vincent Impellitteri, and US Senator Herbert Lehman all sent congratulatory messages. When the former First Lady composed her "My Day" column two days later, she reminded her readers how the neighborhood house Simkhovitch had founded five decades earlier remained such an important part of people's lives. What started to help people adjust to a new country had become a helping hand to people adjusting to a new world.[64]

On November 15, 1951, three weeks after that column appeared, Mary Kingsbury Simkhovitch died.

A reenactment of Simkhovitch's funeral was broadcast a few months later when the National Broadcasting Company (NBC) presented a radio play titled "She Knew Us." The play's narrator described standing in sleet and rain outside the church on the day of Simkhovitch's funeral and watching a large gathering of 300 or so children. Unable to fathom what they were doing there, he asked one boy if he had known Mrs. Simkhovitch. "No, Mister," came the reply. "We didn't know her… but she knew us."[65]

The reporter/narrator understood exactly what the boy meant, having come to a similar realization when he encountered Simkhovitch several years earlier. As a young man, he had been thrown off Greenwich House's baseball club for misbehaving. He found himself standing miserably in front of 27 Barrow Street when a kindly looking woman invited him inside for tea. As the two sat talking, he realized that she was the director of Greenwich House, and he blurted out, "Holy cats! You run the place and I didn't know you." She replied, "But I knew you".[66]

That remains Simkhovitch's legacy—knowing more about others than they know about her. Her life's work reached far beyond slum housing to include factory conditions, consumer protection, access to jobs, fair pay, infant health, cultural opportunities, recreation, and world peace. The National Housing Conference she founded in 1931 continues to operate, and on its ninetieth birthday, it claimed title to the "oldest and broadest coalition of affordable housing leaders in America." Among its new initiatives was the "30/30" undertaking—to create "3 million net new Black homeowners by 2030." Affordable housing remains one of nation's most serious problems well into the twenty-first century, when millions of America's renter households spend more than half their income on shelter.

With housing prices rising faster than wage growth, even those earning middle incomes have little hope of buying a home, making it unlikely they will provide an inheritance for the next generation. Debates over how the federal government should be involved in the solution—whether in making outright subsidies, offering tax advantages and mortgage guarantees, limiting zoning, or something else—continue to this day. But government's responsibility is not in question. A 2024 headline reporting that the president "Suggests a Bigger Federal Role to Reduce Housing Costs" underlines the fact that it's the size and kind of role that Washington plays, not that it plays at all.[67]

In that letter to Simkhovitch in 1943, FDR noted their shared fight for a "slumless America," and he recognized her preeminent role in putting housing on the nation's permanent agenda. Neither he nor her obituary claimed she solved the housing problem, only that she "made a good fight on slums."[68] That is what the president acknowledged when he wrote, "It must be a great inspiration to know you were a pioneer in the whole task of relating housing to the people's welfare. Pioneers are always needed."

Acknowledgements

In the many years I have looked at the life and legacy of Mary Kingsbury Simkhovitch, I have benefitted from insights offered, support given, and materials provided by more persons and institutions than I can possibly acknowledge here. Interviews in the early period with those who knew her yielded especially helpful information, and I regret so many of those who spoke with me are no longer living and able to read these pages.

Grants from the Research Foundation of the City University of New York and the National Endowment for the Humanities funded research at the Schlesinger Library, Radcliffe College, Harvard University, where the Simkhovitch Papers are housed and at the Tamiment Library and Robert F. Wagner Archives, New York University, where the Greenwich House Records are located. Archivists at both sites responded generously to my many requests and pointed me to additional material. When I began my research, Dorothy Wick headed the Tamiment, and she continued to support this project long after she left New York University.

Tim Bent, executive editor at Oxford University Press, gave careful attention to the text and offered many suggestions. His team followed up, turning manuscript into book, and I want to thank Laura Santo, Egle Zigaite, and Deva Thomas.

After she edited my first book with Oxford University Press, Susan Rabiner became a firm advocate and valued friend, offering advice and agenting other books at other presses. I am immensely grateful she agreed that Simkhovitch's story deserved a hearing.

I am fortunate to participate in several groups that meet regularly to discuss individual writing projects and offer encouragement. As a long-time member of the seminar, Women Writing Women's Lives, and of a smaller group composed of Cathy Alexander, Nora Mandel, and Irene

Tichenor, I have profited in more ways than I can count. The Narrative Writing Group, whose members read every chapter of *Slumless*, deserve special recognition for their expertise and unending support. I am indebted to Patricia Auspos, Ruth Franklin, Barbara Fisher, Dorothy Helly, and Melissa Nathanson.

Members of the Simkhovitch family, while imposing no limitations on what I wrote, have been enormously helpful. Mary's daughter, Helena Simkhovitch Didisheim, and son-ion-law Frank Didisheim welcomed me to the Mansion House in Maine and then followed up with countless meetings in New York City. Their son, Dr. Paul Didisheim, contributed countless stories of time spent with his remarkable grandmother. After his death, his daughter, Andrea Didisheim, delivered to me four boxes of family papers and photographs that had not yet been inventoried or archived. Mary's other grandson, Stephen, died in 2013, and I never spoke with him, but his son Ronald, daughter Judith, and Glenda Geraci shared with me his recollections of his grandmother.

In all my earlier books, Livio Caroli had a significant role, and for this volume, he deserves special credit for leading me to the subject. Soon after he started teaching oboe at Greenwich House, he heard about "Mary K" who had founded the institution decades earlier. It didn't take him long to convince me she deserved a book.

I am so glad he did, although neither of us realized how many years it would take.

Notes

During the many years I worked on this book, the two main archives holding Simkhovitch papers reorganized the files and changed their identification codes. I have tried to update the location of all files I cite, but hope that the description of material suffices to find it even if the designations on the folders are outdated.

ABBREVIATIONS USED IN THE NOTES

ER	Eleanor Roosevelt
FDR	Franklin Delano Roosevelt
GH	Greenwich House
GHRTA	Greenwich House Records, Special Collections, New York University
HSD	Helena Simkhovitch Didisheim
MKS	Mary K. Simkhovitch
NPHC	National Public Housing Conference
NYC	New York City
SIMSCH	Simkhovitch Papers, Schlesinger Library, Harvard University
VG and VGS	Vladimir Gregorivitch Simkhovitch

CHAPTER 1

1. While much of Newton, on the western edge of Boston, remained farmland at the time of Mary's birth, it comprised a string of villages, including East Newton, later known as Chestnut Hill, where her parents lived.
2. MKS, *Here Is God's Plenty* (Harper & Bros., 1949), 25.
3. The separate city of Brooklyn had a population of 396,099.
4. Plymouth, the town, was in domain of the Patuxet, who were part of the Wampanoag tribal confederation. See David Bushnell, "Treatment of Indians in the Plymouth Colony," *New England Quarterly* 26, no. 2 (June 1953): 193–218. This article does not mention Roger Conant, who arrived in 1624 and later became governor of the area.
5. MKS, *Neighborhood* (Norton & Co., 1938), 22.
6. MKS, *Neighborhood*, 22.
7. MKS, *Neighborhood*, 24.
8. Jonathan Platt to Laura Holmes, July 14, 1852, SIMSCH, box 6, folder 105.
9. Jonathan Platt to Laura Holmes, July 16, 1857, SIMSCH, box 6, folder 105.
10. Jonathan Platt to Laura Holmes, July 16, 1857, SIMSCH, box 6, folder 105.
11. Letters from Laura Holmes to her sister, Ellen Holmes, emphasize Laura's popularity at Yarmouth and how much pleasure she took in the attention paid her. SIMSCH, box 6, folder 104.

12. Arthur C. Cole, *A Hundred Years of Mt. Holyoke College* (Yale University Press, 1940), 11, notes that Ipswich was judged one of the best seminaries at the time, and page 37 notes that Mt. Holyoke Seminary copied Ipswich's program when it first opened.
13. MKS, *Neighborhood*, 13.
14. Very few four-year colleges in the United States admitted women in the 1850s. Oberlin, in Ohio, opened in 1833, enrolling Blacks and whites, women and men. The land grant colleges were coeducational, but they did not start until 1862. Albert G. Boyden, *History and Alumni Record of the State Normal School, Bridgewater, Mass, to July 1876* (Noyes and Snow, 1876).
15. Frank's full name was Isaac Franklin Kingsbury, and he was often identified as I. F. Kingsbury. In family letters, he is Frank, and that is how he is identified here. He was the son of Isaac Kingsbury (died January 27, 1886) and the father of Isaac William, Mary's brother, who went by "Will" for most of his life. In his later years, he preferred Isaac, and his relatives called him "Ike."
16. Information on Frank's family comes from his letters to Laura during their courtship.
17. Frank Kingsbury to Laura Holmes, August 26, 1859, SIMSCH, box 6, folder 107.
18. Frank Kingsbury to Laura Holmes, February 14, 1861, SIMSCH, box 6, folder 107.
19. Laura Holmes to parents, February 22, 1862, SIMSCH, box 6, folder 104.
20. Oren Ford, "A History of the Bounty System Used During the Civil War," thesis, University of the Pacific, 1933. According to Ford, Massachusetts started paying bounties in 1863, but the amount varied widely by district because some sections of the state had more trouble than others meeting the required number of recruits. The bounties increased and decreased over the course of the war, going from nothing in some districts and years to $400 in others. In some states, the bounty rose to triple that of a neighboring state, giving incentive from residents of one state to enlist in another.
21. Frank Kingsbury to Laura Holmes, September 25, 1860, SIMSCH, box 6, folder 107.
22. Frank Kingsbury to Laura Holmes, July 22, 1862, SIMSCH, box 6, folder 108.
23. Author's interview with Helena Didisheim, July 29, 1982, Robbinston, Maine. When Newton Center celebrated its 275th anniversary in 1939 and used the occasion to dedicate a memorial to local men who served in the Civil War, Mary Simkhovitch was invited to speak, and she included the fact that her father volunteered. See *Newton Graphic*, October 20, 1939.
24. Emma Lincoln, May 5, 1926, letter to Laura Holmes Kingsbury on her birthday, SIMSCH, box 7, folder 121.
25. Military records for Frank Kingsbury obtained from National Archives and Records Administration, Washington, DC.
26. *Harper's Weekly*, December 27, 1862, 818.
27. As quoted in Shelby Foote, *The Civil War: A Narrative*, vol. 2 (Random House, 1958–1974), 43.
28. James M. McPherson, *Battle Cry of Freedom*, (Oxford University Press, 1988), 574, footnote 13, attributes this quote to a letter from William H. Wadsworth to Samuel L. M. Barlow, December 16, 1862, Barlow Papers, Henry E. Huntington Library, San Marino, California.
29. Frank Kingsbury to Laura Holmes, December 28, 1862, SIMSCH, box 6, folder 108.
30. Frank Kingsbury to Laura Holmes, no date, SIMSCH, box 6, folder 110. Although Frank made no mention of it in the letter to Laura, other white men agreed to lead Black troops after the Secretary of War Stanton ordered raising of troops, including "persons of color" in January 1863. Robert Gould Shaw gained fame for leading the Massachusetts 54th regiment, although he died in battle after less than a year. Thomas Wentworth Higginson commanded the 1st South Carolina Volunteers of Blacks and survived the war.

31. Frank Kingsbury to Laura Holmes, November 5, 1862, SIMSCH, box 6, folder 108.
32. Frank Kingsbury to David H. Mason, December 4, 1866, SIMSCH, box 6, folder 117.
33. Frank Kingsbury to David H. Mason, December 4, 1866, SIMSCH, box 6, folder 117.
34. Frank Kingsbury to Laura Holmes, June 1, 1864, SIMSCH, box 6, folder 110.
35. Marriage certificate, SIMSCH, box 5, folder 96.
36. Frank Kingsbury to Laura Holmes, December 29, 1864, SIMSCH, box 5, folder 93.
37. Laura Kingsbury to sister Nellie, January 29, 1865, SIMSCH, box 6, folder 104.
38. Laura Kingsbury to brother Frank, March 4, 1865, SIMSCH, box 6, folder 103.
39. Laura Kingsbury to Ellen Holmes, May 25, 1866, SIMSCH, box 6, folder 104.
40. President Lincoln was shot at Ford's Theater in Washington, DC, on the evening of April 15 and died the next day. After a funeral on April 19, his body (along with that of a son who had died earlier) was transported by train to Springfield, Illinois, where he was buried on May 4. The train made multiple stops along the way so that Americans could mourn their slain leader. After leaving Philadelphia early on April 24, the train reached Jersey City about 10 a.m. and the president's coffin was transferred by ferry to Manhattan at Desbrosses Street, then across Canal Street to Broadway and south to City Hall where it was open for mourners to view for the rest of April 24 and the next morning. Early in the afternoon the procession started north, viewed by an estimated one million along the way. At 34th Street, the hearse moved westward to the Hudson River and the coffin was returned to the train station in Jersey City. The procession of bands and other mourners continued, however, for several hours.
41. Laura Kingsbury to Ellen Holmes, undated letter, SIMSCH, box 6, folder 104.
42. David Oshinsky, *Bellevue: Three Centuries of Medicine and Mayhem of America's Most Storied Hospital* (Doubleday, 2016), 107.
43. Oshinsky, *Bellevue: Three Centuries*, 106.
44. Carroll Smith-Rosenberg, entry for Mary Kingsbury Simkhovitch, *Notable American Women*, vol. 4, 648–651.
45. Laura Kingsbury to Ellen Holmes, undated letter, SIMSCH, box 6, folder 104.
46. Laura Kingsbury to "sister Nellie," March 21, 1865, SIMSCH, box 6, folder 104.
47. Laura Kingsbury to sister, October 12, 1872, SIMSCH, box 6, folder 104.
48. Frank Kingsbury was not alone in preferring his military title. After his presidency ended in 1909, Theodore Roosevelt liked to be called Colonel Roosevelt.
49. *Newton Graphic*, September 24, 1887, 28.
50. Frank M. Grant, *Annual Report of the City Clerk of Newton for Year Ending December 31, 1911*, summarizes Frank Kingsbury's life and career.
51. Letter from "Celia," of the Newton High School, to author, June 7, 1982, reported that school ledgers for 1881–1882 showed Mary Kingsbury and her brother Willie, with address on Hammond Street (no number), attending a Newton school both years. The entry for 1882 was the last one for Mary since the school did not keep records of students after they turned "14 or 15 years old." That may have been because schooling past fourteen was not required. Mary remained until 1886, which is the year she gave for her high school graduation.
52. MKS, *Neighborhood*, 14.
53. Laura Kingsbury to Ellen Holmes, October 12, 1872, SIMSCH, box 6, folder 104. Laura did not take any satisfaction in reporting Mary's comment to her sister, writing, "I regret to say she could think of nothing but a hand organ and a monkey!" Illustrations of immigrant men playing the instrument (later known as the accordion) were common by the 1870s (see *New York Times*, July 14, 1871, 4), and many New Yorkers objected to both

the men and the monkeys. See "The Italians and the Organ Grinders: A Mass Meeting for the Abolition of Street Music," *New York Times*, September 2, 1871, 2.
54. Laura Kingsbury to Ellen Holmes, no date, SIMSCH, box 6, folder 104.
55. MKS, *Neighborhood*, 28.
56. Author's interview with Helena Didisheim, July 29, 1982, Robbinston, Maine.
57. Clippings at her death in 1932 report Laura was a lineal descendant of Roger Conant; over fifty when she learned German; about sixty "when she acquired an extensive knowledge of French literature; and at eighty she turned to Italian." Didisheim Papers. Courtesy of Andrea Didisheim.
58. MKS, *Neighborhood*, 29.
59. *New York Herald Tribune*, March 4, 1946.
60. MKS, *Neighborhood*, 25 and 27.
61. Two doctoral dissertations are examples: Domenica Maria Barbuto, "The 'Matrix of Understanding': The Life and Work of Mary Kingsbury Simkhovitch," Ph.D. diss., State University of New York, 1992, 10; Tracey Briggs, "Twenty Years at Greenwich House," Ph.D. diss., University of Toledo, 2008. Carroll Smith-Rosenberg's entry for MKS in *Notable American Women*, vol. 4, 648–649, identifies the "Kingsbury's considerable wealth" as coming from "large real estate holdings in the Boston area."
62. Stephen Kalberg, "The Commitment to Career Reform: The Settlement Movement Leaders," *Social Service Review* 49, no. 4 (December 1975): 614.
63. MKS, *Neighborhood*, 18.
64. MKS, *Neighborhood*, 18.
65. John H. Spiers, "Landscaping the Garden City: Transportation, Utilities and Parks in Newton, Massachusetts, 1874–1915," *Historical Geography* 39 (2011): 248–274.

CHAPTER 2

1. MKS, *Neighborhood*, 31.
2. Alice Hayes, "Can a Poor Girl Go to College?" *North American Review* 152 (1891): 624–630.
3. Warren O. Ault, *Boston University: The College of Liberal Arts* (Boston University, 1973), 6. Ault notes (56) that an equal number of scholarships was available to men and women, and that 69 percent of Mary's freshman class received remission of tuition, which was $100 per year.
4. MKS, *Neighborhood*, 34.
5. MKS, *Neighborhood*, 36.
6. MKS, *Neighborhood*, 32.
7. St. Augustine's moved to a new building on Phillips Street, just behind Beacon Hill, in 1892, but Mary apparently became acquainted with it earlier, as part of the Episcopal Church's outreach to Boston Blacks.
8. MKS, *Neighborhood*, 15.
9. MKS, in Louis Finkelstein, ed., *American Spiritual Autobiographies: Fifteen Self Portraits* (Harper & Bros., 1948), 141.
10. I. W. Kingsbury, MD, "Concerning Mrs. Mary K. Simkhovitch," June 27, 1951, to Mary's attending physician, SIMSCH, box 7, folder 103.
11. For many women, the years following college graduation were filled with indecision. See Joyce Antler, "After College, What: New Graduates and the Family Claim," *American Quarterly* 32 (Fall 1980): 409–434. One young woman described how she felt as though she had been "flung into space." Marion Talbot, who graduated from

Boston University in 1880, recalled that she felt ostracized by her friends, most of whom wanted nothing more than to marry quickly, while she sought a "definite occupation" (411). Vida Scudder experienced a "semi-invalid summer after college" and then went to Europe (416).

12. Helena Didisheim told author that Berenson courted Mary but did not make a hit with her younger brother, Will, who disliked him intensely. Interview with author, July 29, 1982, Robbinston, Maine.
13. Employment record for Mary Kingsbury obtained from Margaret T. Brennan, Somerville Public Schools, July 6, 1982. Salary and dates of service are taken from the annual reports for 1892–1894 and from the minutes of the Board of Education meeting for January 25, 1892.
14. MKS, *Neighborhood*, 41. Mary admitted she had been "an impatient teacher" who took interest in only the brightest students. See MKS, in Finkelstein, ed., *American Spiritual Autobiographies*, 141.
15. MKS, in Finkelstein, ed., *American Spiritual Autobiographies*, 144, describes how she wrote her thesis on "The Supine in 'u' as a Dative."
16. MKS, statement for *Boston University News*, January 1949.
17. MKS, in Finkelstein, ed., *American Spiritual Autobiographies*, 137–138.
18. Cynthia Nash Wolfe to author, September 13, 1982.
19. *New York Times*, November 7, 1912, 13.
20. Rev. Edward Staples Drown, Sermon at Memorial Service for Henry Sylvester Nash, St. John's Memorial Chapel, January 28, 1913.
21. MKS, letter to *Evening Post*, November 23, 1912.
22. Sermon at Memorial Service for Henry Sylvester Nash, January 28, 1913.
23. As an example of the information that appeared giving the wrong birth dates for Mary's children, see Radcliffe Alumni Directory questionnaire in which she listed Stephen as born in December 1902 and Helena in February 1904. Helena told author that her mother had a long infatuation with a married man in her church but that she would never have engaged in a romantic or sexual liaison with a married man.
24. MKS, *Neighborhood*, 43.
25. Daniel T. Rodgers, *Atlantic Crossings: Social Politics in a Progressive Age* (Harvard University Press, 2000), 64.
26. Boston's population increased from 250,5256 in 1870 to 448, 477 in 1890.
27. Allen F. Davis, *Spearheads of Reform: The Social Settlements and the Progressive Movement, 1890–1914* (Oxford University Press, 1967), 11, quoted by Stephen Kalberg, "The Commitment to Career Reform: The Settlement Movement Leaders," *Social Service Review* 49, no. 4 (December 1975): 612.
28. Robyn Muncy, *Creating a Female Dominion in American Reform, 1890–1935* (Oxford University Press, 1991).
29. Muncy, *Creating a Female Dominion*, xi.
30. Mary named her daughter Helena, but family lore did not tie that to Dudley. Helena thought both she and Stephen were named "just because Mary and Vladimir liked the names."
31. Helena Dudley, "Relief Work Carried on in the Wells Memorial Institute," *Annals of American Academy of Political and Social Science* (November 1894).
32. Anne O'Hagan, article in *The Woman Citizen*, November 1927, 11–13.
33. O'Hagan, *The Woman Citizen*, November 1927, 11–13.
34. Radcliffe College Archives, *Annual Report*, 1894–95, 16.

35. Paul Buck, "Harvard Attitudes Toward Radcliffe in the Early Years," *Massachusetts Historical Society* 74 (1962): 46. Buck notes that Radcliffe was primarily local in the early years because socially conscious women preferred Bryn Mawr.
36. MKS, *Neighborhood*, 44.
37. Radcliffe College Archives, *Annual Report*, 1894–95, 51.
38. *Radcliffe College Catalogue, 1894–95*, 50.
39. Walter Crosby Eells, "Earned Doctorates for Women in the Nineteenth Century," *Bulletin of the American Association of University Professors* 42 (Winter 1956): 644.
40. Patricia Graham, "Expansion and Exclusion: A History of Women in Higher Education," *Signs* 3 (Summer 1978): 766.

CHAPTER 3

1. Laura Kingsbury to Frank Kingsbury, July 20, 1895, SIMSCH, box 6, folder 111.
2. Frank's father, Isaac Kingsbury, died in 1886, leaving an estate of $70,374, of which $42,850 was in real estate and $26,087 was in cash, bonds, and "mortgage notes."
3. Laura Kingsbury to Frank Kingsbury, December 29, 1895, SIMSCH, box 6, folder 112.
4. Laura Kingsbury to Frank Kingsbury, July 25, 1895, SIMSCH, box 6, folder 111.
5. Laura Kingsbury to Frank Kingsbury, November 18, 1895, SIMSCH, box 6, folder 112.
6. Laura Kingsbury to Frank Kingsbury, January 6, 1896, SIMSCH, box 6, folder 113.
7. Ida M. Hyde, "Before Women Were Human Beings: Adventures of an American Fellow in German Universities of the '90s," *Journal of the American Association of University Women* 31 (June 1938): 226.
8. Laura Kingsbury to Frank Kingsbury, August 2, 1895, SIMSCH, box 6, folder 111.
9. Laura Kingsbury to Frank Kingsbury, August 7, 1895, SIMSCH, box 6, folder 111.
10. Laura Kingsbury to Frank Kingsbury, August 18, 1895, SIMSCH, box 6, folder 111.
11. Laura Kingsbury to Frank Kingsbury, August 23, 1895, SIMSCH, box 6, folder 111.
12. Friedrich-Wilhelms-Universität was located in Mary's time in Unter den Linden, in the section later known as East Berlin. Subsequently renamed Humboldt-Universität, it had no connection with Free University of Berlin, founded in 1948, according to a letter to author from Lutz Richter, office of the president, Freie Univeristät Berlin, Altensteinstrasse 40, Berlin 33, written June 14, 1982.
13. Laura Kingsbury to Frank Kingsbury, October 23, 1895, SIMSCH, box 6, folder 111.
14. Mary Kingsbury to Frank Kingsbury, no date, SIMSCH, box 6, folder 111.
15. Laura Kingsbury to Frank Kingsbury, October 4, 1895, SIMSCH, box 6, folder 111.
16. Laura Kingsbury to Frank Kingsbury, October 20, 1895, SIMSCH, box 6, folder 111.
17. Laura Kingsbury to Frank Kingsbury, January 19, 1896, SIMSCH, box 6, folder 113.
18. Laura Kingsbury to Frank Kingsbury, October 4, 1895, SIMSCH, box 6, folder 111.
19. Laura Kingsbury to Frank Kingsbury, October 28, 1895, SIMSCH, box 6, folder 111.
20. Mary Kingsbury to Frank Kingsbury, no date, SIMSCH, box 6, folder 111.
21. *New York Times*, January 7, 1949, 20, article on the fiftieth wedding anniversary of Mary and Vladimir reported that they met in Adolf Wagner's course on socialism in Berlin.
22. MKS, *Neighborhood*, 52.
23. Rodgers, *Atlantic Crossings*, 91.
24. Barbara Levy Simon, "Berlin's Municipal Socialism: A Transatlantic Muse for Mary Simkhovitch and New York City." In *The Settlement House Movement Revisited: A Transnational History*, ed. John Gal, Stefan Köngeter, and Sarah Vicary. (Bristol University Press, Policy Press, 2021), 35–50. https://doi.org/10.2307/j.ctv19cwb3k. Accessed March 19, 2024.

    Rodgers, *Atlantic Crossings*, chap. 4, also uses the term "municipal socialism."

25. Simon, "Berlin's Municipal Socialism: A Transatlantic Muse for Mary Simkhovitch and New York City."
26. Rodgers, *Atlantic Crossings*, 13. One section of the Paris Exposition focused on women's work and institutions, with special attention to those connected to "social maternalists."
27. Emily Balch to "Dear Old Boy" (her father), September 29, 1895, in Emily Greene Balch Papers (DG 006) Swarthmore College of Peace Collection or Microfilm Edition, Reel 5.
28. MKS, Tribute to Emily Balch, 1946, SIMSCH, box 1, folder 16.
29. Laura Kingsbury to Frank Kingsbury, November 9, 1895, SIMSCH, box 6, folder 112.
30. Emily Balch to "Dearest Father," no date, Emily Greene Balch Papers (DG 006) Swarthmore College of Peace Collection or Microfilm Edition, Reel 5.
31. Laura Kingsbury to Frank Kingsbury, October 20, 1895, SIMSCH, box 6, folder 111.
32. Laura Kingsbury to Frank Kingsbury, February 17, 1896, SIMSCH, box 6, folder 113.
33. Emily Balch to "Dearest Papa," February 16, 1896, Emily Greene Balch Papers (DG 006) Swarthmore College of Peace Collection or Microfilm Edition, Reel 5.
34. Vladimir Simkhovitch to "Mary, Du, meine Geliebte," February 1896, SIMSCH, box 1, folder 8.
35. Laura Kingsbury to Frank Kingsbury, no date, SIMSCH, box 6, folder 111.
36. Laura Kingsbury to Frank Kingsbury, November 14, 1895, SIMSCH, box 6, folder 112.
37. Laura Kingsbury to Frank Kingsbury, October 10, 1895, SIMSCH, box 6, folder 111.
38. Laura Kingsbury to Frank Kingsbury, January 6, 1896, SIMSCH, box 6, folder 113.
39. Laura Kingsbury to Frank Kingsbury, December 29, 1895, SIMSCH, box 6, folder 112.
40. Letter of January 4, 1896, from Laura to Frank on their 31st wedding anniversary, SIMSCH, box 6, folder 113.
41. Laura Kingsbury to Frank Kingsbury, January 14, 1896, SIMSCH, box 6, folder 113.
42. Laura Kingsbury to Frank Kingsbury, January 6, 1896, SIMSCH, box 6, folder 113.
43. Laura Kingsbury to Frank Kingsbury, January 6, 1896, SIMSCH, box 6, folder 113.
44. Mary Kingsbury to Frank Kingsbury, August 16, 1895. SIMSCH, box 6, folder 111.
45. Mary Kingsbury to Frank Kingsbury, October 3, 1895, SIMSCH, box 6, folder 111.
46. Laura Kingsbury to Frank Kingsbury, no date, SIMSCH, box 6, folder 113.
47. Laura Kingsbury to Frank Kingsbury, March 15, 1896, SIMSCH, box 6, folder 114.
48. Laura Kingsbury to Frank Kingsbury, March 15, 1896, SIMSCH, box 6, folder 114.
49. Laura Kingsbury to Frank Kingsbury, March 18, 1896, SIMSCH, box 6, folder 114.
50. Laura Kingsbury to Frank Kingsbury, March 29, 1896, SIMSCH, box 6, folder 114
51. Laura Kingsbury to Frank Kingsbury, April 4, 1896, SIMSCH, box 6, folder 114.
52. MKS, *Neighborhood*, 55.
53. Laura Kingsbury to Frank Kingsbury, February 19, 1896, SIMSCH, box 6, folder 113.
54. Laura Kingsbury to Frank Kingsbury, October 23, 1895, SIMSCH, box 6, folder 111.
55. The fact that both photos remained in Mary's personal papers after her death suggests she never mailed them. Both showed a good-looking young man, and he had inscribed the one to Miss Anne O'Hagan, "As a sign of good friendship, a bad photo from Vladimir." On the photo he inscribed to Ida, his message implies a previous interaction with her: "As a remembrance of the silks I gave you." Both photos are in possession of Andrea Didisheim, and the author is grateful that she shared them.
56. Inscription is dated March 24, Berlin, but Mary was touring Italy with her mother at that date. It is possible that Vladimir used spring break to visit his family and retrieve the photo he wanted to give Mary when she returned to Berlin.

57. The photo came from the Warsaw studio of Jan Mieczkowski, who apparently went bankrupt later in the year and moved his studio to Paris. The picture of Vladimir shows a serious boy sitting on a bed of dry leaves. Warsaw, with multiple cultural institutions, was about eighty miles from Vladimir's birthplace, Ciechanowiec, which was part of Russia at the time of his birth but is currently in Poland. I am grateful to Susan Salm and Arianna Kalian for help in translating the inscription.
58. Mercedes M. Randall, *Improper Bostonian* (Twayne, 1964), 89–90.
59. Emily Balch to "Dearest Papa," February 16, 1896, Emily Greene Balch Papers (DG 006) Swarthmore College of Peace Collection or Microfilm Edition, Reel 5.
60. MKS, *Neighborhood*, 55.

CHAPTER 4

1. Passenger list shows MMKingsbury left Southampton on September 8, 1896.
2. MKS, *Neighborhood*, 58.
3. Anne O'Hagan married Francis Shinn in 1908, and many biographical sources refer to her as Anne O'Hagan Shinn. MKS lists some of O'Hagan's "delightful companions" that she met, including James Ford and Richard Aldrich, in *Neighborhood*, 57.
4. MKS, in Finkelstein, ed., *American Spiritual Autobiographies*, 147.
5. I found no evidence that Mary's parents thought Vladimir was Jewish. He attended Episcopal services with Mary; their wedding was in an Episcopal chapel, and he was buried after a Christian funeral service. His grandson reported that he never heard a reference to Vladimir's Jewish upbringing while he was alive, but the family found a menorah among his belongings when he died, and they "assumed" he was Jewish. The town where he was born was more than 50 percent Jewish.
6. *Columbia University: A History* (Columbia University, 1904), 277.
7. James Harvey Robinson, *The New History: Essays Illustrating the Modern Historical Outlook* (Macmillan & Co., 1912).
8. Annette Lopes, assistant registrar, Columbia University, letter to author, May 17, 1993.
9. Hester Dorsey Richardson, "The College Settlement," *Lippincott's Monthly Magazine* 47 (January 1891): 785–786.
10. Jane E. Robbins, "The First Year at the College Settlement," *Survey* 27 (February 24, 1912): 802.
11. *New York Times*, October 27, 1894, 5, reported Robbins's speech at the Women's Municipal League on October 26, 1894.
12. See *Records of College Settlement*, vol. 1, September 1, 1897, to November 1, 1898, Sophia Smith Collection of Women's History, Smith College.
13. John P. Rousmaniere, "Cultural Hybrid in the Slums, College Women and the Settlement House, 1889–1894," *American Quarterly* 22 (Spring 1970): 61.
14. Edward Cummings, "University Settlements," *Quarterly Journal of Economics* (April 1892): 257–279.
15. Vida Scudder, "The Place of the College Settlement," *Andover Review* 18 (October 1892): 341.
16. Scudder, "The Place of the College Settlement," *Andover Review*, 350.
17. Helena Dudley, born in 1858 in Nebraska, and Ida Scudder, born in 1861 in India, formed a bond that lasted more than four decades. After Scudder and Dudley, both Episcopalians like Mary, formed the female Society of the Companions of the Holy Cross to provide fellowship and an annual retreat for meditation and exchange of ideas among equals, Mary became a devoted member.

18. Vida Dutton Scudder, *On Journey* (E. P. Dutton & Co., 1937), 212. Nan Bauer Maglin discusses Scudder's book in "Vida to Florence: 'Comrade and Companion,'" *Frontiers* IV, no. 3 (1979): 16.
19. Mary Kingsbury, "Women in New York Settlements," *Municipal Affairs*, vol. II (September 1898): 458–462.
20. Kingsbury, "Women in New York Settlements," 462.
21. MKS, *Neighborhood*, 71.
22. MKS, in Finkelstein, ed., *American Spiritual Autobiographies*, 148.
23. Elizabeth Ogg, article on Mary's run for New York City Council in 1937, GHRTAM, box 18, folder 26.
24. MKS, *Neighborhood*, 78.
25. MKS, *Neighborhood*, 59. Passenger lists show MMKingsbury sailed to England on the *Manitoba*, leaving New York on May 30, 1897. She left London on August 18 to return to New York.
26. Helena Didisheim to author, July 29, 1982, Robbinston, Maine. VGS returned very few times to Europe after immigrating to the United States in 1898, but his passport application of 1927 includes evidence that he traveled in England and Germany from June to September 1913.
27. Inscription on back of the photograph, "To our Künftiger Americaner…Halle, March 31, 1898." I am indebted to Susan Salm and Arianna Kalian for help in translating the inscription.
28. Mary L. McClure to MKS, January 7, 1949, SIMSCH, box 1, folder 20.
29. Vida Scudder to MKS, January 7, 1949, SIMSCH, box 1, folder 20.
30. The two photos, inscribed in German, one to Anne O'Hagan, January 12, 1897, and the other to Ida Davis Ripley, December 16, 1896, are currently in the possession of Andrea Didisheim.
31. Michael T. Florinsky, "Memorial Minutes Presented at the Meeting of the Faculty of Political Science," Columbia University, April 22, 1960, SIMSCH, box 1, folder 8.
32. Annie F. Ware to friend, SIMSCH, box 2, folder 21.

CHAPTER 5

1. The average salary for a teacher in New York City in 1900 was $600 for females and $900 for males. Mary's $1,000 salary was equivalent to about $32,000 in today's dollars.
2. See *Annual Report of Friendly Aid*, Columbia University. The suite designated for the head worker at Friendly Aid was inviting enough. On the quiet, garden side of the main floor, it had its own sitting room, along with a bedroom. Resident workers would sleep in small bedrooms on the top two floors and socialize in the large parlor on the street side of the main floor. Everyone ate together in a dining room on ground/basement level.
3. Friendly Aid had previously operated a social center in another location but without a resident head worker.
4. Domenica Maria Barbuto, "The Matrix of Understanding: The Life and Work of Mary Kingsbury Simkhovitch," Ph.D. diss., State University of New York at Stony Brook, 1991, 2.
5. When Taylor retired as director of the Chicago Commons in 1922, his daughter took his place, and the Commons continued to operate into the twenty-first century.
6. Katherine Kish Sklar, *Florence Kelley & the Nation's Work: The Rise of Women's Political Culture, 1830–1900* (Yale University Press, 1995), 96.

7. Sklar, *Florence Kelley & the Nation's Work*, 167–168.
8. Halle-Wittenburg resulted from the merger in 1817 of two older universities, Halle and Wittenberg. It was located in Halle, about one hundred southwest of Berlin. *Columbia Alumni News*, October 19, 1917, 88, noted Halle-Wittenburg's superb reputation at the time Vladimir studied there. His dissertation, titled "The Field Association in Russia: A Contribution to Social History and to the Knowledge of the Current Economic Condition of Russian Peasants," treated an important topic at a time of rapid industrialization, and a German publisher, Jena, was issuing it in print. Eugen Diederichs Verlag started Jenna in 1896 to help scholars get attention for their work. Gary D. Stark wrote an article on Verlag in 2014, and when the author queried Stark on May 12, 2020, he replied that VGS's name did not turn up in his research as one who received help from Verlag.
9. Lucy Sprague Mitchell, *Two Lives* (Simon and Schuster, 1953), 90.
10. Mitchell, *Two Lives*, 91.
11. VGS's opinion of Professor Conrad, in response to Farnam Survey, is reported in Rodgers, *Atlantic Crossings*, 531, endnote 32.
12. Author's interview with Barbara Moravec, January 6, 1986, Ancient House, Manningtree, England.
13. MKS, *Neighborhood*, 87.
14. The Chapel of the Incarnation, a small Episcopal house of worship with an outstanding organ, was near the Friendly Aid settlement. The building is no longer standing, having been replaced in 1904. Mary had other Episcopal ties in the city, as illustrated by the fact that Percy Stickney Grant, rector from 1893–1924 of the Church of the Ascension, at Fifth Avenue and 10th Street, sent her as a wedding present a handsome *Book of Common Prayer*, which she later gifted to the wife of her grandson Paul Didisheim. I am grateful to Andrea Didisheim, current owner of the book, for sharing this information with me.
15. Nash was not a resident of New York, and it is possible he was not licensed to officiate at weddings.
16. Marion R. Taber to MKS, January 13, 1949, SIMSCH, box 1, folder 15.
17. *The Villager*, January 6, 1949, 1. The marriage certificate, obtained from the Department of Records and Information Services, Municipal Archives, 31 Chambers Street, New York, New York, lists both Ernest L. Bogart and Mary's brother, Isaac William Kingsbury, as witnesses, and Henry R. Wadleigh, vicar of the Chapel of the Incarnation, 240 East 31st Street, as performing the marriage. The Kingsbury family minister, Henry Nash, is not listed.
18. *New York Times*, June 30, 1901, reported on its front page that 200 horses had died from heat, and 18 dead horses were currently lying in the streets around Bellevue Hospital, not far from Friendly Aid.
19. MKS, *Neighborhood*, 83.
20. MKS, *Neighborhood*, 83.
21. A 1912 map of Manhattan shows St. Gabriel Park running from 35th to 36th Street and from First to Second Avenue. Its name was later changed to St. Vartan Park.
22. MKS, *Neighborhood*, 86.
23. Single women did not easily find housing in New York City at that time. See Harriet Fayes, "Housing of Single Women," *Municipal Affairs* 3 (1899): 95–107. Fayes argued that women married earlier than they otherwise would have because they could not find acceptable housing as single women. She wrote that if the "smart, clever businesswoman" had "clean safe housing," she would not jump at the first marriage proposal but would wait to make a "good marriage."

24. MKS, *Neighborhood*, 81–82.
25. Author's interview with Paul Didisheim, Washington, DC, June 25, 1987.
26. VGS review of *Geschichte der Russische Fabrik*, in *Political Science Quarterly* 16 (March 1901): 153–155.
27. The author is indebted to Susan Abele, Newton, Massachusetts, for information on the history of the Social Science Club and the town of Newton.
28. In addition to the article already published in *Municipal Affairs* in 1898, MKS had also finished "Friendship and Politics," scheduled for publication in *Political Science Quarterly* 17 (June 1902).
29. *Newton Graphic*, April 26, 1901, 6.
30. *Newton Graphic*, April 26, 1901, 6.
31. MKS, *Here Is God's Plenty*, 25.
32. Letter from Advisory Board to Mrs. Vladimir G. Simkhovitch, June 4, 1901, SIMSCH, box 2, folder 27.
33. MKS to Elsie Clews Parsons, December 25, 1901, in Elsie Clews Parsons Papers, Rye Historical Society, Rye, New York. I am grateful to Patricia Auspos for sharing this source.
34. EK to MKS, no date, SIMSCH, box 2, folder 27.
35. MKS to Elsie Clews Parsons, May 20, 1902, Elsie Clews Parsons Papers, Rye Historical Society, Rye, New York. Shared with author by Patricia Auspos.
36. MKS wrote to Elsie Clews Parsons, probably June 5, 1902, that "his empty bed makes horrid fancies in one's head." Letter is in Elsie Clews Parsons Papers, Rye Historical Society, Rye, New York. Shared with author by Patricia Auspos.
37. MKS to Elsie Clews Parsons, May 28, 1902, Elsie Clews Parsons Papers, Rye Historical Society, Rye, New York. Shared with author by Patricia Auspos.
38. MKS, *Neighborhood*, 82.
39. MKS, *Neighborhood*, 86.
40. Richard H. Evansley to MKS, May 10, 1902, SIMSCH, box 2, folder 27.
41. David Klaassen to author, September 29, 1982. Minnesota's collection of papers from the National Federation of Settlements and Neighborhood Centers includes Friendly Aid records from the early twentieth century, when MKS worked there. Columbia University holds more complete records of the Goddard-Riverside Community Center, the umbrella group under which Friendly Aid operated, and Columbia's description notes that the annual reports (subseries I.4) document the work of Mary Simkhovitch before she started Greenwich House. The description does not clarify that Simkhovitch's name is mentioned in the original reports.
42. Josephine Shaw Lowell to MKS, undated letter, SIMSCH, box 2, folder 27.
43. EK to MKS, no date, SIMSCH, box 2, folder 27.
44. MKS to EK, no date, SIMSCH, box 2, folder 27.
45. EK to MKS, no date, SIMSCH, box 2, folder 27.
46. Although the incorporating papers for the Cooperative Social Settlement Society were filed in 1902, Mary, with her usual disregard for dates, gets this wrong in *Neighborhood*, when she writes on page 90, "It was in May, 1901, that the Cooperative Social Settlement Society was founded."
47. James Sheerin, *Henry Codman Potter, an American Metropolitan* (Fleming H. Revell Co., 1933), 177. Potter also had access to money, having married Elizabeth Scrivin Clark, widow of Alfred Corning Clark, who died in 1896 leaving an immense estate for the time, $25 million. On Clark's wealth, see Jack Buckman, *Unraveling the Threads* (Dog Ear Publishing, 2016) on the Singer Sewing Machine fortune that Clark's father inherited.

48. Howard B. Radest, *Towards Common Ground: The Story of the Ethical Societies in the United States* (Ungar, 1969), gives Felix Adler prime place in starting such organizations.
49. Constitution of the Co-operative Social Settlement Society of the City of New York, dated May 26, 1902, GHRTAM, box 1, folder 1.
50. Meredith Hare, treasurer, initial report on Greenwich House, SIMSCH, box 2, folder 27.
51. MKS, "Friendship and Politics," *Political Science Quarterly* xvii, no. 2 (June 1902).
52. MKS to Else Clews Parsons, June 27, 1902. Elsie Clews Parsons Papers, Rye Historical Society, Rye, New York. Shared with author by Patricia Auspos.
53. MKS to Elsie Clews Parsons, no date, Elsie Clews Papers, Rye Historical Society, Rye, New York. Brought to author's attention by Patricia Auspos.
54. Paul Kennaday to MKS, July 29, 1902, GHRTAM, box 21, folder 8.
55. William Potts to MKS, July 28, 1902, GHRTAM, box 21, folder 10.
56. See comments by MKS in *New York Times Magazine*, May 22, 1932, 12.
57. MKS to Meredith Hare, August 4, 1902, GHRTAM, box 21, folder 10. When MKS deemed work being done with Italians as "relatively very little," she was referring to the West Side Branch that her friends at University Settlement had opened at 38 King Street in December 1900. Under the aegis of James B. Reynolds, the West Branch had not done well. Reynolds was disappointed with Edith Thomas, the head worker whom he had assigned to the West Branch, and by March of 1901, he was planning to replace her. He had asked MKS for suggestions, specifying that he wanted someone "neither too young, too handsome, nor too stylish but a fair amount of all these qualities will not be an objection...someone who has for some time been devoted to good works but would like to continue that devotion at sweat shop wages." (Source is Reynolds to MKS, March 13, 1901, University Settlement Society Papers, reel 6.) When Edith Thomas heard she was being replaced, she was devastated, and on May 14, 1901, she shot herself in her second-floor bedroom at the King Street settlement while her husband and Reynolds were conversing on the floor below. The *New York Herald* carried the story the next day with the headline "Lived to Aid Others, Dies by her Own Hand," and the *New York Evening Journal* ran a photo of Thomas with the headline "Writer Who Shot Herself Is Mourned by the Poor." The West Side Branch catered to the heavily Italian population, with a gym, dozens of clubs and classes, a library, and penny savings bank. For information on Edith Thomas and the West Side Branch, see Gerald W. McFarland, *Inside Greenwich Village: A New York City Neighborhood, 1898–1918* (University of Massachusetts Press Books, 2001), 52–53. Reports of the University Settlement Society can be seen on HathiTrust. The West Side Branch was separated from University Settlement in 1903, but the larger organization continued to pay the rent for a year so that a group could reopen as Richmond Hill House at 28 MacDougal Street and use the house on King Street as residential hall for its staff. Richmond Hill continued to be important to the Italian community, and in 1910, when the Russell Sage Foundation initiated a study of Italian women in industry, Richmond Hill House supplied many of the informants and a home base for the investigators. See MacFarland, *Inside Greenwich Village*, 58. In 1901 MKS checked with University Settlement about opening a second settlement in Greenwich Village and was encouraged to proceed.
58. MKS to Meredith Hare, August 18, 1902, GHRTAM, box 21, folder 10.
59. MKS to Elsie Clews Parsons, mid-September 1902, Elsie Clews Parsons Papers, Rye Historical Society, Rye, New York. Shared with author by Patricia Auspos.

60. Kathryn Kish Sklar, "Who Funded Hull House?" in Kathleen McCarthy, *Lady Bountiful Revisited: Women, Philanthropy, and Power* (Rutgers University Press, 1990). See 95ff on how Addams inherited a sizable estate—about $50,000 in 1881—and used part of this inheritance to fund Hull House in the early years, contributing a total of $14,684 in the first four years.
61. MKS to Elsie Clews Parsons, no date, but internal evidence places it early fall, 1902, Elsie Clews Parsons Papers, Rye Historical Society, Rye, New York. Shared with author by Patricia Auspos.
62. MKS to Elsie Clews Parsons, September 1902, Elsie Clews Parsons Papers, Rye Historical Society, Rye, New York. Shared with author by Patricia Auspos.
63. Annual Report, 1902–03, GHRTAM, box 1, folder 16.
64. O'Hagan, *The Woman Citizen*, November 1927, 13.

CHAPTER 6

1. MKS, *Neighborhood*, 95.
2. "Dr. Simkhovitch Recalls," *The Villager*, April 30, 1942, 10.
3. S. J. Wolf, "Thirty Years of Work for 'The Village': Mrs. Simkhovitch of Greenwich House Gives the Results of an Experiment in Friendship and Neighborliness," *New York Times*, May 22, 1932, 12.
4. MKS, *Neighborhood*, 138.
5. Seventh Avenue opened to traffic below 14th Street in 1912. The Sixth Avenue subway line was completed in 1926, and the street opened to vehicular traffic in 1927.
6. McFarland, *Inside Greenwich Village*, 62.
7. In discussing Italian immigration, it is important to remember that US Immigration officials classified as Northern Italians only those from the three northern regions of Italy. All others, including Tuscans and Romans, were listed as Southern Italians. Using that definition, Northern Italians dominated early immigration to the United States. In New York City, they marked their presence by establishing the St. Anthony of Padua parish in 1886, at the intersection of Houston and Sullivan Streets. As Southern Italians increased in numbers, soon dwarfing the Northern Italians, they wanted a church named for one of their saints. They proceeded gradually, first renting space on Bleecker Street and then acquiring a building farther west with a history reflecting the changing population. After starting as a meeting place for Unitarian Universalists, it became a place of worship for African Americans in 1883, and then a Roman Catholic church in 1898, with a name reminiscent of the congregants' origins in southern Italy—Our Lady of Pompeii. That building was destroyed when Sixth Avenue was extended in 1927, and the current Church of Our Lady of Pompeii was built at the intersection of Bleecker and Carmine Streets.
8. MKS, *Neighborhood*, 92–93.
9. MKS *Neighborhood*, 96.
10. MKS, *Neighborhood*, 96.
11. Annual Report, 1902–03, GHRTAM, box 1, folder 16.
12. Report in February 1903, GHRTAM, box 1, folder 16.
13. Report in February 1903, GHRTAM, box 1, folder 16.
14. Annual Report, 1902–03, GHRTAM, box 1, folder 16.
15. Director's Report, GHRTAM, box 1, folder 1.

16. Meredith Hare, treasurer, statement of principles and appeal for funds, no date, SIMSCH, box 1, folder 29.
17. Mr. I. F. Morton, 32 Jones Street, attended his first meeting of the GH board on January 21, 1904. GHRTAM, box 1, folder 17.
18. MKS, *Neighborhood*, 94.
19. Minutes of GH board, May 18, 1904, GHRTAM, box 1, folder 17.
20. MKS, *Neighborhood*, 157, reported that the music school had its beginnings on the parlor floor of 18 Jones Street, purchased in 1909, then moved to 44 Barrow Street when that building was purchased in 1913. Pottery classes moved to 18 Jones Street; 20 Jones Street became the men's residence. See MKS, *Neighborhood*, 179.
21. Reports of meetings in 1905: May 24, June 21, October 18, and November 22, GHRTAM, box 1, folder 18.
22. Director's Report, GH board meeting, April 20, 1904, GHRTAM, box 1, folder 17.
23. Crystal Eastman to Max Eastman, no date, Crystal Eastman Papers, Schlesinger Library, Radcliffe Institute, Harvard University, folder 169.
24. *The Villager*, April 30, 1942, 9, summarizes the operation of the Greenwich House nursery school over several decades.
25. Minutes, June 1903, GHRTAM, box 1, folder 16.
26. Minutes, November 1903, GHRTAM, box 1, folder 16.
27. Minutes, November 1903, GHRTAM, box 1, folder 16. Also see Second Annual Report, 1904, 7–8, in box 1, folder 17.
28. Annual Report, 1, 1902–1903, GHRTAM, box 1, folder 16.
29. On discussion of the "colored [sic] population," see minutes of board meeting, November 18, 1903, including the director's report of nightly fighting on Cornelia Street. Also minutes of the Greenwich House Board meeting, January 21, 1904, including the director's request for investigation into the need for social work among the "colored [sic] community." Also Annual Report, 2, 1903–04. The death rate in 1901 for the city was 20.69 per thousand, much lower than in the Black neighborhood, where it reached 28.68 per thousand. GHRTAM, box 1, folders 16–17.
30. Board meeting minutes of March 15, 1905, GHRTAM, box 1, folder 18.
31. Annual Report, October 1907, lists 5 visits to "colored" [sic] families, 145 visits to Italians, and 90 visits to Irish. GHRTAM, box 1, folder 6.
32. MacFarland, *Inside Greenwich Village*, chap. 2, "For Their Mutual Benefit," 62, notes that "no African American was included among the incorporators or, for that matter, on any other board of the fledgling settlement." MacFarland continues, however, that "this did not indicate any antipathy on Simkhovitch's part toward the settlement's black [sic] neighbors." She "expressed admiration for the 'dignified manners' of African American 'ministers from the South' who lodged at a boardinghouse across the street from Greenwich House."
33. Elisabeth Lasch-Quinn, *Black Neighbors: Race and the Limits of Reform in the American Settlement House Movement, 1890–1945* (University of North Carolina Press, 1993), 1.
34. Allen F. Davis, *Spearheads for Reform* (Oxford University Press, 1967), 95.
35. Lasch-Quinn, *Black Neighbors*, 3.
36. Dorothy Salem, *To Better Our World: Black Women in Organized Reform, 1890–1920* (Carlson, 1990), 65–100.
37. Judith Trolander, *Professionalism and Social Change: From the Settlement House Movement to Neighborhood Centers, 1886 to the Present* (Columbia University Press, 1987), 137–40.

38. Jacqueline Anne Rouse, *Lugenia Burns Hope: Black Southern Reformer* (University of Georgia Press, 1989), 90.
39. Director's Report, June 18, 1903, GHRTAM, box 1, folder 16.
40. Minutes, October 19, 1904, GHRTAM, box 1, folder 17.
41. Director's Report, June 18, 1903, GHRTAM, box 1, folder 16. According to McFarland, Hunter from University Settlement had formed a Child Labor Committee in 1902, comprising MKS from Friendly Aid, Lillian Wald from Henry Street, and others. They lobbied Albany in 1903, and four regulatory measures were passed that were among the strongest in the nation, although not as strong as the Child Labor Committee wanted. See Briggs, "Twenty Years at Greenwich House," 36.
42. Nancy Schromm Dye, *As Equals & As Sisters: Feminism, Unionism, and the Women's Trade Union League of New York* (University of Missouri Press, 1980), 21.
43. Dye, *As Equals & As Sisters*, 24, reports that in 1903, women made up only 3.7 percent of New York City's unionists. On 17, Dye writes that when the WTUL formed, 350,000 women were employed in the city. The majority had service jobs, as servants, domestic workers, waitresses, laundresses, and clerks. In 1900 132,535 women worked in factories, and it was to these semiskilled and unskilled that the WTUL directed its efforts.
44. Mary Dreier bestowed on O'Reilly a lifetime annuity that freed her to work full time in labor organizing. See Susan Ware, "Overlooked No More: Leonora O'Reilly, Suffragist Who Fought for Working Women," *New York Times*, August 21, 2020.
45. Dye, *As Equals & As Sisters*, 117. A document in the Didisheim Papers, written at the time of MKS's death in 1951, confirms that she continued to pay dues long after she had ceased to be active in the WTUL.
46. MKS to Elsie Clews Parsons, undated, 1903, Elsie Clews Papers, Rye Historical Society, Rye, New York. Shared with author by Patricia Auspos.
47. MKS to Elsie Clews Parsons, July 13, 1903, Elsie Clews Parsons Papers, Rye Historical Society, Rye, New York. Shared with author by Patricia Auspos.
48. MKS to Elsie Clews Parsons, October 17, (year not clear), Elsie Clews Parsons Papers, Rye Historical Society, Rye, New York. Shared with author by Patricia Auspos.
49. Crystal Eastman, letter to her mother, December 5, 1906, Crystal Eastman Papers, Schlesinger Library, Radcliffe Institute, Harvard University, folder 168.
50. Amy Aronson, *Crystal Eastman: A Revolutionary Life* (Oxford University Press, 2019), 86.
51. Aronson, 86, quotes Annis's letter to Crystal and concludes that the romance ended in June 1909 without Mary ever knowing about it.
52. VGS to Crystal Eastman, no date, Crystal Eastman Papers, Schlesinger Library, Radcliffe Institute, Harvard University, folder 196.
53. VGS to Crystal Eastman, no date, Crystal Eastman Papers, Schlesinger Library, Radcliffe Institute, Harvard University, folder 196.
54. VGS to Crystal Eastman, no date, Crystal Eastman Papers, Schlesinger Library, Radcliffe Institute, Harvard University, folder 196.
55. Crystal Eastman to her mother, March 29, 1907, Crystal Eastman Papers, Schlesinger Library, Radcliffe Institute, Harvard University, folder 169.
56. Author interview with Helena Didisheim, July 29, 1982, Robbinston, Maine.
57. Telegram from Prince Lvoff to VGS from St. Petersburg, April 11, 1907. Didisheim Papers. Courtesy of Andrea Didisheim. I am indebted to Alla Roytberg Esq. for rendering in English the transliteration from Russian of the original telegram asking Professor Simkhovitch to assist in forwarding to Prince Lyoff the money collected in America.

58. Franz Boas to "My dear Dr. Simkhovitch," May 11, 1903, Boas Collections at the American Philosophical Association.
59. Minutes, December 17, 1903, treasurer's report notes gift from Professor Seligman to the Greenwich House Committee on Social Investigations. GHRTAM, box 1, folder 16.
60. MKS brought Emily Dinwiddie to Greenwich House in March 1903, before the Committee on Social Investigations was formed. See Briggs, "Twenty Years at Greenwich House," 47. The manual did not sell enough copies to produce money for Greenwich House.
61. The definition was later amended to three families or more.
62. The structure at 31–33 Cornelia Street was built about 1859 on a double lot. Its ground floor had two storefronts on street level, with two apartments at the back and four families on each of the top three floors.
63. Frances Perkins, oral history, Columbia University, 393.
64. For Mary's views, see minutes of Greenwich House Board meeting, January 19, 1906, GHRTAM, box 3, folder 5.
65. Louise Bolard married while working at Greenwich House, and she occasionally published as Mrs. Charles More. See her report to Greenwich House Board at meeting on January 19, 1906, GHRTAM, box 3, folder 5.
66. Louise Bolard More, *Wage-Earners' Budgets: A Study of Standards and Cost of Living in New York City* (Henry Holt and Co., 1907; reprinted by Arno Press, Inc., 1971), 64.
67. More, *Wage-Earners' Budgets*, 62. Also see M. L. Nassau's *Old Age Poverty in Greenwich Village* (1913) and MKS's book *The City Worker's World in America* (1917) All pointed to settlement houses as helping to improve working conditions. These and other books documented the unsafe conditions in sweatshops, health hazards, and lengthy hours of factory work.
68. Franz Boas to "My dear Dr. Simkhovitch," March 15, 1906, Boas Collection at the American Philosophical Association.
69. Greenpoint Settlement, a model tenement building on 23rd Street in Brooklyn.
70. Mary White Ovington, *The Walls Came Tumbling Down* (Harcourt Brace, 1947), 13.

CHAPTER 7

1. *Sunday Evening Star*, May 23, 1909, 1.
2. Proceedings of the First National Conference on City Planning, May 21–22, 1909, published by the American Society of Planning Offices, 1313 East 60th Street, Chicago, September 1967, 101–103.
3. Proceedings of the First National Conference on City Planning, May 21–22, 1909, 101–103.
4. Corinne Rieder, secretary of the Trustees of Lowe Memorial Library, Columbia University, supplied these records to author, April 1988.
5. Annual Report, 1907/08, and Annual Report, 1908/09, GHRTAM, box 1, folder 6.
6. MKS, *Neighborhood*, 132, gives the New Jersey address of the farm as Whitehouse.
7. Laura Kingsbury to "My dear Mary," November 8, 1908, SIMSCH, box 7, folder 124.
8. Laura Kingsbury to MKS, no date, SIMSCH, box 7, folder 124.
9. Laura Kingsbury to MKS, no date, SIMSCH, box 7, folder 124.
10. Laura Kingsbury to MKS, no date, SIMSCH, box 7, folder 124.
11. Deed for 108-acre property Mary Simkhovitch purchased from Anna Mary Burkey, April 14, 1909, in Readington Township, Hunterdon County, New Jersey, is at SIMSCH, box 1, folder 7.

12. MKS, *Neighborhood*, 133–134.
13. MKS, *Neighborhood*, 133. MKS wrote that she bought the farm in 1908 and sold it in 1925, but the deed shows purchase in early 1909.
14. MKS, *Neighborhood*, 134.
15. MKS, *Neighborhood*, 134–135.
16. Author's interview with Helena Didisheim, July 29, 1982, Robbinston, Maine.
17. Laura Kingsbury to MKS, no date, SIMSCH, box 7, folder 124.
18. Laura Kingsbury to MKS, no date, SIMSCH, box 7, folder 124.
19. The Didisheim Papers, in possession of Andrea Didisheim, include eleven ribbons for first prize from the Paterson, New Jersey, Poultry Association and four from the Easton Poultry Association. VGS also picked up two first prizes and one second prize from the Empire Poultry Association and another first at Madison Square Garden.
20. MKS to Frank Kingsbury, no date, SIMSCH, box 7, folder 124.
21. The two courses were "Economic and Social Evolution of Russia since 1800" in the fall semester and "Radicalism and Social Reform as Reflected in the Literature of the 19th Century" in the spring semester.
22. MKS to Frank Kingsbury, no date, SIMSCH, box 7, folder 124.
23. MKS to Laura and Frank, from Orlanova, no date, SIMSCH, box 7, folder 24.
24. MKS to Frank Kingsbury, no date, SIMSCH, box 7, folder 124.
25. Words of song sung at Thanksgiving Dinner, November 22, 1915, in GHRTAM, box 2, folder 7.
26. Laura Kingsbury to MKS, undated letter, SIMSCH, box 7, folder 124.
27. Helena Simkhovitch to Frank Kingsbury, April 7, 1917, SIMSCH, box 1, folder 10.
28. Helena Simkhovitch to Laura Kingsbury, May 9, 1916, SIMSCH, box 1, folder 10.
29. Bess Child to MKS, no date, SIMSCH, box 1, folder 10.
30. Helena Didisheim to author, July 29, 1982, Robbinston, Maine. Elisabeth Israels Perry, who visited the Didisheims earlier to assess the value of the Simkhovitch Papers for the Schlesinger Library, reported to author she heard similar complaints from Helena Didisheim.
31. Florence Kelley to MKS, October 4, 1912, GHRTAM, box 18, folder 52.
32. Author's interview with Gerry McGerr, August 20, 1981, Riverdale, New York.
33. Merlo Pusey, *Eugene Meyer* (Knopf, 1974), 26.
34. Olivia Howard Dunbar, "A Great Profession for women—Social Service," *New York Times*, July 31, 1910, 11.
35. William M. Ivins Jr. in a condolence letter to Helena Didisheim at the death of VGS. Didisheim Papers. Courtesy of Andrea Didisheim.
36. See the Didisheim Papers for documents showing that VGS attended the club's banquet in 1906, with Mary's brother, Will Kingsbury, as his guest.
37. VGS to Frank Kingsbury at 73 Perkins Street, West Newton, Massachusetts, December 31, 1903, SIMSCH, box 1, folder 9.
38. VGS, *Marxism Versus Socialism* (Henry Holt and Co., 1913), xv.
39. VGS, *Education Review*, May 1907, 486–522. He specifically recommended less authoritarianism (separating the school from the police department) and better treatment of teachers (especially in regulations and pay).
40. VGS, *Bookman*, March 1907; VGS, *International*, July 1905.
41. "The Russian Peasant and Autocracy" in *Political Science Quarterly*, March 1905; "Russia's Struggle with Autocracy," in *Political Science Quarterly*, December 1906. *Political Science Quarterly* 23, no. 2 (June 1908): 123–129.
42. Author's interview with Helena Didisheim, July 29, 1982, Robbinston, Maine.

43. The Morgan Library did not become a public institution until 1924.
44. See *Wasau (WI) Daily Herald*, October 14, 1913, 7, for evidence of Morgan arranging with VGS for the collection of early church manuscripts and books to be put on exhibition in Wisconsin. The Morgan Archives also list communications between VGS and Belle da Costa Greene on how exhibitions should be publicized. She "objected violently" to a decision in one instance.
45. Born in Virginia in 1883, Greene attended Northfield Seminary for Young Ladies and briefly Amherst before taking a job in the Princeton library in 1901, under the supervision of Charlotte Martins in the Purchase Department. Her father, Richard Theodore Greener, had separated from his family when she was young, and both she and her mother underscored the break by deleting the final "r" to their last name. Belle added a middle name, da Costa, and attributed it to a Portuguese grandmother, thus accounting for her dark complexion. Belle's father had won acclaim as the first African American to graduate from Harvard, but she wanted nothing of that identification, and both she and her mother passed as white.
46. With the backing of Grace Dodge, who knew Greene at Columbia, Greene attended Northfield Seminary for Young Ladies and then took a summer course in library science at Amherst. A catalog published to accompany the 2024 exhibition on Greene at the Morgan Library explores her life and contributions: *Belle da Costa Greene: A Librarian's Legacy*, ed. Erica Ciallela et al. (Delmonico Books/Morgan Library and Museum, 2024).
47. Century's website lists both Woodbridge and Grant as VGS's sponsors when they proposed him for membership in March 1906. Others who signed in support of VGS were a mixed lot: merchant, chemist, author, lawyer, real estate developer, and two professors. I am grateful to Tim DeWerff for directing me to this source.
48. Quoted in Heidi Ardizzone, *An Illuminated Life* (W. W. Norton & Co., 2007), 103. Letter written January 25, 1909, in Archives of the Morgan Library, Morgan Collections Correspondence ARC1310.
49. *New York Tribune*, March 27, 1915, 9.
50. Mike Wallace, *Greater Gotham, 1898–1919* (Oxford University Press, 2017), 262.
51. Eugenie Ladner Birch, "Edith Elmer Wood and the Genesis of Liberal Housing Thought, 1910–1942," Ph.D. diss., Columbia University, 1975, 182.
52. *New York Times*, March 29, 1908, pt. 2, 8.
53. MKS, speech reported in *Proceedings of the First National Conference on City Planning*, Washington, DC, 1909, 101–104, https://catalog.hathitrust.org/Record/102357784. Accessed March 21, 2024.
54. In 1852 Carola's maternal grandmother, Anna Uhl, assumed full control of the *Staats-Zeitung* after her husband died, leaving her with very little money and six children to support. For a while, she managed on her own, but in 1859 she married Oswald Ottendorfer, an editorial writer on the paper, and together they converted it to a profitable enterprise. Anna Ottendorfer then turned to philanthropy, endowing a home for aged German American women, German reading rooms, and hospitals. Her daughter, Anna, also became a supporter of many causes. She married Wall Street banker Charles Woerishoffer, and Carola was the younger of two daughters born to them.
55. VGS's *Marxism Versus Socialism* was published in book form in 1913, after Woerishoffer's death, but the essays included had appeared earlier in *Political Science Quarterly*. See xv for VGS's praise for both Carola Woerishoffer and MKS. MKS credited an early resident of Greenwich House, Henry Mussey, for directing Carola Woerishoffer to the settlement. Mussey taught at Barnard and Bryn Mawr, where Carola was a student.

56. Mrs. V. G. Simkhovitch, "Standards and Tests of Efficiency in Settlement Work," *Conference of Charities and Corrections*, 1911, 299–305.
57. Director's Report, October 20, 1909, GRHTAM, box 1, folder 22. Also see records on the purchase of these three buildings in GHRTAM, box 7, folder 5. The front of 16 Jones was torn down, and the rear turned over to Maude Robinson and Camilla Mason for pottery classes. Number 20 became a dormitory for male volunteers.
58. Briggs, "Twenty Years at Greenwich House," 124, notes the appointment came in November 1909. The St. Louis conference took place in 1910, and Jane Addams presided. New York Governor Charles Evans Hughes named Mrs. V. Simkhovitch to the State Commission on the Distribution of the Population in October 1910. See *New York Times*, October 17, 1910, 6.
59. MKS, "Statement on Behalf of the Equal Franchise Society," GHRTAM, box 22, folder 32.
60. Mary Donovan, "We Develop Through Inter-relatedness: A Study of the Social Service Networks of Mary Kingsbury Simkhovitch." Didisheim Papers. Courtesy of Andrea Didisheim.
61. Donovan, "We Develop Through Inter-relatedness."
62. Briggs, "Twenty Years at Greenwich House," 124, citing minutes of March 1910.
63. *Pittsburgh Gazette Times*, September 20, 1913, 3: "I became a suffragist through my work…during the last 15 years I became convinced of the need for woman's vote to improve conditions in the neighborhoods [in which] we work."
64. *Washington Post*, October 27, 1914, 7.
65. Annual Report, 1914/15, GHRTAM, box 1, folder 8.
66. "Meeting of Federation of Graduate Clubs of American Universities," (Baltimore) *Sun*, December 30, 1896, 6.
67. *Boston Globe*, October 26, 1897, 4.
68. *Yonkers Statesman*, March 16, 1898, 1.
69. For details of Carola Woerishoffer's life, see Roderick W. Nash, "Emma Carola Woerishoffer," in *Notable American Women*, vol. 3, 639–641. Also see *Carola Woerishoffer: Her Life and Work* (Class of 1907 of Bryn Mawr College, Bryn Mawr, 1912), for tributes by Ida Tarbell, Vladimir and Mary Simkhovitch, and others.
70. Anna Woerishoffer to VG and MKS, December 23 (no year). Didisheim Papers. Courtesy of Andrea Didisheim.
71. Minutes of a Special Meeting of the Board of Managers, February 3, 1912, GHRTAM, box 4, folder 4.
72. MKS to Frank Kingsbury, January 11, 1914, when Frank was staying in Hartford at 4 Atwood Street. Didisheim Papers. Courtesy of Andrea Didisheim.
73. *New York Tribune*, January 23, 1919, 11, reported Vincent Pepe, a local real estate agent, had leased the apartment to VGS, W. R. Browne, and another man whose name is not clear in the newspaper article. In registering for the draft in 1917, Vladimir gave his residence as 103 Waverley Place. Two years later, he was renting an apartment at 66 West 12th Street.

CHAPTER 8

1. Robert M. Fogelson, *The Great Rent Wars, New York, 1917–1918* (Yale University Press, 2013). Chapter 1 is titled "The Great Rent Strikes."
2. Fogelson, *The Great Rent Wars*, 111. Fogelson is quoting from Lockwood hearings, vol. 2.
3. Fogelson, *The Great Rent Wars*, 142.

4. Fogelson, *The Great Rent Wars*, 111, citing *Proceedings of the 7th National Conference on Housing*, 1918, 291.
5. Roy Lubove, *The Progressive and the Slums: Tenement House Reform in New York City, 1890–1917* (University of Pittsburgh Press, 1962) 151ff, section titled "Age of Veiller." For more on Veiller's impact, see Roy Lubove, "Lawrence Veiller," *Mississippi Valley Historical Review* 47, no. 4 (March 1961): 659–677.
6. Edith Elmer Wood, *The Housing of the Unskilled Wage Earner: America's Next Problem* (Macmillan Co., 1919).
7. Birch, "Edith Elmer Wood."
8. Nicholas Dagen Bloom and Matthew Gordon Lasner, eds., *Affordable Housing in New York: The People, Places, and Policies That Transformed a City* (Princeton University Press, 2016). Kindle edition.
9. Author interview with Charles Woolley, November 9, 1982, 26 Jones Street, NYC.
10. Clare Sheridan, *My American Diary* (Boni and Liveright, 1922), 73.
11. Twenty-seven Barrow Street is near what became the intersection of Christopher Street and Seventh Avenue, and Seventh Avenue was being extended below 14th Street about the time the lots that became 27 Barrow were acquired.
12. In 1914 Delano and Aldrich completed a home at Fifth Avenue and 94th Street for Willard Straight, the young investment banker who had married Dorothy Payne Whitney (born 1887), one of the wealthiest women in the world after her father, William Collins Whitney, died in 1904.
13. MKS's instructions to architects, reported in *Neighborhood*, 180.
14. Although transfer of offices and activities occurred in the late fall, the official opening was in January 1918.
15. Dorothy Mackamer, quoted in Director's Report, October 18, 1923, GHRTAM, box 2, folder 1.
16. The meeting room next to the director's apartment was named the "Mary Kingsbury Room."
17. Description of GH is in Annual Report, 1916/1917. GHRTAM, box 1, folder 8.
18. Dorothy Mackamer, quoted in Director's Report, October 18, 1923, GHRTAM, box 2, folder 1.
19. Charles Woolley conducted the author on a tour of his apartment at 26 Jones Street on November 9, 1982. He pointed out that the kitchen, obviously an addition to the building, was "probably illegal." Other information on Woolley comes from his obituary, *New York Times*, November 13, 1986.
20. Author's interview with Gerald McGerr, August 20, 1981, Riverdale, New York. A record of his residence at GH is at GHRTAM, box 15, folder 14.
21. Information on Theodore Barbato was furnished to the author by his daughter, Eleanor Jenkins, and by Robert M. Belmonte, Bethlehem, Pennsylvania. August Belmonte, father of Robert, was also a member of the Stoic Club.
22. Females did not get the right to vote in national elections in Italy until 1945, although participation in some local elections was permitted earlier.
23. MKS, "A New Social Adjustment," *Proceedings of the Academy of Political Science of New York City* I, no. 1 (October 1910): 81–90, discusses ethnic differences among Jewish, Irish, and Italian women who came to Greenwich House. MKS wrote that the Italian "girl" differed from the Irish "girl" in that she had been "constantly chaperoned and is going from a carefully controlled situation to an uncontrolled one—a difficult change. All immigrant women who work need proper opportunities for pleasure, a living wage, and the cultivation of independence, self-respect, and idealism."

24. Helen Josephine Ferris and Virginia Moore, *Girls Who Did: Stories of Real Girls and their Careers*. (E. P. Dutton & Co., 1927), 253–269.
25. Annual Report, 1915/1916, GHRTAM, box 1, folder 8.
26. Director's Report, November 21, 1918, GHRTAM, box 1, folder 31.
27. Annual Report, 1915/1916, GHRTAM, box 1, folder 8.
28. Allen F. Davis, *American Heroine: The Life and Legend of Jane Addams* (Oxford University Press, 1973), 223.
29. MKS, *The City Worker's World in America* (Macmillan Co., 1917; reprint by Arno & New York Times, 1971).
30. MKS, *The City Worker's World*, 18.
31. MKS, speech at Boston University, June 8, 1916, SIMSCH, box 3, folder 60.
32. MKS, "A Settlement War Program," *Survey*, May 5, 1917, gives a summary of the results of her poll of settlements, revealing what settlement workers thought they should be doing after the United States entered the war in April 1917.
33. Robert K. Murray, *Red Scare: A Study in National Hysteria, 1919–1920* (University of Minnesota Press, 1955), 98.
34. *New York Times*, May 10 and May 15, 1921.
35. MKS to A. E. Stevenson, counsel to the Lusk Committee, November 18, 1919, GHRTAM, box 19, folder 16.
36. MKS to A. E. Stevenson, November 18, 1919, GHRTAM, box 19, folder 16.
37. MKS to A. E. Stevenson, December 1, 1919, GHRTAM, box 19, folder 16.
38. Copy of letter to Mary Simkhovitch from the Committee of Seven, asking her to join in their effort, January 10, 1920, GHRTAM, box 17B, folder 98, has "Done" in her handwriting across the top.
39. *New York Times*, May 26, 1923, on Governor Al Smith's signing the bills that revoked the Lusk laws.
40. MKS to James J. Walker, undated memo, GHRTAM, box 22, folder 49.
41. MKS, memorandum re: Lusk Bills, May 20, 1920, GHRTAM, box 19, folder 16.
42. MKS, memorandum re: Lusk Bills, May 20, 1920, GHRTAM, box 19, folder 16.
43. *Forest Hills Garden Bulletin*, March 19, 1921, 1. I am grateful to Nora Mandel for providing me with this bulletin.
44. *Forest Hills Garden Bulletin*, March 19, 1921.
45. *New York Times*, October 17, 1918, 20.
46. *New York Times*, November 1, 1918, 7.
47. MKS, "Church and Woman Suffrage," GHRTAM, box 22, folder 47.
48. Donovan, "We Develop Through Inter-relatedness," 12, cites as sources MKS to Mrs. Victor Morawetz, June 14, 1917; and *New York Times*, November 8 and November 24, 1917.
49. Percy Stickney Grant was rector of Church of the Ascension, 10th Street and Fifth Avenue, from 1893–1924.
50. Author's interview with Helena Didisheim, Robbinston, Maine, July 29, 1982.
51. Author's information on history of the Society of the Companions of the Holy Cross came from Ruth S. Leonard, archivist of the Society, 370 Longwood Avenue, Boston, Massachusetts. A statement supplied by Leonard clarified that the society is "not a religious order" but a society of about 700 members (in 1982) "who are bound together in 'companionship'... with special concern for social justice, Christian unity, and the mission of the [Anglican] church." Membership is by invitation only. MKS joined in 1916.
52. Accession records at the Metropolitan Museum of Art show it acquired from Vladimir Simkhovitch eleven works of art in 1918, including tapestries, paintings, and Chinese scrolls. Amount paid is not recorded, but several of the Chinese scrolls were originally

attributed to earlier dynasties and then revised to later periods. William M. Ivins, VGS's friend in his early days at Columbia, abandoned a career in law in 1916 and became curator of the Met's new Department of Prints, where he remained until 1946.
53. Author's interview with Paul Didisheim, June 25, 1987, Washington, DC.
54. Helena Didisheim to author, July 29, 1982.
55. Helena described her brother as "acting like a prince."
56. Author's interview with Charles Woolley, November 9, 1982, at 26 Jones Street, NYC.

CHAPTER 9

1. Muncy, *Creating a Female Dominion*.
2. Muncy, *Creating a Female Dominion*, 30.
3. Richard A. Meckel, *Save the Babies: American Public Health Reform and the Prevention of Infant Mortality, 1850–1929* (Johns Hopkins University Press, 1990).
4. Meckel, *Save the Babies*, 212.
5. Meckel, *Save the Babies*, 222.
6. MKS, *Neighborhood*, 198.
7. MKS, *Neighborhood*, 199.
8. In 2023 two bars operated in New York City using the Raines name: the Raines Law Room at the William Hotel, 24 East 39th Street, and the Raines Law Room, an "upscale cocktail bar" at 48 West 17th Street. The latter functioned like a speakeasy, and clients pushed a doorbell to be admitted.
9. John J. Peters, "The Story of the Committee of Fourteen of New York," *Journal of Social Hygiene* (July 1918): 358.
10. Letter signed "Very respectfully, a father" to Committee of Fourteen, July 28, 1908, GHRTAM, box 17B, folder 98.
11. Clipping, Records of Committee of Fourteen, GHRTAM, box 17B, folder 98.
12. Robert E. Humphrey, *Children of Fantasy: The First Rebels of Greenwich Village* (John Wiley & Sons, 1978). Christine Stansell, *American Moderns: Bohemian New York and the Creation of a New Century* (Metropolitan Books, 2000) does not include the Simkhovitches.
13. June Sochen, *Movers and Shakers: American Women Thinkers and Activists, 1900–1970* (Quadrangle/The New York Times Book Co., 1973), 79.
14. Director's Report, December 18, 1919, GHRTAM, box 1, folder 31.
15. Briggs, "Twenty Years at Greenwich House," 257.
16. The change occurred in 1928, and 18 Jones Street eventually became a highly respected pottery school, with its products going into the collections of major museums.
17. Gene Tunney won the light heavyweight title in 1922 and 1923, and then held the heavyweight title from 1926 to 1928. He later recounted how he came to Greenwich House at age sixteen and learned the fundamentals of boxing from Willie Green. SIMSCH, box 2, folder 22.
18. MKS, *Neighborhood*, 123–124, names Tunney as a boxing hero. ER mentioned Tunney's time at GH in her "My Day" column, October 25, 1951. None of Tunney's children followed his route to success. John Varick Tunney (1934–2018) was a US representative and US senator from California from 1965 to 1977. Son Gene became US district attorney for Sonoma County. The one daughter, Joan, convicted of murdering her husband, was committed to McClean Hospital on June 6, 1970, when she was thirty-one.
19. MKS ("Molly") to Laura Kingsbury, no date, SIMSCH, box 1, folder 11.

20. Although Stephen wrote about returning to the Taft School and his grandmother believed he was enrolled there, the school has no record of his attendance. Email from Christina Esmiol, assistant director of Annual Fund, Taft School, February 26, 2021.
21. I could not find Stephen Simkhovitch listed in Princeton directories online, but Glenda Geraci sent me a copy of Princeton Bric-A-Brac, freshman class, 1922, showing on page 63 that Stephen Kingsbury Simkhovitch, of 27 Barrow Street, New York City, was enrolled as a freshman. I am grateful to Glenda Geraci for this information.
22. Stephen Simkhovitch to Laura Kingsbury, postmarked September 1921. Didisheim Papers. Courtesy of Andrea Didisheim.
23. This may have been a reference to the money given to him and his sister by Carola Woerishoffer's mother after Carola's death. Laura Kingsbury had made a will in 1919, leaving $500 to Stephen, payable when he came of age. But he would not collect that until after her death.
24. Diary entry of Laura Kingsbury, May 12, 1923, SIMSCH, box 5, folder 101.
25. Dr. Salmon died at age fifty-one in the Long Island Sound after he fell from his forty-foot yacht and drowned in August 1927.
26. VGS to MKS, September 3, 1927, Didisheim Papers. Courtesy of Andrea Didisheim.
27. Stephen's whereabouts remain unclear. Although Princeton Bric-A-Brac listed him as a freshman in September 1922 (when he would have been twenty years old), his grandmother noted in her diary that he had done well on a test at Columbia six months later.
28. This was his grandson's later assessment. Glenda Geraci to author, email, July 15, 2020.
29. Quoted online in "Broadway and Hollywood Movies, 1932."
30. Tea Room, GHRTAM, box 24, folder 56, contains records of fundraising to open the tearoom and a summary of training to be offered.
31. Rumor persisted that Sonja had some money, the result of a settlement with a married man whose child she bore. But that child, Mary Jane, appears only as a ghostlike figure in Sonja's life. In one online entry, Mary Jane recalls playing under the tables in the tearoom where Sonja worked. That same online entry reports that Sonja sent Mary Jane to live with people she knew in Minnesota and ignored her for the rest of her long life.
32. Laura Kingsbury to MKS, February 26, 1931, Didisheim Papers. Courtesy of Andrea Didisheim.
33. Laura Kingsbury to MKS, February 28, 1931, Didisheim Papers. Courtesy of Andrea Didisheim.
34. Sonja Stockstad was not the only one who did not know where Stephen Simkhovitch was. It is not clear that he ever went to Brazil or picked up the checks his grandmother sent to him there. Very soon, however, he had settled in the Los Angeles area to work as a Hollywood writer.
35. Helen Murphy, letter to author, November 9, 1982.
36. Helen Murphy, letter to author, November 9, 1982.
37. Helen Murphy's papers, at the Tamiment Library, New York University, include photos, correspondence, and evidence of her training and of her work at Greenwich House over the time she worked there, 1922–1951.
38. *Daily News*, December 21, 1923, 30.
39. Eugene O'Neill to Helena Simkhovitch, September 15, 1924, and copy of letter from O'Neill to "Jimmy," September 24, 1924. Didisheim Papers. Courtesy of Andrea Didisheim.

40. Helena Simkhovitch to Laura Kingsbury, October 31, 1925, announced that Helena planned to sail in December or January. Didisheim Papers. Courtesy of Andrea Didisheim.
41. Helena Simkhovitch to Laura Kingsbury, October 31, 1925. Didisheim Papers. Courtesy of Andrea Didisheim.
42. Letter dated March 15, 1928, in Didisheim Papers, from editor of the *Nation* rejects Helena's piece on "literary news" because *Nation* does not publish that kind of article. Editor suggests taking the piece to the *Times* or *Tribune*. Another long letter in the Didisheim Papers from unsigned person indicates Helena is trying a writing career—she intends to write a book.
43. MKS to George Palmer Putnam, Earhart's husband, on September 30, 1938. Mary frequently mentioned that Vladimir knew some of the young, attractive residents at Greenwich House better than she did. Copy of letter is at SIMSCH, box 1, folder 13.
44. *Philadelphia Inquirer*, April 11, 1937, 102.
45. In addition to the MKS letter to Putnam, see Ariel Kates, "Amelia Earhart: Aviatrix, Feminist, Fashionista, Villager," Greenwich Village Society for Historical Preservation, *Newsletter*, July 24, 2019. Also see Fred Goerner, *The Search for Amelia Earhart* (Doubleday, 1966), 16.
46. Copy of telegram is in the Didisheim Papers. Original is in the Amelia Earhart Papers at Purdue University Libraries, Archives and Special Collections.
47. Obituary for Marion Tanner, *New York Times*, October 31, 1985.
48. The School of Philanthropy, sponsored by the Charity Organization Society, had offered courses in philanthropy from 1898, but it changed its name in 1917 to the New York School of Social Work. It later affiliated with Columbia and began offering a master's degree in social work in 1940.
49. Director's Report, January 18, 1924, GHRTAM, box 2, folder 2.
50. Director's Report, February 15, 1923, GHRTAM, box 2, folder 1.
51. Director's Report, April 17, 1924, GHRTAM, box 2, folder 2.
52. Unsigned letter to Mr. Parsons and Mr. Merritt, April 9, 1923, GHRTAM, box 20, folder 33.
53. Director's Report, May 31, 1923, GHRTAM, box 2, folder 1.
54. Memo, dated January 12, 1923, from secretary of MKS to "My dear Mr. Pepe" asking the real estate agent to indicate persons "that might be of help financially." GHRTAM, box 7, folder 2.
55. *New York Tribune*, January 8, 1922, 16, announced sale, and same paper on January 14 reported sales totaled $12, 225.50.
56. *New York Tribune*, January 14, 1922, 9.
57. MKS to Gerard Swope, February 20, 1924, GHRTAM, box 20, folder 52.
58. Marshall Field III, 1893–1954, was heir to the department store fortune. See *New York Times*, May 28, 1939, for information on his opening the garden at his country estate for the benefit of Greenwich House.
59. MKS to Cutting, January 15, 1925, GHRTAM, box 19, folder 24.
60. MKS to Cutting, January 15, 1925, GHRTAM, box 19, folder 24.
61. Director's Report, February 16, 1922, GHRTAM, box 1, folder 35.
62. MKS to Gerard Swope, January 29, 1925, GHRTAM, box 20, folder 53.
63. The offer is made in a letter from VGS to Gerard Swope, March 12, 1929, and that offer is referred to in a letter from Gerard Swope to Mrs. Robert J. F. Schwarzenbach, March 12, 1929. VGS had made four separate sales of Chinese paintings and scrolls to the Metropolitan Museum of Art in the 1920s according to accession records. I found no evidence that he gave the $10,000 or that matching funds materialized.

64. Greenwich House's association with Columbia University is documented in GHRTAM, box 21, folders 25–28.
65. "Women in Government," *New York Times*, November 12, 1987.
66. Caroline F. Ware, *Greenwich Village, 1920–1930* (Houghton Mifflin, 1935; reprint by University of California Press, 1994).
67. Ware, *Greenwich Village*, 119.
68. MKS to Professor MacIver, October 29, 1934, GHRTAM, box 4b, folder 18.
69. R. M. MacIver to Dr. Caroline F. Ware, October 30, 1934, GHRTAM, box 4b, folder 18.
70. Caroline F. Ware to author, July 7, 1988.
71. Ware, *Greenwich Village*, 89.
72. Ware, *Greenwich Village*, 373–374. Ware failed to give credit to Simkhovitch for incorporating the third "attitude" into Greenwich House's program. She had added a psychiatrist to the settlement house staff in 1927 but had to discontinue that service after two years because of lack of funding.
73. Susan Ware, *Partner and I: Molly Dewson, Feminism, and New Deal Politics*. (Yale University Press, 1987), 138.
74. Ware, *Partner and I*, 138 and footnote 19 on page 290.
75. HSD to MKS, no date, Didisheim Papers. Courtesy of Andrea Didisheim.
76. VGS to MKS, September 17, 1927, SIMSCH, box 1, folder 9.
77. VGS to MKS, September 3, 1927, Didisheim Papers. Courtesy of Andrea Didisheim.
78. VGS to MKS, September 3, 1927, Didisheim Papers. Courtesy of Andrea Didisheim.
79. VGS to MKS, September 5, no year, Didisheim Papers. Courtesy of Andrea Didisheim.
80. VGS to MKS, September 5, no year, Didisheim Papers. Courtesy of Andrea Didisheim.
81. Elisabeth Israels Perry, *After the Vote, Feminist Politics in La Guardia's New York* (Oxford University Press, 2019), 6.
82. Birch, "Edith Elmer Wood," 106.
83. Nicholas Dagen Bloom, *Public Housing That Worked: New York in the 20th Century* (University of Pennsylvania Press, 2009), 17.

CHAPTER 10

1. When White died in an ice-skating fall through the ice in 1921, he left his daughter $15 million. See *New York Times*, February 20, 2021, E1.
2. *New York Times*, quoted in Bloom and Lasner, eds., *Affordable Housing in New York*,. Kindle edition.
3. Eugenie Birch and Deborah Gardner, "The Seven Percent Solution, A Review of Philanthropic Housing, 1870–1910," *Journal of Urban History* (August 1981): 403–438. Provides an overview of attempts at philanthropic housing and how they failed.
4. *New York Times*, "Health and Profit," November 29, 1896, 13.
5. MKS, *Neighborhood*, 131.
6. Wood, *The Housing of the Unskilled Wage Earner*, 7.
7. Lubove, *The Progressive and the Slums*, 179.
8. MKS, *The City Worker's World*, 169.
9. Birch, "Edith Elmer Wood," 203, cites her interview with Woodbury, June 2, 1975.
10. Susan Ware, speaking at Greenwich House Conference, March 1, 1987, held at Greenwich House.
11. Bloom, *Public Housing That Worked*, 14. The proposed apartments would rent for $7.50 a room and were intended for wage earners, not relief recipients.

12. Bloom and Lasner, eds., *Affordable Housing in New York*, Kindle edition.
13. Paul Blanshard to MKS, January 22, 1932, GHRTAM, box 10, folder 43.
    Blanshard did not mention in that letter what MKS almost certainly knew—that Edith Elmer Wood had been first choice for the job but had turned it down.
14. PHC later changed its stationery to proclaim a subtly different objective: "to promote slum clearance and low rent housing through an established federal local service."
15. "Statement of Public Responsibility for Low Income Housing," GHRTAM, box 22, folder 89.
16. Conference held December 2–5, 1931.
17. Lawrence Veiller, *The Housing Problem in the United States* (NHA Publication #61, March 1930), 12–13, quoted in Birch, "Edith Elmer Wood," 188.
18. Peter Marcuse, "The Beginnings of Public Housing in New York," *Journal of Urban History* 12 (August 1986): 355.
19. Edith Elmer Wood, *Recent Trends in American Housing* (Macmillan Co., 1931), 2.
20. Charles Ascher to Eugenie Ladner Birch, October 21, 1974, cited in Birch, "Edith Elmer Wood," 190.
21. MKS to HSD, February 12, no year. Didisheim Papers. Courtesy of Andrea Didisheim.
22. Letter from Pennsylvania Museum of Art, November 18, 1930, enclosing check for $20,000 "covering purchase by the museum of The Red Robed Man" is in the Didisheim Papers. Courtesy of Andrea Didisheim. In the archives of the Philadelphia Museum of Art, a long correspondence between VGS and Horace H. F. Jayne, curator of sculpture, attests to the attempts to reach Kevorkian throughout 1928 and 1929 to clear Kevorkian's claim to the painting. Documents supplied to author, April 22, 2021, by Marge Huang, Martha Hamilton Morris Archivist at the Philadelphia Museum of Art.
23. Document in the Didisheim Papers. Courtesy of Andrea Didisheim.
24. Author's interview with Helena Didisheim, July 29, 1982, Robbinston, Maine. Since accession records at the Metropolitan Museum of Art show that Vladimir had no dealings with the museum between 1923 (when he sold three different batches of art works) and 1947, he had plenty of time to see what the private market would bear.
25. In 1934 the *New York Times* published seven articles with Mary's name in headlines before Vladimir's name appeared in November 1934. One article refers to her work on housing (May 2, 1934); two refer to funding for Greenwich House (May 15 and November 7); and five refer to honors for MKS (March 19, May 9, November 4, November 5, and November 16).
26. MKS to "My dear Mr. Mayor," March 31, 1932, GHRTAM, box 10, file 43.
27. MKS to "My dear Mr. Mayor," March 31, 1932, GHRTAM, box 10, file 43.
28. MKS letter, dated June 20, 1932, appeared in the *New York Times* on June 23.
29. MKS, to the *New York Times*, June 23, 1932.
30. MKS, "Detroit Address on Housing," June 11, 1933, in GHRTAM, box 22, folder 80.
31. MKS, "Housing Management in England," GHRTAM, box 30, folder 49.
32. Catherine Bauer, *Modern Housing* (Houghton Mifflin Co., 1934).
33. *Time*, August 19, 1935.
34. *Charlotte Observer*, August 12, 1935, 3; (Baltimore) *Sun*, August 12, 1935, 3.
35. *San Francisco Examiner*, August 12, 1935, 1.
36. *Boston Globe*, August 12, 1935, 11.
37. *Richmond Times Dispatch*, August 13, 1935, 7.
38. *The Bee*, Danville, Virginia, August 13, 1935.

39. Newspaper clipping from unidentified source. Didisheim Papers. Courtesy of Andrea Didisheim.
40. *Time*, August 19, 1935.
41. *Daily News*, June 28, 1932.
42. Stephen Simkhovitch married Dorothy Cowan on November 2, 1935.
43. Medical superintendent, Patton State Hospital, to MKS, July 27, 1937. Didisheim Papers. Courtesy of Andrea Didisheim.
44. Medical Superintendent Webster to MKS, July 22, 1937. Didisheim Papers. Courtesy of Andrea Didisheim.
45. MKS to Edward W. Stitt Jr., August 24, 1937. Didisheim Papers. Courtesy of Andrea Didisheim.
46. MKS to Arthur Pinover, August 24, 1937. Didisheim Papers. Courtesy of Andrea Didisheim.
47. MKS to Walter Hyams and Company, August 24, 1937. Didisheim Papers. Courtesy of Andrea Didisheim.
48. Dorothy Simkhovitch to MKS, "Saturday morning." Didisheim Papers. Courtesy of Andrea Didisheim.
49. Walton, Bannister & Stitt, 40 West 40th Street, New York, NY, to MKS, July 24, 1937. Didisheim Papers. Courtesy of Andrea Didisheim.
50. Stephen Simkhovitch to MKS, Labor Day 1937. Didisheim Papers. Courtesy of Andrea Didisheim.
51. MKS to HSD, July 12, 1939. Didisheim Papers. Courtesy of Andrea Didisheim.
52. MKS to HSD, July 12, 1939. Didisheim Papers. Courtesy of Andrea Didisheim.
53. MKS to HSD, July 12, 1939. Didisheim Papers. Courtesy of Andrea Didisheim.
54. Frank Didisheim to HSD, July 8, 1939. Didisheim Papers. Courtesy of Andrea Didisheim.
55. The "Find a Grave" website shows a tombstone for Stephen in Westwood Memorial Park, Los Angeles, California, so it is possible some of the ashes remained with Stephen's wife, Ruth, and were buried there. That site lists a son for the deceased: Steven Stockstad Simkhovitch, 1931–2013.
56. Mary's support for her daughter's art was not misplaced. Helena, who used Simkhovitch for her work, began receiving favorable reviews, and in 1950 she was one of the "New York Six" women who exhibited at the Petit Palais in Paris. The other five were Doris Caesar, Rhys Caparn, Minna Karkavy, Helen Phillips, and Arline Wingate. Among the museums that added Helena Simkhovitch's creations to their collections are the Whitney in New York and the Pennsylvania Academy of Fine Arts.
57. Undated letter from MKS to HSD, but interior evidence places it early July 1939. Didisheim Papers. Courtesy of Andrea Didisheim.
58. MKS to HSD, July 12, 1939. Didisheim Papers. Courtesy of Andrea Didisheim.
59. MKS to Eric Bender, July 17, 1939, GHRTAM, box 5b, folder 24.

CHAPTER 11

1. *New York Herald Tribune* reported on the speech on March 9, 1935. Along with MKS, whom the First Lady identified as a "social economist," she named Amelia Earhart, Frances Perkins, Jane Addams, and Lillian Wald.
2. *Dayton Daily News*, November 9, 1934, 11.
3. *Morning Telegraph*, June 12, 1937, 4.

4. *Atlanta Constitution*, December 19, 1936, 13, singled out Lillian Wald and MKS as two women who "mother whole sections of New York City and enter into the Christmas joy of hundreds and hundreds of families."
5. Timothy L. McDonnell, *The Wagner Housing Act: A Case Study of the Legislative Process* (Loyola University Press, 1957), 29.
6. McDonnell, *The Wagner Housing Act*, 55.
7. Frances Perkins told Wagner's biographer, J. Joseph Huthmacher, that reformers learned to "head straight for Wagner's door" as early as 1915. See J. Joseph Huthmacher, *Senator Robert Wagner and the Rise of Urban Liberalism* (Athenaeum, 1968), 39. In 1913 Wagner introduced a bill in the New York State Legislature calling for a state referendum on giving the vote to women. See Huthmacher, 29.
8. Birch, "Edith Elmer Wood," 196.
9. Eugenie Ladner Birch cites letter, on 196, as coming from Helen Alfred to Edith Elmer Wood, May 22, 1933, Edith Elmer Wood Collection, box 39B, Columbia University.
10. Birch, "Edith Elmer Wood," 208.
11. *New York Times*, May 2, 1934, 23.
12. Birch, "Edith Elmer Wood," 212.
13. Rosalie Genevro, "Site Selection and the NYC Housing Authority, 1934-1939," *Journal of Urban History*, August 12, 1986, 334.
14. *New York Times*, February 14, 1934, 21.
15. *New York Times*, February 18, 1934, 3.
16. Genevro, "Site Selection," 343.
17. *New York Times*, May 2, 1934, 23.
18. See Malvina T. Schneider (secretary to ER) to "My dear Mrs. Simkhovitch," May 6, 1936, explaining that ER had received MKS's letter "and she is giving it to the President." FDR Presidential Library, Digital Franklin Collection.
19. See, for example, MKS to ER, March 28, 1936, in FDR Presidential Library, Digital Franklin Collection.
20. MKS to ER, no date, FDR Presidential Library, Digital Franklin Collection. In that letter, MKS protested the appointment of John Ihlder as housing director as "unsuitable, in fact tragic."
21. On June 7, 1933, ER wrote MKS that she wanted to come to the Simkhovitches' Maine house for a party, but that FDR would "get off the boat" for a very brief time, and "any party at all…will have to be on our own front lawn." FDR Presidential Library, Digital Franklin Collection.
22. MKS to ER, July 2, 1934, GHRTAM, box 20, folder 43.
23. MKS to ER, July 2, 1934, GHRTAM, box 20, folder 43.
24. MKS to ER, July 2, 1934, GHRTAM, box 20, folder 43.
25. Frank LiCausi, quoted in *New York Times*, December 18, 1995, B1, on his moving into First Houses in 1935. He was still living there sixty years later.
26. *New York Times*, December 1, 1935. Some accounts give the number of apartments as 125. Others say 123. Two apartments could be combined to accommodate a large family.
27. "Housing Problems Will Be Discussed," *New York Times*, December 1, 1935, 8. Subtitle: "Mary K. Simkhovitch Is Head of Sponsoring Group for Tuesday's Conference."
28. MKS, "Housing as a Permanent Municipal Service," radio address on WEAF, February 19, 1934. GHRTAM, box 22, folder 92.
29. MKS, "The Church—Better Housing, in the Spirit of Missions," GHRTAM, box 22, folder 93.

30. MKS, "What a Slum Is and What a Slum Does," GHRTAM, box 22, folder 74.
31. MKS, "Slum as a Social Menace," GHRTAM, box 23, folder 13.
32. McDonnell, *The Wagner Housing Act*, 88.
33. McDonnell, *The Wagner Housing Act*, 92–95.
34. *New York Times*, May 5, 1935, Part III, 8.
35. *New York Times*, January 31, 1936, 1.
36. Quoted in *New York Times*, January 31, 1936, 1.
37. *New York Times*, January 31, 1936, 20.
38. McDonnell, *The Wagner Housing Act*, 132.
39. Birch, "Edith Elmer Wood," 212.
40. McDonnell, *The Wagner Housing Act*, 71.
41. FDR to Senator Wagner, October 28, 1935, in FDR Presidential Library, Digital Franklin Collection.
42. MKS, "Statement to Members of Congress on the Wagner-Ellenbogen Bill," GHRTAM, box 30 folder 49.
43. MKS, "Slums as a Social Menace," GHRTAM, box 23, folder 13.
44. FDR sent the telegram to MKS, in her capacity as president of the NPHC, and it is quoted in *New York Times*, June 26, 1936, 2, in article titled "President Spurs Housing."
45. *New York Times*, October 20, 1936, 1 and 20, on the president's visit to New York City.
46. Birch, "Edith Elmer Wood," 221.
47. Birch, "Edith Elmer Wood," 245.
48. Marcuse, "Beginnings of Public Housing," 369.
49. MKS, as member of Executive Board of National Urban League, "Report to President Roosevelt on general conditions of Negroes in the U.S. in 1937," SIMSCH, box 3, folder 52.
50. Minutes of the meeting of the Harlem Advisory Committee and Members of the New York City Housing Authority, November 6, 1939, are in the authority's papers, a copy of which can be found in GHRTAM, box 17F4, folder 11.
51. Frank Didisheim, Mary's son-in-law, was employed by the NCHA, and he accompanied her to this meeting and supported her view of the statistics and their application to selection of tenants.
52. See copy of minutes of meeting, November 6, 1939, in GHRTAM, box 4, folder 31.
53. Robert C. Weaver, "Negroes Need Housing," *The Crisis*, May 1940, 138.
54. Robert C. Weaver, "Racial Policy in Public Housing," *Phylon* 1, no. 2 (2nd Quarter, 1940): 156.
55. For fuller discussion of how distinctions were made on political, economic, and social rights in late nineteenth-century America, see Charles Postel, *Equality: An American Dilemma, 1866–1896* (Farrar, Straus and Giroux, 2019).
56. Jennifer Guglielmo, *Living the Revolution: Italian Women's Resistance and Radicalism in New York City, 1880–1945* (University of North Carolina Press, 2010), 263–264.
57. Nicholas Dagen Bloom, "Mary Kingsbury Simkhovitch," in *Affordable Housing in New York*. Kindle edition.
58. Papers of Catherine Fox Lansing were generously shared with author by her niece, Frances Lansing.
59. Bloom, "Mary Kingsbury Simkhovitch," in *Affordable Housing in New York*. Kindle edition.
60. Bloom, "Mary Kingsbury Simkhovitch," in *Affordable Housing in New York*. Kindle edition. Bloom also praised Simkhovitch in an earlier book, *Public Housing That Worked*.
61. Bloom and Lasner, eds., *Affordable Housing in New York*, preface.

CHAPTER 12

1. Eugenie L. Birch, "Woman-Made America: The Case of Early Public Housing Policy," *Journal of the American Institute of Planners* 44, no. 2 (1978): 130–144. http://dx.doi.org/10.1080/01944367808976886. Accessed March 2, 2024.
2. Wood, *Recent Trends*, 39.
3. Wood, *Recent Trends*, 40.
4. Wood, *Recent Trends*, 40.
5. Rixt Woudstra, "Exhibiting Reform: MoMA and the Display of Public Housing (1932–1939)," *Architectural Histories* 6, no. 1 (2018): 11. http://doi.org/10.5334/ah.269. Accessed August 16, 2025.
6. *New Yorker*, February 27, 1932, 49.
7. Barbara Penner, writing in foreword to 2020 edition of Catherine Bauer, *Modern Housing* (University of Minnesota Press, 1934), ix.
8. Catherine Bauer, "Machine-Age Mansions for Ultra Moderns," *New York Times Magazine*, April 15, 1928, 10.
9. Catherine Bauer, *New Republic*, March 2, 1932, 74.
10. Bauer, *Modern Housing*, 126–127. This includes data on England and Wales, Scotland, Germany, Holland, Belgium, France's Paris and environs, Austria's Vienna, Denmark's Copenhagen, 280 towns of Sweden, and 5 towns in Norway and in Switzerland (Zurich). The total number was 4,587,000 dwellings, which amounted to about 70 percent of the total built. Public authorities built 1,321,400 of that number, and public utility companies built the rest (1,755,100) to house nearly 16 percent of the population in the areas where they were located.
11. Barbara Penner, writing in foreword to Bauer, *Modern Housing*, 2020 edition, xvi.
12. Jessica Fletcher, "Where Tenants and Tenets Don't Agree: Elisabeth Coit and the Planning Practices of the New York City Housing Authority (1934–51)." *Buildings and Landscapes Journal of the Vernacular Architectural Forum* 28, no 2 (Fall 2021): 71–95.
13. Joyce Milambiling, *Skyscraper: The Many Lives of Christadora House* (New Village Press, 2023), for overview of Christadora House. For Catherine Lansing's relationship with Simkhovitch, information comes from author's multiple interviews with Frances Lansing, niece of Catherine Lansing.
14. Jessica Fletcher quotes Catherine Lansing's "Study of Community Planning," on how kitchens are used.
15. *New York Times*, February 12, 1939, 56.
16. *New York Times*, March 26, 1946, 21.
17. Author's interview with Frances Lansing, Venice, Italy, November 5, 2023.
18. Kristina Marie Borrman, "Planning the American Neighborhood: The Science of Sociability at the Dawning of Desegregation, 1933-1965," Ph.D. diss., University of California, Los Angeles, 2020, 8. Lansing married Duncan Oats in 1946, and Borrman cites her as Catherine Oats, although the publication mentioned was written in 1937. "Studies of Community Planning in the Terms of the Span of Life" (New York City Housing Authority, 1937).
19. See chapter 6 on Atlanta's Neighborhood Union.
20. Jacqueline Anne Rouse, *Lugenia Burns Hope: Black Southern Reformer* (University of Georgia Press, 1989), 124.
21. "Lugenia Burns Hope" entry in *Encyclopedia Britannica*.
22. Robert G. Barrows, "'The Homes of Indiana': Albion Fellows Bacon and Housing Reform Legislation, 1907–1917," *Indiana Magazine of History* 81, no. 4 (December 1985): 309–350.

23. Darrek E. Bigham, "Work, Residence, and the Emergence of the Black Ghetto in Evansville, Indiana, 1865-1900," *Indiana Magazine of History* 75, no. 4 (December 1980): 287-318. Statistics on home ownership on page 310.
24. Wood, *The Housing of the Unskilled Wage Earner*, 85.
25. Mrs. Ernest P. Bicknell, "The Home-Maker in the White House: Mrs. Woodrow Wilsons's Social Work in Washington," *Survey* 33 (October 3, 1914): 19-22.
26. Betty Boyd Caroli, *First Ladies: From Martha Washington to Michelle Obama* (Oxford University Press, 2010), 143.
27. Bicknell, "The Home-Maker in the White House," 19-22.
28. Frances Perkins to MKS, April 18, 1949, SIMSCH, box 1, folder 18.
29. Emily Sweetser Alford, "Tribute to MKS" delivered to Fortnightly members after MKS's death. Didisheim Papers. Courtesy of Andrea Didisheim.
30. Annual Report 1929/30 notes that the purchase of the seventy-seven acres was the high point of the past year. Nine miles east of Poughkeepsie, the camp could be reached by motor or by boat to Poughkeepsie and then by motor. GHRTAM, box 1, folder 12.
31. *The Villager*, April 30, 1942, 8.
32. For example, the Metropolitan Museum of Art website notes that the *Gathering of Philosophers*, initially attributed to 1222-1304, was later identified as from the Quin dynasty (1644-1911). The *Immortal and the Sages*, formerly attributed to 1041-1106, was later attributed to the Ming dynasty (1368-1644). As for Vladimir's expertise, a document in the Didisheim Papers, dated April 18, 1923, on stationary of the Joseph Brummer Gallery at 43 East 57th Street, is signed by VGS and one other, signature unclear but appears to be Joseph Dunnsley, who notes that a "small silver statue of Venus…considered by me as forgery (which Prof. Simkhovitch thinks is genuine)" is being exchanged "on equal terms" with "a life-sized marble head of Heria belonging to him." Vladimir's confidence in his own judgment is unusual for a major collector, and it prompted questions after his death. Felice Fischer, who curated an exhibition of his collection at the Philadelphia Museum of Art in 1993, queried this author: "How did he become interested in Chinese painting? Where did he buy his Chinese art? Did he have an advisor for his purchases?"
33. A Belgian woman had seen his Chinese collection and had "gone mad over it," VGS wrote his daughter, Helena. After lining up "a great Bulgarian collector" to buy it for $260,000, the Belgian asked only 15 percent as her commission. Vladimir explained that "a clever dealer could make a cold million over and above" what he was asking, but he was eager to get back to his "scientific work" and willing to settle for a "respectable figure & let a dealer make all the profits he can." Vladimir had refused to bring parts of his collection with him on the European trip because of problems he might encounter at border crossings. Some of the artwork weren't even accessible, because he had stored them "in the vaults of Columbia University and Fogg Art Museum to whom I loaned a number of paintings for the opening of their new building…on June 20." Letter of July 18, 1927. Didisheim Papers. Courtesy of Andrea Didisheim.
34. VGS to HSD, July 18, 1927. Didisheim Papers. Courtesy of Andrea Didisheim.
35. Ethel Gillespie, "The Chinese Paintings in the Simkhovitch Collection," *Art and Archaeology* (October 1932): 237. Clipping in the Didisheim Papers. Courtesy of Andrea Didisheim.
36. Handwritten note, January 28, no year. Didisheim Papers. Courtesy of Andrea Didisheim.
37. MKS to HSD, February 12, no year, but ca. 1929. Didisheim Papers. Courtesy of Andrea Didisheim.
38. MKS to HSD, February 12, no year, but ca. 1929. Didisheim Papers. Courtesy of Andrea Didisheim.

39. MKS, "A Comment on the Social Justice Conference," August 1937, provided to author by Ruth S. Leonard, archivist for Society of the Companions of the Holy Cross.
40. *New York Times*, October 19, 1937, 16.
41. *New York Times*, October 6, 1937, 24; October 10, 1937, 98.
42. Harlem's *New York Age*, October 30, 1937, cited by Perry, *After the Vote*, 215. Perry also cites *New York Times*, September 27, 1937.
43. Marshall Field served as campaign treasurer and sent out letters asking for donations for MKS's campaign. See his letters in GHRTAM, box 17b, folder 38.
44. Perry, *After the Vote*, 216. Earle won one of Brooklyn's nine seats, but only after receiving the votes from another candidate who had too few votes to proceed. Earle had long, distinguished service, but she had never joined a political club. She would not have won without support from a candidate who garnered fewer votes than she. Earle served on the city council until 1947, and after hiring a Black secretary, she gained credit with African Americans.
45. Author's interview with Paul Didisheim, June 25, 1987, Washington, DC.
46. Carolyn G. Heilbrun, *Writing a Woman's Life* (Norton & Co., 1988), 24, cites Conway's essay, "Convention Versus Self Revelation: Five Types of Autobiography by Women of the Progressive Era." Project on Women and Social Change, Smith College, June 13, 1983. Other women in the survey were Ida Tarbell and Charlotte Perkins Gilman. Addams came in for special censure. Conway found her account "sentimental and passive—her cause finds her rather than the other way round." Wald's books deserve the same judgment. Anecdotal accounts of the people who came to Henry Street fill most of her pages, and she pointed to her co-workers who built the house and made it what it was.

    Compared with the books by Wald and Addams, *Neighborhood* looks academic. Instead of dozens of drawings and illustrations offered in the books on Hull House and Henry Street, *Neighborhood* has only four black-and-white photos—two of its founder (one a youthful Mary, the other middle-aged) and two of Greenwich House. Wald's humor is missing in *Neighborhood*, and it is unlikely that the serious, scholarly Mrs. Sim would have sympathized with Wald's scoffing at statistics. One story relayed in *Windows on Henry Street* shows its author's disdain for academics by reporting how one man responded to a professor's question on the death rate in his community. He allowed it was "about one per person." Lillian Wald, *Windows on Henry Street* (Little Brown, 1934), 11.
47. MKS, *Neighborhood*, 93, 102, 168, 173.
48. "This book is for you. Perhaps you may like to read the first chapter now, and the others later on. You remember your great grandmother, and she remembered her great-grandfather Samuel Shaw, who fought with Washington at Valley Forge. So you see, it takes only two steps to go back to the beginnings of our country. This book is a tiny chapter in that history. M.K.S."
49. Robert F. Wagner Collection, box 129, folder 1876. LaGuardia and Wagner Archives, LaGuardia Community College, City University of New York.
50. *New York Times*, September 15, 1960, 62.
51. In a very few NYCHA records, the complex is listed as both Simkhovitch Houses and Gouverneur Gardens.
52. Lasner, "Stabilizing the Middle," in *Affordable Housing in New York*, writes that the limited income cooperative resulted from "an increased interest in below market subsidized housing not just for the poor but also moderate income families." Kindle edition.
53. Bloom, *Public Housing That Worked*, 24.

54. Bloom, *Public Housing That Worked*, 28.
55. Catherine A. Paul, "The Progressive Era," *Social Welfare History Project*. https://socialwelfare.library.vcu.edu/eras/civil-war-reconstruction/progressive-era/. Accessed March 7, 2024.

CHAPTER 13

1. Jill Lepore, *Secret History of Wonder Woman* (Knopf, 2014), 222.
2. Lepore notes that copies are hard to find. See Greenwich House's website entry for Women's History Month, 2023. The idea for the series on historical figures apparently resulted from a chance meeting of Alice Marble, the top woman tennis player in the world, and William Moulton Marston, a psychologist and sometime writer of *Wonder Woman*. According to Lepore, the two met at a cocktail party where all the talk was about the success of the fictional Wonder Woman, and Marble asked Marston why he didn't write about real women like Clara Barton and Eleanor Roosevelt. Both Marble and Marston wrote some of the sketches of women to be included, but authors for most of the series remain unknown. Lepore speculates that many entries were the work of a Washington, DC, editor Dorothy Roubicek. Although Marston's involvement was significant, much of his story remained hidden. Not only did he invent the lie detector test, he also lived for decades with two women. One was an attorney and the other a former student of his. Both women bore his children, and the two women continued living together after his death. The younger one was the niece of Margaret Sanger. Florence Nightingale was featured in the first issue of *Wonder Woman of History*; MKS appeared in 1952.
3. Lepore, 228, cites "America's Wonder Women of Tomorrow," Wonder Woman #7 (Winter 1943).
4. Lepore, 220, citing an article by William Moulton Marston: "Noted Psychologist Revealed as Author Best Selling 'Wonder Woman,' Children's Comic," press release, typescript, June 1942, in Marston letters at the Smithsonian. William Moulton Marston, "Why 100,000,000 Americans Read Comics," *American Scholar* 13, no. 2 (Spring 1944): 247–252.
5. *Herald Tribune*, November 24, 1942, 25.
6. Copy of instructions to the Alien Enemy Hearing Boards, issued December 13, 1941, by the attorney general. SIMSCH, box 3, folder 44.
7. Request to Serve, SIMSCH, box 3, folder 44. The wired request was dated December 16, 1941, and stated the terms of service and compensation.
8. Records obtained by author under the Freedom of Information Act, December 15, 1997.
9. *The Villager*, April 30, 1942, 7.
10. Greenwich House Report, GHRTAM, box 2, folder 28.
11. *The Villager*, April 30, 1942, 9.
12. MKS, letter to the *New York Times*, March 14, 1943, 21.
13. MKS to Marshall Field, January 20, 1943, SIMSCH, box 2, folder 27.
14. National Public Housing Conference, *Public Housing Progress*, March 1943.
15. MKS, "A Woman's View of Housing," *New York Herald Tribune*, October 28, 1945.
16. *New York Times*, January 11, 1946, 15.
17. *New York Times*, February 16, 1947, 34.
18. *New York Times*, May 22, 1946, 2.
19. *New York Times*, February 29, 1948, 34.

20. *New York Post*, November 3, 1943.
21. *New York Post*, November 3, 1943.
22. MKS to Mrs. Charles T. Zahn, July 24, 1939, GHRTAM, box 5b, folder 24.
23. MKS to Lou Molloy, November 2, 1945, SIMSCH, box 2, folder 32.
24. MKS to Lou Molloy, November 2, 1945, SIMSCH, box 2, folder 32.
25. MKS to Lou Molloy, November 2, 1945, SIMSCH, box 2, folder 32.
26. MKS to Max Lerner, May 16, 1946, SIMSCH, box 2, folder 32.
27. Unidentified clipping in the Didisheim Papers has a photo of Mary at the time of her marriage and a picture of Vladimir.
28. SIMSCH, box 5, folder 89.
29. MKS to Ordway Tead, March 31, 1947, SIMSCH, box 5, folder 89.
30. MKS, *Here Is God's Plenty*, preface.
31. *Kirkus Reviews*, August 15, 1949, 458.
32. The entire manuscript for *Green Shoots* is at SIMSCH. The discussion of woman's role in the family is in chapter 2. Unlike MKS's previous books, this does not include much autobiographical material.
33. MKS, typescript of article, SIMSCH, box 4, folder 74.
34. James J. Kirk to MKS, May 16, 1948, SIMSCH, box 1, folder 18.
35. MKS to "Friends" undated letter at end of World War II, SIMSCH, box 1, folder 17.
36. *New York Sun*, January 30, 1946.
37. Published as letter to editor, *New York Times* and *New York Herald Tribune*, November 12, 1949.
38. MKS to VGS, March 3, 1946, SIMSCH, box 1, folder 9.
39. In June 1946 MKS tried to engage a literary agent to sell two articles she had written, one on Guatemala and the other on family allowances in Canada. After modestly listing her own accomplishments ("you might recall the fact that I am Vice Chairman of the NYCHA and have written three or four books,") she added a P.S.: "I'd love to earn a little money." SIMSCH, box 4, folder 74.
40. Author's interview with Helena Didisheim, Robbinston, Maine, July 29, 1982.
41. MKS to James Lindsay, May 7, 1947, SIMSCH, box 1, folder 18.
42. Eleanor Roosevelt's typed note with signature in her hand, dated September 20, 1935. Didisheim Papers. Courtesy of Andrea Didisheim.
43. William (Billie) Ivins to VGS, 1947. Didisheim Papers. Courtesy of Andrea Didisheim.
44. Sarah McNear to Andrea Didisheim, February 2021, reported VGS was vice president from at least 1936–1940. McNear, a curator of photos, reported she is working on a book about Steichen and delphiniums.
45. Letter in Didisheim Papers, July 3, no year. Courtesy of Andrea Didisheim.
46. *Courier News*, Bridgewater, New Jersey, May 15, 1915, 7.
47. "Paulot" to his parents, July 1944. Didisheim Papers. Courtesy of Andrea Didisheim.
48. Paul Didisheim to his father, July 4, 1944. Didisheim Papers. Courtesy of Andrea Didisheim.
49. Paul Didisheim to his father, July 4, 1944. Didisheim Papers. Courtesy of Andrea Didisheim.
50. Author's interview with Paul Didisheim, Washington, DC, June 25, 1987.
51. Paul Didisheim to Frank Didisheim, July 4, 1944. Didisheim Papers. Courtesy of Andrea Didisheim.

52. Board of deacons at First Congregational Church to VGS, June 12, 1951. Didisheim Papers, Courtesy of Andrea Didisheim. Author found no evidence that VGS accepted the invitation to speak.
53. "A Maine girl" to MKS, no date, SIMSCH, box 1, folder 5.
54. Clipping, SIMSCH, box 1, folder 5.
55. See letter of October 28, 1929, from Hodson to MKS, wishing her well on her sinus surgery and recuperation in Hartford. William Hodson Papers, Brooke Astor Rare Books and Manuscripts, New York Public Library, box 1. Also note of July 11, 1939, on death of MKS's son, box 1.
56. Edward W. Stitt Jr. (Simkhovitch attorney) letter to Zagon & Aaron (attorneys for Stephen's estate in Los Angeles) quoting William Hodson, September 20, 1939. Didisheim Papers. Courtesy of Andrea Didisheim.
57. Edward W. Stitt Jr. to MKS, October 20, 1939. Didisheim Papers. Courtesy of Andrea Didisheim.
58. Stockstad may very well have taken the census taker's question as asking what job she held. Or she may have considered the weekly payments to be withdrawals from an account rather than income.
59. Author's correspondence with Glenda Geraci and with Steven Simkhovitch's son and daughter, who all had warm memories of Sonja Stockstad.
60. Glenda Geraci to author, September 29, 2020.
61. Information on the savings bond came from Glenda Geraci. Mary's will, made in 1939, named VGS as executor, and designated one-third of her estate to each of these three: VGS, HSD, and Paul Didisheim. VGS left no will, and Frank Didisheim was appointed his executor.
62. Author's interview with Helena Didisheim, Robbinston, Maine, July 29, 1982.
63. Vladimir to "Dearest Molly," August 31, 1951, SIMSCH, box 1, folder 9.
64. ER, "My Day," October 25, 1951.
65. Virginia Mazer, radio play broadcast May 18, 1952, script in the Didisheim Papers. Courtesy of Andrea Didisheim.
66. Pamphlet of script for radio play, written by Virginia Mazer, and broadcast May 18, 1952. Didisheim Papers. Courtesy of Andrea Didisheim.
67. *New York Times*, March 21, 2024.
68. *New York Times*, November 17, 1951, 16.

Index

For the benefit of digital users, indexed terms that span two pages (e.g., 52–53) may, on occasion, appear on only one of those pages.

A. A. Frazar Company 4–6
Ackerman, Frederick L. 179–80
Addams, Jane 16, 24, 43, 57, 70
   College Settlement and 26
   honorary degree 105
   inheritance 73–4
   Nobel Peace Prize 35
   pacifism of 126
   politics and 53
   Social Welfare History Project and 204–5
   Toynbee Hall and 22
Adler, Felix 54, 69–70
affordable housing 203
alcohol 139–40, 155–6
Aldrich, Chester Holmes 120
Alford, Emily Sweetser 198–9
Alfred, Helen 175–6, 181
Allen, Mary E. 101–3
The Alley (Herzfeld) 92
Alley Bill 198
Amalfi coast 39
American Delphinium Society 218
American Economic Association 106
American Gynecological Society 137–8
American Legion 215
American Scientific Association 78
Annals of the American Academy of Political and Social Science 25
Antietam Creek 6
antisemitism 32–3
Arkwright Club 106
Aronovici, Carol 193–4
Art Institute of Chicago 150–1
Ashcan School 140–1
Ashley, William 26–7
Association of College Women 69

Association of Neighborhood Workers 63, 85
Atlanta Baptist College 84–5

Bacon, Albion Fellows 196–7
Bacon, Hilary E. 196
Balch, Emily 25, 32, 35, 126
   in London 41–2
   on Simkhovitch, V. 36, 40–1
   Staatswissenschaftlicher Verein and 38
   on suitors 36
Barbato, Theodore 123, 125
Barnard College 98, 152
Barnett, Henrietta 42–3
Barnett, Samuel 42–3
Barrow Street 119–21, 141
Baruch, Bernard 132
Bauer, Catherine 165–6, 183, 192–3, 203–4
Beam, Abraham 179–80
"Before Women Were Human Beings" (Hyde) 31
Berenson, Bernard 18, 109
Berlin, Germany
   arrival in 32
   cultural institutions of 33
   municipal socialism and 34
Berlin Museum of Antiquities 33
Bethune, Mary McLeod 196
"Better Homes Through Better Housing" (Simkhovitch, M. K.) 182–3
Bicknell, Grace Vawter 197–8
Black community 82–3
   Federation of Settlements and 84
   housing and 185–7
   social service centers and 83–4
Blanshard, Paul 161
Bliss, William Dwight Porter 21

Board of Health 9–10
Boas, Franz 89–90, 93
Bogart, Ernest 61, 106
Bolshevik Revolution 128
bolshevism 131
Boynge, Margaret 168
Boston
    Brahmins in 13
    expansion of 14
    slums in 25–6
Boston and Albany Railroad 14
Boston University (BU) 16–17, 19, 127
    doctorate degrees and 27
Bowne, Borden P. 17
Boyce, Neith 140
Bridgewater, Massachusetts 2, 4
Bromley, Dorothy Dunbar 202
Brush, W. Franklin 79–80
Bryan, William Jennings 197
Bryn Mawr 25, 35
Bull Moose campaign 126
Bureau of Industries and Immigration 113
Burlington Magazine 107–8
Burns, Lugenia Hope 84–5

Caecilian Society 11
Cambridge, Massachusetts 19–21
Cambridge Theological School 11
Camp Herbert Parsons 199
Campobello 11–12, 71–2, 174
"Can a Poor Girl Go to College?" (*North American Review*) 16–17
Cannon, Joseph 96, 98
career women 124
Carnegie Foundation 125
Carola Woerishoffer Fund 114
Catholic Charities 186
CCP. *See* Committee on Congestion of Population
Century Association 108–9
Chamberlain, Joseph 34
Charity Organization Society 54, 68, 79–80, 113
Chestnut Hill, Massachusetts 4, 10, 19–21
Chestnut Hill Church 3–4, 39
Chicago Commons 58–9
Child, Bess 103–4
child crop 137
child labor 85, 124–5
Children's Bureau 137

Church of the Redeemer 11
Christian, Joseph J. 179–80
Christodora House 194–5
Cipriani, Lisi 88
Citizens' Committee 215
Citizens Nonpartisan Committee 201
Citizens' Union 210
City Planning Convention (1909) 114–15
The City Worker's World in America (Simkhovitch, M. K.) 126–7, 204
Civil War 1–2, 5–6
Clark, John Bates 47
Clews, Elsie 47–8. *See also* Parsons, Elsie Clews
Coit, Elisabeth 194, 196
Coit, Stanton 21–2
College Settlement 21–2, 49
    focus of 51
    Kingsbury, M. M., becoming head worker at 50
    Kingsbury, M. M., moving to 48–9
    local politics and 53
    Robbins and 50
    volunteer outreach and 49
College Settlement Association 22, 25–6, 48–9, 51–2
Columbia University 41, 46–8, 52
    Dewey and 94–5
    Greenwich House and 152
    Nehru at 216
    Simkhovitch, V., and 64–5, 89–90, 102, 105–6, 152
    Social Science Research Council 154
Commission on Congestion of the Population 109–10
Committee of Fourteen 111–12, 139–40
Committee on Congestion of Population (CCP) 93, 96, 109, 136–7, 159
Committee on Social Education 94–5
Committee on Social Investigations 90, 92–3
The Commonwealth (newspaper) 7
Conant, Roger 2
Conference on Home Building and Home Ownership 161–2
Consumer League 137
Converse, Florence 133–4
Conway, Jill Ker 202
Cooper, Gertrude Sturgis 212
cooperative housing 122

Cooperative Social Settlement Society of
    the City of New York 70–1, 75–6
  Columbia University and 152
  property purchases by 111, 120–1
Copeland, Royal S. 117–18
Cornell University 61
Council of Social Agencies 215
Cowan, Dorothy 167–8
Cox, James M. 132
The Crisis (magazine) 187–8
Cuba 143–4
Cummings, Edward 51
Cutting, Fulton 151–2

Davis, Ida 16, 18
Delano, William Adams 120
Democratic National Campaign
    Committee 24
Denison House 22–3, 25–8, 35, 42, 113, 148
  Harvard Annex and 26
Dennis, Patrick 149
*Design and Construction of the Dwelling
    Unit for the Low-Income Family*
    (Coit) 194
Devine, Edward T. 79–80, 90
Dewey, John 94–5
Dewson, Molly 24, 155–6
Didisheim, Frank 148, 171
Didisheim, Helena. *See* Simkhovitch,
    Helena
Didisheim, Paul 134, 170–1, 202, 218–19
diet 124
dispossess notices 162
doctorate degrees 27
Dodge, Mabel 140
Douglas, Kirk 147
Dreier, Margaret 86
Dreier, Mary 86
Dresden, Germany 37
Dryden, John 213–14
Dudley, Helena 22, 25, 51–2
Dunbar, Olivia Howard 105

Earhart, Amelia 148–9
Earle, Genevieve B. 202
Eastman, Annis 88
Eastman, Crystal 81, 88–9
East Newton, Massachusetts. *See* Chestnut
    Hill, Massachusetts
East Side 54

education
  music 3–4, 141–2, 212–13
  Normal Schools 4
18th Amendment (Prohibition) 155–6
88 Grove Street 80–1
Eisenach, Germany 31
Ellenbogen, Henry 183
Elliott, John 63
Elmira Academy of Science 50
Enemy Alien Hearing Board 208
Episcopal Suffrage Association 111–12
Episcopal Theological School 19–20
Equal Franchise Society 111–13
ethnic groups
  conflicts among 82
  household budget differences and 93
  Simkhovitch, M. K., relations with 123–4
Evansville, Indiana 196–7
evictions, limitations on 117

Fabian Socialists 41–2
factory workers, female 86
Family Allowance program (Canada) 215
family budgets 93
Federal Home Loan Bank Act 161–2
Federal Housing Administration (FHA) 178
Female Seminary 3
FHA. *See* Federal Housing Administration
Field, Marshall 201
Field, Marshall (Mrs.) 151–2
Fine, Jean 22
First Houses 179–81, 204
Fredericksburg 6
freedom of speech 130
French, Daniel Chester 140–1
Friedrich der Grosse (ship) 55
Friendly Aid Society 57–8, 60–1
  activities and services provided by 62
  Association of Neighborhood
      Workers and 63
  census records of 63–4
  O'Hagan and 63–4
  residency requirements 59–60
  Simkhovitch, M. K., contract
      renewal with 66
  Simkhovitch, M. K., leaving 67–9
  Simkhovitch, M. K., work at 62–4
  Simkhovitch, V., and 64
"Friendship and Politics" (Simkhovitch,
    M. K.) 71

Gabrilowitsch, Ossip 142
Germany
  studying in 31
  urbanization in 34
Gettysburg 7
Giddings, Franklin 47, 90
Girls Who Did 124
Goddard, Warren 58–9, 69
Gompers, Samuel 132
Gophers (gang) 73, 91–2
Gouverneur, Abraham 203
Gouverneur Gardens 203
Grace Church 69–70
graded rents 185
Grant, Percy Stickney 108–9, 132–3
Grant, Zilpah 3
Great Depression 160–2
  housing movement and 165
Great Migration 116
Great Red Scare 128
Great War of 1914–1918 (World War I) 114, 116, 126–7
Greene, Belle da Costa 108–9
Green Shoots (Simkhovitch, M. K.) 214
Greenwich House
  arts at 140–1, 147
  Arts Committee 140–1
  Barrow Street building 119–21, 141
  board of managers 79–80
  Carnegie Foundation evaluation of 125
  charter 80
  classes and clubs at 81
  Columbia University and 152
  Committee on Social Investigations 90, 92–3
  Earhart at 148–9
  finances of 79, 198–9
  founding of 70
  funding 73–4, 78–9, 150–2, 199
  intervention failures 124–5
  Lusk Committee and 129
  membership program 79
  move to new building 116
  music education program 141–2, 212–13
  opening of 77–8
  Ovington and 94
  racial segregation in 83
  research institute in 94–5
  securing location for 73
  services provided by 78, 82
  Simkhovitch, V., and 89–90
  space allotments in 80
  staff of 87–8
  successor for directorship of 211–13
  tearoom 144–5
  Tenants' Manual 90–2, 204
  theater productions 146–7
  Tunney and 142–3
  Wage-Earners' Budgets 93, 98
  Ware, C., on 153–5
  Woerishoffer, C., and 114
  woman suffrage movement and 112–13
  worker recruitment and 149–50
  Zinsser at 81
Greenwich Village 72
  population of 77–8
  road patterns in 77
  Roaring 20s and 136
Greenwich Village, 1920–1930 (Ware, C.) 153, 155
Greenwich Village Improvement Society 85
Grimani Breviary 107–8
"Guatemalan Snapshot" (Simkhovitch, M. K.) 216

Hague peace conference of 1915 126
Half a Man (Ovington) 94
Halle University 41
Hansan, John E. 204–5
Hapgood, Hutchins 140
Harlem Houses 185–7
Harper & Brothers 213
Hartley House 52
Hartridge (school) 104
Hartwick, Thomas W. 128
Harvard Annex 19–20, 22–3, 27–8
  Denison House and 26
  faculty at 26–7
Hayes, Rutherford B. 70
health, housing and 117–18
Henry Street 59, 70, 94–5, 125, 161
Here Is God's Plenty (Simkhovitch, M. K.) 213–14
Herzfeld, Elsa 92, 94–5
Hill, Octavia 189
Hitchcock, Henry Russell 192–3
Hodson, William 220–1

INDEX

Holmes, Laura 2–3, 5–6. *See also* Kingsbury, Laura
    Kingsbury, F., letters to 4–5, 7–8
    Kingsbury, F., proposing marriage to 5, 8
    marriage 8
Holmes, Oliver Wendell, Jr. 128
home finishers 85–6
homelessness, Great Depression and 160–1
Hoover, Herbert 161–2, 164–5
Hope, Lugenia Burns 196
housing. *See also* public housing
    activism for 157, 159
    affordable 203
    crowding in 23–4, 91
    government funding and 160–2
    Great Depression and reform movement for 165
    health and 117–18
    Hoover and 161–2
    as human right 118–19, 160, 191
    immigrants and 91
    laws and 117
    minimum requirements 160
    MoMA exhibit on 192–4
    National Industrial Recovery Act and 175–6
    socialism and 160, 165
    vocabulary for 90–1
Housing Act (1937) 185, 189–90
The Housing of the Unskilled Wage Earner (Wood, E. E.) 119
Hovde, Carl 209
Howard, Ebenezer 14–15
How the Other Half Lives (Riis) 48, 70, 194
Hudson Dusters (gang) 73, 91–2
Hudson Guild 63
Hudson Park 85, 105
Hughes, Charles Evans 111–12
Hull House 22, 59, 70, 73–4
Hyde, Ida 31

Ickes, Harold 176, 187–8
immigrants
    College Settlement outreach to 49
    housing and 91
immigration 14, 23, 116
    changes in law and 150
    Kingsbury, M. M., studying 52
individualism 161

industrialization 23
    housing vocabulary and 90–1
    slums and 181
infant mortality rate 137–9
inflation 116
integration 187–8
International Socialist Workers and Trade Union Congress 41–3
International Style 192–3
International Workers of the World ("Wobblies") 128
intervention failures 124–5
Israels, Belle. *See* Moskowitz, Belle Israels
Italian community 123–5, 154
    diet of 124
    immigration law changes and 150
Ivins, William M. 105–6

James, Henry 76–7
James, William 26
"Jekal & Mr. Simkhovitch" (*Time*) 165–6
Johnson, Philip 192–3
Jones Street 73, 77–8, 121, 123
    cooperative housing and 122–3
    Cooperative Social Settlement Society purchases on 111
    descriptions of 76–7
    disease risks in 98
    living conditions in 96–7
    racism on 82
    streetlights on 81

Kalberg, Stephen 13–14
Kappa Kappa Gamma 17
Kelley, Florence 24, 59, 104, 109–10, 136–7
Kennaday, Paul 72–7
Kevorkian, Hagop 163–4
Kingsbury, Frank 1, 10, 30
    career 10
    marriage 8
    military service 1–2, 5–8
    moving to Bridgewater 4
    proposal of marriage 5, 8
    public service and 13–14
    relationship with daughter 13
    retirement 11
    Simkhovitch, V., and 61
    visiting Orlanova 104
    woman suffrage and 11
Kingsbury, Isaac William, "Will," 10, 18

Kingsbury, Kenneth 143
Kingsbury, Laura 1, 10, 12
  antisemitism 32–3
  arrival in Berlin 32
  on Berlin cultural institutions 33
  on cost of Berlin 36–7
  death 220
  on farm purchase 99–100
  in Germany 31–2
  household tasks and 12
  intellectual pursuits of 13–14
  in Italy 38–40
  marriage 8
  Simkhovitch, S., and 143–6
  Simkhovitch, V., and 46, 61, 100–1
  on suitors 36
  travel to Europe 29–31
  visiting New York City 9, 44
  visiting Orlanova 104
Kingsbury, Mary Homer 3–4
Kingsbury, Mary Melinda
  arrival in Berlin 32
  arrival in New York City 44–5
  becoming head worker at College
    Settlement 50
  birth of 1
  Boston Brahmins and 13
  changes after year in Europe 35
  childhood 2
  College Settlement and 48–9
  Columbia University and 46–8
  decisions about further studies in
    Europe 40–1
  Denison House and 22–3, 27–8
  Dewson and 24
  engagement to Simkhovitch, V. 55–6
  financial background 13–14
  first exposure to slum housing 18
  first publications 52
  in Germany 31–2, 40
  graduate study and 30–1
  at Harvard Annex 19–20, 22–3, 26–8
  health 18, 37
  household tasks and 12
  in Italy 38–40
  in London 41–2
  marriage 61
  meeting Roosevelts 11–12
  Nash influence on 20
  New York City and 46
  politics and 53–4
  relationship with father 13
  return to New York 43–4
  Simkhovitch, V., meeting 36
  sororities and 17
  Staatswissenschaftlichter Verein and 38
  starting teaching 18–19
  studying German 31
  studying immigrants 52
  studying Yiddish 52
  suitors 36
  Tiffany and 21
  Toynbee Hall and 42–3
  travel to Europe 29–31
  volunteering at St. Augustine's 17–18
  Wagner lectures and 33–4
  working for Friendly Aid 57–9, 61
Kirk, James J. 215
Klaassen, David 68

labor law 85
labor unions 86
LaGuardia, Fiorello 161, 163, 180, 200–1
  public housing and 177
Lake Como 39–40
Lama, Alfred 203
landlords 116–17
  laws and 117–18
  profit limit proposals on 159–60
  resistance to 117
Lansing, Catherine 189, 194–6
Lansing, Frances 195–6
Lathrop, Julia 137
Le Corbusier 192–3
Leffingwell, Russell 151–2
Lerner, Max 212
Liberator (journal) 81
Liberty Loan Campaign 121
LiCausi, Frank 180
Lincoln, Abraham 6, 8–9
Lindsay, James 217
Lindsay, Thomas 16–17
Lippincott's Monthly Magazine 48–9
living conditions 96–7
Low, Seth 53–4
Lowell, Josephine Shaw 54, 68
Lusk, Clayton 128
Lusk Committee 128–30, 135
Lvoff, Georgy 89–90
Lyon, Mary 3

"Machine-Age Mansions for Ultra
  Moderns" (Bauer) 192–3
MacIver, Robert M. 153–4

Manitoba (ship) 54–5
Manning, William Thomas 111–12
Mansion House 71–2, 134–5, 169–70, 174, 218, 222
Marciana Library 107–8
Marsh, Benjamin 96, 109–10
Marston, William Moulton 206–7
Marx, Karl 41–2
Marxism Versus Socialism (Simkhovitch, V.) 107, 110
Massachusetts Institute of Technology 25
Mayer, Albert 177–8
Mayo-Smith, Richmond 46–7
McClure, Mary 55
Metropolitan Health Act (1866) 9–10
Metropolitan Museum of Art 134, 163, 199
Meyer, Eugene 105
Millay, Edna St. Vincent 138–9
Miller, Nathan 130
Minetta Lane 82–3, 92
Mitchell, MacNeil 203
Mitchell, Wesley Clair 60
Mitchell-Lama formula 203
Modern Housing (Bauer) 165, 193
Molloy, Lou 211
MoMA. *See* Museum of Modern Art
Moore, E. Roberts 177, 186
More, Louise Bolard 92–5, 98
Morgan, J. Pierpont 107–8
Morgan, Junius 108
Morgan Library 108
Morgenthau, Henry 96
Moskowitz, Belle Israels 54, 157
Moskowitz, Henry 54
Mumford, Lewis 165, 192
Municipal Affairs (journal) 52
Municipal Art Society 109–10
municipalization 34
municipal socialism 34
Murphy, Helen 146–7
Museum of Modern Art (MoMA) 192–4, 200
Museum of Natural History 109–10
music education 3–4, 141–2, 212–13

NAACP. *See* National Association for the Advancement of Colored People
Nash, Henry Sylvester 11–12, 19–20, 61, 71–2
National Association for the Advancement of Colored People (NAACP) 94, 196
National Civic Federation 197–8
National Conference of Charities 111–12
National Conference on City Planning and the Problems of Congestion 96
National Consumers' League 24, 104
National Federation of Settlements 83–4
National Housing Conference 204, 223–4
national housing law 53
National Industrial Recovery Act (1933) 175–6
National Public Housing Conference (NPHC) 161, 164, 175, 180, 183–4, 194–5, 209
National Urban League 186, 188
National Youth Administration (NYA) 196
"Negroes Need Housing" (Weaver) 187–8
Negro Plantations 76–7
Nehru, Jawaharlal 216
Neighborhood (Simkhovitch, M. K.) 69, 100, 142–3, 202, 213–14
Neighborhood Guild 21–2
Neighborhood Union 84–5
Neighborhood Workers' Association 96–7
Neighborship Settlement 52
New Deal 24, 155, 157–8
New Jersey State Housing Authority 176
New Moon (boat) 71–2
Newton, Massachusetts 1, 9–10
  Boston expansion and 14
  growth of 14–15
  Social Science Club 65–6
Newton Graphic 10
New Villagers 140–1, 150
New York City 9, 44–5
  Eighth Ward 53
  Great Depression and 162
  Great Red Scare and 128
  grid pattern in 77
  heat wave of 1902 62
  housing funding in 176
  immigrants arriving in 14
  Kingsbury, M. M., and 46
  Ninth Ward 54, 150
  public housing in 177–81
New York City Council 201–2
New York City Housing Authority (NYCHA) 177–80, 185–7, 194–5, 198–9, 202–4, 209–10
  MoMA exhibit and 193–4
New York Infirmary 50
New York Society of Ethical Culture 54, 69–70

New York State
  housing board 157
  landlords limited by 118
  Tenement House Law (1867) 91
  women voting in 131–2
New York State Housing Board 177
New York University 152
Noordland (ship) 29–30
Normal School 4
North American Review 16–17
North Perry, Maine 11–12, 20, 71–2, 87, 174
Notable American Women 10
NPHC. *See* National Public Housing Conference
Nurses' Settlement 51–2
NYA. *See* National Youth Administration
NYCHA. *See* New York City Housing Authority
Nye, Carole S. 63–4

O'Brien, Ruth 169–71
OCD. *See* Office of Civilian Defense
O'Dwyer, William 210
Office of Civilian Defense (OCD) 208
O'Hagan, Anne 17–18, 25–6, 40, 48, 56
  Friendly Aid and 63–4
  in New York City 45–6
  Simkhovitch, V., and 45–6
  26 Jones Street and 75
O'Reilly, Leonora 86
Orlanova (farm) 100–1, 114–15
  staff changes at 103
Our Lady of Pompeii church 77–8
overcrowding 96–7
Ovington, Mary White 93–4
Oxford University 42–3

pacifism 35, 126–7
Paris Universal Exposition (1900) 34–5
Parsons, Elsie Clews 67, 72–4, 87
Parsons, Herbert 67
Pepe, Vincent 120, 150
Perkins, Frances 91–2, 95, 133–4, 198–9, 207
PhDs 27
Philadelphia Museum of Art 200
"philanthropy plus 5%" concept 159–60
Philbin, Eugene 69–70
Pink, Louis 177, 181
Platt, Jonathan 2–3
play spaces 63

political campaigning 53–4, 126, 131–2
political machines 53
Political Science Quarterly (journal) 64–5, 71, 107
politics
  Addams and 53
  College Settlement and local 53
  Scudder and 53
  Simkhovitch, M. K., and 126, 131–2, 200–2
  Simkhovitch, M. K., writing on 71
Porter, Polly 155–6
Post, Langdon 177–8
Potter, Henry C. 69–70, 113
Powers, Maxwell 212
"A Predecessor of the Grimani Breviary" (Simkhovitch, V.) 107–8
Primrose club 17–18
Prince, Diana 75, 206–7
Princeton University 108
Progressive movement 136, 189–90, 202
Prohibition 155–6
Promotion of the Welfare and Hygiene of Maternity and Infancy Act (Sheppard–Towner Act) (1921) 137–8
prostitution 139–40
public housing 174–5, 183–5, 204
  integration and 187–8
  LaGuardia and 177
  in New York City 177–81
  racial segregation and 186–8
  rent collection in 189
  Wood, E. E., on standards for 191–2
Public Housing Conference 161
"Public Housing Progress" (bulletin) 183
public parks 63
Public Works Administration (PWA) 176, 178, 187, 189
Puritan (magazine) 63–4
Putnam, George 149

racial segregation 83, 187–8
  public housing and 186–7
racism 82
Raines, John 139
Raines law 139–40
Rand, Helen 22
Rand School 128
Readington Township, New Jersey 100–2
Real Estate Board 117

INDEX

Recent Trends in American Housing
    (Wood, E. E.) 162, 191
Red Cross 121
Red Robed Man (painting) 163
Reform Judaism 69–70
refrigeration 81
Reid, William 202–3
religion
    settlement house movement and 42, 58
    Simkhovitch, M. K., and 132–3, 217
rent collection 189
rents 62
    graded 185
    industrialization and 23
rent strikes 117
Riis, Jacob 48, 70, 194, 202–3
Ripley, Ida 40, 56, 103, 106, 216
Ripley, William 18
Rivington Street. *See* College Settlement
Roaring 20s 136
Robbins, Ira 181
Robbins, Jane 50
Robbinston, Maine 134
Robinson, James Harvey 47
Robinson, Maude 199
Rockefeller, Abigail Aldrich 200
Rockefeller, John D. 128
Rockefeller Foundation 153
The Rookery 91–2
Roosevelt, Eleanor 24, 71–2, 157, 163–4, 217
    at Campobello 174
    Cooper and 212
    NPHC and 180
    Simkhovitch, M. K., and 174–5, 178–9
Roosevelt, Franklin Delano 11–12, 71–2, 132, 164–5, 208, 224
    at Campobello 174
    death of 217
    election of 165
    housing bill and 182–4
    public works projects and 176
    taking office 175
Roosevelt, James 11–12
Roosevelt, Sara Delano 11–12, 207
Roosevelt, Theodore 126, 137
Rous, Marion 142
Rouse, Jacqueline Anne 84–5
Russell, Bertrand 35
Russian Soviet Bureau 128

Salmon, Thomas 144
Sanger, Margaret 206–7
Sanitary Conditions of the City 9–10
Santayana, George 26
Schiff, Jacob 151
Schlesinger Library 89, 100
Schlueter, Edward Henry 132–3
School and Society (Dewey) 94–5
Schurz, Carl 70
Scudder, Vida 22, 24–5, 43, 51, 69, 133–4
    on Kingsbury, M. M., engagement 55
    politics and 53
Seager, Henry 90, 94
Seligman, Edwin R. 47, 90, 106
Seneca Falls convention 2–3
settlement house movement 21–4
    common threads through 51
    racial segregation and 83
    religion and 42, 58
    in United States 21–2
    uniting workers in 63
settlement houses
    focuses of 51
    gender separation and 43
    married couples and families in 58–60
    politics and 53
    volunteer work and 149–50
sewer socialism 34
shaft loophole 91–2
sharecropping 90–1
Shaw, George Bernard 41–2
Sheppard–Towner Act. *See* Promotion of the Welfare and Hygiene of Maternity and Infancy Act
Sheridan, Clare 120
Sherman, Mary 72–3, 79–80
Simkhovitch, Helena 87, 114, 156, 222
    art and 172, 220
    birth of 78
    on childhood 104
    in Europe 147–8
    Mansion House and 134–5
    on Orlanova 101
    theater and 147
Simkhovitch, Mary Kingsbury 10, 15, 76, 224. *See also* Kingsbury, Mary Melinda
    Addams and 126–7
    on American citizenship 131
    articles by 71
    Barnard College and 98, 152

Simkhovitch, Mary Kingsbury (*Continued*)
  on Berlin 29
  at Campobello 174
  Carnegie Foundation evaluation of 125
  on causes of congestion 97
  Committee of Fourteen and 139–40
  cooperative housing and 122
  Cowan and 168
  death 223
  death of son 170–1
  Dewey and 94–5
  diet and 124
  ethnic groups and 123–4
  on family finances 102
  family problems 103
  farm purchased by 99–101
  federal housing bill and 181–4
  finances 152, 211
  freedom of speech and 130
  Friendly Aid and 63–4
  fundraising by 150–2, 199
  government-funded housing and 161–2
  Great Depression and 160–1
  health 207–8
  heat wave reactions and 62
  honorary degrees 202
  housing activism by 157, 164–5, 182–3
  on housing as right 160
  housing conference and 96
  on housing remedies 97–8
  income distribution programs and 215
  infant mortality rate and 138–9
  Kelley working with 136–7
  leaving Friendly Aid 67–9
  Lusk Committee and 129
  in Maine 87, 218–19
  moving to Greenwich Village 78
  NPHC and 161, 175, 180, 183, 209
  NYCHA and 177–9, 185–6, 198–9, 204, 209–10
  O'Brien and 170–1
  on Orlanova 100–1
  politics and 126, 131–2
  pregnancy 66–7, 72, 78
  publications 111, 213–14
  public housing advocacy by 174–5, 180–1, 183–4
  public speaking and 113
  on racial mixing 187
  racism resisted by 82
  religion and 132–3, 217
  retirement 212–13
  Roosevelt, E., and 174–5, 178–9
  Roosevelt, F. D., and 174
  running for political office 200–2
  Salmon and 144
  settlement workers' associations and 63
  slum investigations and 91–2
  Social Science Club talk 65–6
  starting new settlement 69
  Stockstad and 167
  successor at Greenwich House to 211–13
  suffrage movement and 111–13, 157
  on teachers 47–8
  Wagner, R., and 175
  Ware, C., and 153–5
  World War I and 126–7
  World War II and 208
  WTUL and 86
Simkhovitch, Stephen 69, 72, 114, 143–7, 220–1
  alcohol problems 167
  birth of 67
  death of 169–71
  finances 168–9
  health of 87, 98
  Mansion House and 134–5
  O'Brien and 169
  Salmon and 144
  Stockstad and 144–6, 167
  temperament in childhood 103–4
  trust fund 144
  Willard and 165–7
Simkhovitch, Steve 171, 221–2
Simkhovitch, Vladimir 36, 40–1, 43–4, 76, 152, 168–9, 222
  alcohol and 155–6
  American Economic Association and 106
  art and 107–9, 150–2, 163, 199–200
  Columbia University and 64–5, 102, 105–6, 152
  Cornell University and 61
  death of son 170
  delphiniums raised by 218
  descriptions of 41, 60
  Dewey and 94–5
  Didisheim, P., and 218–19
  Eastman, C., and 88–9
  engagement to Kingsbury, M. M. 55–6
  family 56

farming by 101–2
farm purchased by 99
Friendly Aid and 64
on Jones Street 76–7
Kingsbury, L., and 46, 100–1
Mansion House and 134, 218
marriage 61
misrepresentation charge against 163–4
Morgan breviary and 107–8
moving to Greenwich Village 78
moving to New York 54–5
O'Hagan and 45–6
publications 106–7
rural areas and 98–9
on Simkhovitch, S. 144
Staatswissenschaftlichter Verein and 38
visiting family 156
wandering eye of 102–3
Woerishoffer, A., and 119–20
Woerishoffer, C., and 110
Simkhovitch Houses proposal 202–3
Sloan, John 140–1
slum clearance 118–19, 140–1, 177–8, 183, 185
Slum Clearance Committee 177–8
slum housing 18, 91–2, 159–60
 minimum requirements and 160
 Wood on 119
Slums and Blighted Areas in the U.S. (Wood, E. E.) 184
Smith, Al 119, 130–2, 157
Smith, Alys 35
social gospel 21–2, 43
socialism 33, 35, 41–2, 129–30
 housing and 160, 165
 municipal 34
 sewer 34
 state 33
Socialist Assembly 117
Socialist Party 161, 176, 201
Social Science Club 65–6
Social Security Act (1935) 138
social services
 settlement houses and 53
 Ware, C., on 155
Social Welfare History Project 204–5
social work, professionalization of 149
Society of the Companions of the Holy Cross 133–4, 201
Soldiers' and Sailors' Civil Relief Act 117
sororities 17

Spanish-American War 64
Sprague, Ethel 104
Sprague, Joseph 104
Staatswissenschaftlichter Verein (Political Science Club) 38, 40
Standard Oil of California 143
Starr, Ellen 43
State Housing Act (1926) 157–8
State Reconstruction Commission 119
state socialism 33
St. Augustine's (school) 17–18
Stein, Clarence S. 119
Stein, Gertrude 26
Stockstad, Sonja 144–6, 167, 220–1
Stoic Club 123, 125
Straus, Nathan 210
suffrage 11, 111–13, 131–2, 157
Sumner, Charles 25
Swope, Gerard 151–2, 201

Taft, William Howard 137
Tammany Hall 53
Tanner, Marion 149
Taylor, Graham 58–9
teaching 4
Tead, Ordway 213
telephones 134
tenant farmers 90–1
tenants 90–1
tenants leagues 117
Tenants' Manual (Greenwich House) 90–2, 204
Tenement House Commission 62–3
Tenement House Law (1867) 90–1
tenements 9–10
 defining 90–1
 dumbbell shape in 91
 overcrowding in 62–3
 reform efforts for 118
 regulation of 62–3
Thomas, Norman 161
Tiffany, Francis 21, 27–8
Time (magazine) 165–6
Toynbee, Arnold 42–3
Toynbee Hall 21–2, 42–3, 49, 149–50
Triangle Shirtwaist fire 113
Tunney, Gene 142–3
26 Jones Street 72–3, 88, 121–3
 condition of 74–5
 space allotments in 80

Union Carbide 123
Unitarian Church 69, 159–60
United Nations 217
United Neighborhood Houses of
    New York 63, 128, 157
United States
    immigration to 14
    urbanization in 34
United States Housing Authority (USHA)
    185–7, 194
University Settlement 21–2
Up from Slavery (Washington) 94
urbanization 34
    housing vocabulary and 90–1
    slums and 181

Van Pelt, John V. 117–18
Vatican Square 39
Veiller, Lawrence 62–3, 118, 160–2
Venice 38
Vers Une Architecture (Le Corbusier) 192–3
Vladeck, Charney 177–8, 202–3

Wage-Earners' Budgets (Greenwich House)
    93, 98
Wagner, Adolph 33–4, 41–3
Wagner, Robert 175–6, 180–4, 202–3
Wald, Lillian 16, 51–2, 57, 59, 70, 85, 94–5,
    109–10, 125, 151, 161, 201–3
Walker, Jimmy 130, 164
Warburg, Felix 79
Warburg, Frieda 79
Ware, Annie 56
Ware, Caroline 153–5
Ware, Susan 155–6, 160–1
Washington, Booker T. 94
Washington Square 54, 72, 76–7
Washington Square (James, H.) 76–7
Weaver, Robert C. 187–8
Webb, Beatrice 41–2
Webb, Sidney 41–2
WEIU. *See* Women's Educational and
    Industrial Union
West Side Rookery (Herzfeld and
    Simkhovitch, M. K.) 92
"What a Slum Is—What a Slum Does"
    (Simkhovitch, M. K.) 181
White, Alfred Tredway 159–60
Whitechapel (neighborhood) 42–3
Whitehouse, New Jersey 100–1, 103–4
White House Conference on the Care of
    Dependent Children 137

Whitney, Gertrude 79, 141, 152
Whitney, Harry Payne 141
Whittier House 52
Willard, Ralph 165–7
Williamsburg Houses 186–7
Wilson, Ellen Axson 197–8
Wilson, Woodrow 197–8
Wischnewetzky, Lazare 59
Woerishoffer, Anna 114, 119–20, 144, 152
Woerishoffer, Carola 110–11, 113–14
Woman's Medical College 50
Woman's Peace Party 126
woman suffrage 11, 111–13, 131–2, 157
women
    doctorate degrees and 27
    working conditions of 85–6
Women's Christian Temperance Union 59
Women's City Club 157
Women's Club of Forest Hills Gardens
    131
Women's Conference (Zurich, 1919) 126
Women's Educational and Industrial
    Union (WEIU) 24
Women's Municipal League 50
Women's Trade Union League
    (WTUL) 86
Wonder Woman (comic) 206–7
Wood, Edith Elmer 175–6
    on Bacon, A. F. 197
    documenting housing conditions
        118–19, 160, 184–5
    housing campaigns and 157, 162
    New Jersey State Housing
        Authority and 176
    on public housing standards 191–2
    USHA and 185
Wood, Reuben T. 181–2
Woodbridge, Frederick J. E. 108–9
Woodbury, Coleman 160–1
Woolley, Charles 122–3
working conditions, of women 85–6
World War I 114, 116, 126
World War II 208
Wright, Frank Lloyd 193–4
WTUL. *See* Women's Trade Union League
Wurster, William 203–4

Yale, doctorate degrees and 27
Yiddish 52

Zahn, Charles T. 211
Zinsser, Hans 81